PETERHEAD
ROLL OF HONOUR
1914-1918

This book is dedicated to the 487 men from Peterhead who sacrificed their lives for this country.

Family History Society of Buchan

22 Harbour Street

Peterhead

AB42 1DJ

Scottish Registered Charity SC039533

In 1922 the people of Peterhead donated money to build an elegant Great War memorial which is now located on the South Road. The Memorial dominates the entrance to the town and any visitor cannot fail to be impressed by its grandeur. However beautiful the memorial is - it sadly commemorates 368 of the townsfolk who fell during the Great War. The names engraved upon its four huge granite plaques are only part of the story. Many more names do not appear on the memorial but have equal justification to be there.

The soldiers, sailors, airmen and civilians honoured in this book either have their name engraved on the War Memorial or are included in the Buchan Observer's Roll of Honour for Peterhead and the immediate vicinity, published in 1919. Those names that appear on the 1919 Roll of Honour but are not engraved on the War Memorial are suffixed with an asterisk *. Where men have been identified as a native of Peterhead but do not appear on either the War Memorial or the 1919 Roll of Honour their Service details are listed in the epilogue to this book.

Each entry includes the serviceman's military details, family particulars and the memorial or cemetery, which honours his sacrifice. The latter details are taken directly from the Commonwealth War Graves Commission.

This book has been extensively researched, using many local and national resources but there is the possibility that some details have been missed. In this case, please contact the Society and any new details will be included in a future re-print.

Alan L Fakley

ACKNOWLEDGEMENT

The following agencies/publications were extensively used in the research for this book and without each and every one of them this book would not have been possible. Particular thanks go to Anne Park, Carolyn Morrisey and Douglas MacDonald for all their help and enthusiasm in seeing this book completed.

Carolyn Morrisey
Anne Park
Aberdeenshire Museums Service, Mintlaw
Commonwealth War Graves Commission
The National Archives at Kew
The General Records Office of Scotland
The Canadian, Australian and South African National Archives
The Buchan Observer Newspaper
The Peoples Journal Newspaper
Aberdeen Daily Journal Newspaper
Aberdeen University Roll of Honour
Members of the Family History Society of Buchan
49th Bn. Canadian Expeditionary Force (Alberta) Nominal Roll 1915
People of Peterhead who kindly donated their stories and photographs
Mr Douglas MacDonald for his knowledge of local spellings and for proof reading this book

Abbreviations

2Lt	Second Lieutenant	Maj	Major
		MIA	Missing in Action
AB	Able Seaman (Rank of)	MGC	Machine Gun Corps
A/Cpl	Acting Rank of Corporal	MC	Military Cross
ADJ	Aberdeen Daily Journal	MI	Memorial Inscription
	Newspaper	MM	Military Medal
AIF	Australian Imperial Force	m/s	Maiden Surname
aka	Also Known As	MT	Mechanical Transport
ASC	Army Service Corps	MV	Motor Vessel (Ship)
A/Sgt	Acting Rank of Sergeant		
A&SH	Argyll and Sutherland	NCO	Non Commissioned Officer
	Highlanders	NOK	Next-Of-Kin
		NSW	New South Wales (Australia)
BC	British Colombia (Canada)	NZEF	New Zealand Expeditionary
Bde	Brigade (Army Formation)		Force
Bdr	Bombardier (Rank of)		
BEF	British Expeditionary Force	occ	Occupation
Bn	Battalion		
BO	Buchan Observer Newspaper	PJ	People's Journal Newspaper
Bty	Battery (Army Formation)	Pnr	Pioneer (Rank of)
Capt	Captain	POW	Prisoner of War
		Pte	Private
CB	Confined to Barracks		
CDG	Croix de Guerre (French	QMS	Quartermaster Sergeant
	Gallantry Medal)		
CEF	Canadian Expeditionary Force	RAMC	Royal Army Medical Corps
Coy	Company (Army Formation)	RASC	Royal Army Service Corps
Cpl	Corporal	RFA	Royal Field Artillery
CSgt	Colour Sergeant	RM	Royal Marines
CSM	Company Sergeant Major	RMLI	Royal Marine Light Infantry
CWGC	Commonwealth War Grave	RMSP	Royal Mail Steam Packet
	Commission	RN	Royal Navy
		RNAS	Royal Naval Air Station
DCM	Distinguished Conduct Medal	RNR	Royal Naval Reserve
Div	Division (Army Formation)		
		Sgt	Sergeant/Serjeant
FP	Field Punishment/Fatigue Party	Sgt Maj	Sergeant Major
		SLI	Somerset Light Infantry
Gnr	Gunner (Rank of)	SNWM	Scottish National War Memorial
		Sqn	Squadron
HB	Highland Battalion	Spr	Sapper (Rank of)
HFA	Highland Field Ambulance	SR	Scottish Rifles (as in
HLI	Highland Light Infantry		Cameronians (SR))
HM	His Majesty	SS	Steamship
HMAT	His Majesty's Australian	St	Saint or Street (both used in
	Transport		Street names)
HMD	His Majesty's Drifter		
HMS	His Majesty's Ship	TF	Territorial Force
HMT	His Majesty's Trawler	Tpr	Trooper (Rank of)
KIA	Killed in Action	UK	United Kingdom of Great Britain
KOSB	King's Own Scottish Borderers		and Ireland (as in 1918).
KRRC	King's Royal Rifle Corps		
		V Bn.	Volunteer Battalion
LCpl	Lance Corporal	VAD	Voluntary Aid Detachment
LSgt	Lance Sergeant/Serjeant		
Lt.	Lieutenant	WA	Western Australia
Lt.Col.	Lieutenant Colonel	WAFF	West Africa Frontier Force
Lt.Cmdr.	Lieutenant Commander	WO2	Warrant Officer Class 2

Battles and Incidents - Naval

Many of the local fishing drifters were acquired by the Admiralty to act as minesweepers, anti-submarine vessels, harbour boats or water tankers. A number of these boats were lost during the war and the casualties from Peterhead are recorded in this book. The sinking of the following Royal Navy ships resulted in the death of many Peterhead sailors.

HMS Hawke – 15 Oct 1914. This ship was torpedoed by the German submarine U-9 igniting a magazine causing a huge explosion which sank the ship immediately. Her Commander, 22 Officers and 427 men were lost. Three men from Peterhead were lost that day.

HMS Bulwark – 26 Nov 1914 In terms of loss of life, the loss of the Bulwark remains one of most catastrophic in the history of the Royal Navy. Of its 750 crew, only 17 survived when the ship suddenly exploded whilst moored off the River Medway in Kent. Four men from Peterhead were lost in this tragedy.

HMS Invincible – 31 May 1916 During the Battle of Jutland the Invincible was attacked by two German ships. A 12-inch shell pierced the Q-turret detonating the mid-ships magazines. Of the 1026 crew only six survived. On that day four men from Peterhead and another aboard the ill-fated HMS Queen Mary lost their lives.

HMS Invincible

Battles and Incidents - Army

The Great War was the largest single war ever to have occurred. Therefore, due to the immense number of battles, this list includes only the major battles and incidents where a number of Peterhead men fell.

Givenchy - 18/24 Dec 1914 With the French under considerable pressure at Arras the order was given to attack the Germans at Givenchy to prevent German reinforcements reaching Arras. British casualties ran to over 4000.

Festubert - 15/25 May 1915 More than 16000 Casualties were sustained on the attack at Festubert in support of the much larger offensive to the South at Vimy Ridge.

The Labyrinth - Mar 1916 On relieving the French at The Labyrinth the Gordon Highlanders and other battalions of the 51st Highland Division were subjected to an enormous number of mine explosions and shell bombardments. Mortar and rifle fire remained a constant danger. At least 29 members of the Gordon Highlanders were killed or posted as missing at the Labyrinth.

High Wood - 30/31 Jul 1916 As part of the Battle of the Somme, the attack on High Wood and the subsequent advance on Wood Lane resulted in 227 casualties. This engagement did not result in the capture of High Wood. The objective was finally secured later in mid-September.

Beaumont-Hamel - (Ancre)13/18 Nov 1916 The Beaumont-Hamel Offensive formed part of the Battle of Ancre. Beaumont-Hamel had been one of the major Allied objectives on the first day of the Somme but had proved exceptionally difficult to take. The objective stretched from the Y-Ravine to Beaumont-Hamel, a heavily fortified town. Utilising the new tactic of infantry formations leap-frogging each other, Beaumont-Hamel was taken on the 18 Nov 1916 and was the foundation stone on which the reputation of the 51st Highland Division was built. The day of the 13 Nov 1916 resulted in huge losses for the Gordon Highlanders.

Arras - Apr/May 1917 To coincide with a massive French offensive the British offensive at Arras was intended to foreshorten the war and end hostilities within 48 hours. The British effort was along the wide front between Vimy in the north-west and Bullecourt to the south-east. The Canadians captured Vimy leaving the British to make significant gains up the River Scarpe. Following initial success the Commonwealth forces were engaged in a series of small engagements. Though the Commonwealth forces did make significant gains the breakthrough to end the war was not achieved. The Battle of Arras officially finished on the 16 May 1917.

3rd Battle of Ypres (Passchendaele) - Jul/Nov 1917

Officially the 3rd Battle of Ypres, Passchendaele, was the major Commonwealth offensive of the summer and autumn of 1917. The objective was Passchendaele Ridge which was captured on the 30 Nov 1917 after 4 months of appalling weather conditions of rain, mud and slime. Nearly 400,000 British Empire casualties were inflicted with the same number on the German side.

Menin Road Ridge - 20-25 Sep 1917 The third major offensive by the British as part of the 3rd Battle of Ypres showed the British attack, take and hold the Menin Road Ridge despite strong German counter-attacks. This offensive reinforced the success of the tactic of leap-frogging captured trenches and in good weather could make significant gains.

Cambrai – Nov/Dec 1917 The Battle of Cambrai was the British attempt to penetrate the Hindenberg Line near the Bourton Ridge and then threaten the rear of the German lines. Cambrai is remembered for being a large tank battle with new joint artillery-infantry tactics. Initial gains were soon reversed by German counter-attacks. Nearly 48,000 men lost their lives at Cambrai.

St Quentin – German Offensive Mar/Apr 1918 A major offensive starting on the 21 Mar 1918 resulted in the 5th Bn. Gordon Highlanders sustaining huge losses. With over 440 men killed, missing or prisoners-of-war, the Battalion almost ceased to function. This also followed the very unpopular removal of the 1st/5th Bn. Gordon Highlanders from the prized 51st Highland Division to bolster the rather inferior 61st (2nd South Midland) Division. With only 60 men left in the Battalion the Gordon Highlanders held the bridge at Voyennes and took part in further counter-attacks.

Battle of St Quentin Canal - 29 Sep 1918 Probably the most pivotal battle of the Great War, a joint British, Australian and American attack spearheaded a major offensive that breached the Hindenberg Line. Achieving all its objectives, this offensive convinced the German High Command that any hope of a German victory was lost.

Buzancy – 28 Jul 1918 The attack on the village of Buzancy was fixed for 12:30 hours on the 28 Jul 1918 and 8th Bn Seaforth Highlanders and 1st /5th Bn. Gordon Highlanders would spearhead the assault. The village proved to be an exceptionally difficult target to overcome and was reminiscent of some of the hard slogs on the Somme in 1916. The Division counted this day fighting as one of the most gruelling it had ever undergone. No small words from a unit that had been in the thick of the fighting since the Battle of Loos in Sep 1915.

By 13:30 hours the 15th Scottish Brigade had captured all of its objectives but on their right there was still no sign of the 91st French Regiment. By 15:35 hours, word had got through to General Reed in command of the 15th Division that the 91st French Regiment had been forced back by the strong point in front of it and could make no progress. This left the Highlanders in a precarious position. German counter attacks and barrages were falling on them as they were forced to retire back across the open ground to prevent them being surrounded. Six hours after they had launched their heroic attack the Highlanders found themselves back in their starting lines.

THE FALLEN OF PETERHEAD

Francis R. ADAM MM

Service No: 8531. Rank: Cpl. Regiment: 1st Bn. Cameronian's (Scottish Rifles).

Francis (aka Frank) was the son of Alexander and Mary Adam of 7 Ferryhill Terrace, Aberdeen. Born in the parish of St Nicholas and lived at 39 St Peter St. Peterhead, he worked aboard a herring boat in Peterhead.

Francis enlisted in Aberdeen and travelled to France with the 1st Expeditionary Force in 1914 and was later awarded the Military Medal for bravery.

Francis was killed in action on the 20 Jul 1916 during the Somme Offensive and has no known grave. Francis' sacrifice is commemorated on the Thiepval Memorial.

References:
CWGC Casualty No 772630
Aberdeen City Roll of Honour

Robert ADAMS

Service No: 2120. Rank: Pte. Regiment: 5th Bn. Gordon Highlanders.
Service No: 240432. Rank: Pte. Regiment: 1st /5th Bn. Gordon Highlanders.

Born on the 22 Oct 1886 in Peterhead, Robert was the married son of Alexander and Jane (m/s Thomson) Adams. He was also the brother of Jane, John A., James, George and William Adams. Robert married Janet Christie Reid in Peterhead in 1913 and lived at 41 Maiden St., Peterhead.

Robert enlisted in Peterhead in 1914 and joined C Coy of the 5th Bn. Gordon Highlanders. He was killed in action on the 18 Apr 1917 at Fampoux as apart of the infamous Arras offensive of Apr-May 1917 and has no known grave.

References:
CWGC Casualty No 738205
Buchan Observer: 1914.
Soldier's Will.
Marriage Certificate.

John AHERN

Service No: 2143/TS. Rank: Trimmer.
Service: RNR - HMT Oku.

Born in Cardiff in 1885, John was the son of George and Mary Ann (m/s Redman) Ahern

and was married to Helen Buchan of Peterhead.

John served aboard HMT Oku which was one of a number of trawlers based in Peterhead The role of these boats were to mine sweep the area or to attack German U-boats transiting the Buchan coastline en-route to Scapa Flow. John died of chronic myocarditis on the 13 Nov 1917 at 1 Great Stuart St., Peterhead and he is buried in the Peterhead Cemetery.

References:
CWGC Casualty No 327006
www.naval-history.net

Hugh AIRD

Service No: 9419. Rank: Pte. Regiment: 1st Bn. Scots Guards.

Born in 1895, Hugh Aird was the third son of Hugh Aird, a blacksmith, of Martin Rd., Insch, Aberdeenshire. He was employed at HM Convict Prision in Peterhead, as an apprentice blacksmith. He had 3 brothers all serving in the Army; George (3rd /5th Bn. Gordon Highlanders), Robert (Argyle and Sutherland Highlanders) and his younger brother Hector (2nd /5th Bn. Gordon Highlanders). It is believed that all three brothers survived the conflict.

Hugh joined the 1st Bn. Scots Guards in Aberdeen and after basic training was drafted to France in Dec 1914. Aged 20, Hugh was listed as missing after an engagement with the enemy at La Bassee on the 25 Jan 1915. After a suitable period he was presumed dead by the Army Council and his body was never found. Hugh's sacrifice is commemorated on the Le Touret Memorial at the Pas de Calais.

References:
CWGC Casualty No 823264
Buchan Observer 1915

Alexander John ALEXANDER

Service No: 1778. Rank: Pte. 5th Gordon Highlanders.
Rank: 2Lt. Regiment: 5th Bn. Duke of Wellington (West Riding) Regt.

Alexander was the eldest son of Francis and Helen Ann Alexander of 28 Constitution St., Peterhead. Residing at 11 Back St, Peterhead, he worked for the Buchan Observer newspaper before becoming a cooper in the employment of Messrs Sinclair and Buchan.

Alexander enlisted in 1914 as a Pte and rapid promotion saw him become a Sgt and a signalling instructor. He was later commissioned into the 5th Bn. Duke of Wellington's (West Riding) Regiment. Alexander, now a 2Lt. was killed on the 27 Nov 1917 aged 20, whilst leading his platoon in the attack on Bourlon Village. This attack occurred as part of the Battle of Cambrai. His sacrifice is honoured on the Cambrai Memorial.

References:
CWGC Casualty No 1750753
Buchan Observer: 1914

Alexander Murrison ALEXANDER

Service No: 130255. Rank: Pte. Regiment: 16th Bn. Canadian Infantry (Manitoba Regiment).

Alexander was born on the 18 Jul 1887, the son of George and Elizabeth A. Alexander of 18 St Peter St. Peterhead. Having worked at the Post Office in Peterhead he emigrated to Vancouver in about 1905 where he was employed as a fireman. Alexander enlisted at the giant Canadian Training Camp at Valcartier, Quebec.

He joined the 72nd Overseas Bn. of the Canadian Expeditionary Force (CEF) and was sent to France. He had only been at the front for two weeks when he was killed on the 13 Jul 1916 by a stray bullet whilst behind the lines. He is buried in the Railway Dugouts Burial Ground, Ieper, Belgium. In 1916 this burial ground was used by a nearby advanced dressing station.

References:
CWGC Casualty No 489017
Canadian Archives

Charles ALEXANDER

Service No: 201625. Rank: Pte. Regiment: 4th Bn. Gordon Highlanders.

Born in Peterhead in 1884, Charles was the son of William Birnie and Ann (m/s Noble) Alexander. He was also brother to Mary J., William, Ann, Andrew H. and Jane Alexander. Before the war, he worked for Messrs

Alexander Brothers, fishcurers in Peterhead.

Charles enlisted in Aberdeen and lest for France. On the 1 Jul 1916, supported by a French attack to the south, thirteen divisions of Commonwealth forces launched an offensive on a line from north of Gommecourt to Maricourt. This was to become known as the Battle of the Somme. Charles was killed in action on the 23 Jul 1916. His sacrifice is commemorated at the Thiepval Memorial and he has no known grave.

Reference:
CWGC Casualty No 773046

George ALEXANDER

Service No: 524A. Rank: Gnr. Regiment: 22nd Australian Machine Gun Corps.

Born on the 4 Jun 1880 in Mintlaw, George was the son of Charles, a chemist, and Mary Jane Alexander. The family lived at a number of addresses in Peterhead including 14 Kirk St., 88 Queen St. and 39 Kirk St. Mary later moved to 47 Tullibody Rd. Alloa and changed her surname to Benzie. Prior to the war, George served his apprenticeship with Mr James Simpson, chemist, Peterhead.

George emigrated to Australia to work as a miner. Following his death, correspondence was received from a Miss Annie E Grassie of Brisbane, Queensland seeking clarification of his status.

George enlisted in Stanthorpe, Queensland on the 25 Mar 1916 and in Jan 1917 had arrived in England. By May 1917 George was serving in France only to return to England in the October of that year with a gunshot wound to the right shoulder. In Mar 1918 he returned to the front only to be killed on the 30 Aug 1918. George was buried by his comrades and a simple wooden cross marked the grave. George is listed on the Villers-Bretonneux Memorial. This memorial is the Australian National Memorial erected to commemorate all Australian soldiers who fought in France and Belgium during the First World War.

References:
Australian Government Archives
CWGC Casualty No 1457391

Harry ALEXANDER

Service No: 2733. Rank: Pte. Regiment: 5th Bn. Gordon Highlanders.

Harry was the fourth son of Charles (occ cooper) and Mary (m/s Lovie) Alexander of 39 Kirk St, Peterhead. He was born on the 21 Jan 1898 and enlisted into the 5th Bn. Gordon Highlanders in Peterhead. He had a brother George Alexander.

Harry was listed as missing, believed killed, on the 23 Mar 1916 which was the day of a major enemy bombardment in which the Gordon Highlanders lost a great number of men (78). They were subjected to this very heavy bombardment which included shrapnel, all types of trench-mortar bombs and rifle fire. Their losses were severe: 4 officers (1 killed, 2 wounded, and 1 missing) and 74 other ranks (14 killed, 24 wounded and 36 missing). These unfortunate men who were mainly buried by the falling earth, are commemorated on the Arras Memorial. This memorial commemorates almost 35,000 servicemen from the United Kingdom, South Africa and New Zealand who died in the Arras sector between the spring of 1916 and 7 Aug 1918.

References:
CWGC Casualty No 738367
Carolyn Morrisey

William ALEXANDER

Service No: 3314S. Rank: Stoker. Service: RNR - HMS Invincible.

Born about 1889 in Peterhead, William was the son of William and Elizabeth (m/s Birnie) Alexander of Harbour St. Boddam. He was brother to James J., Mary A., Rose E. and Primrose F. Alexander.

Having already seen action at Helgoland and the Falkland Islands, William was lost at the Battle of Jutland when HMS Invincible was lost.

The date of this disaster was the 31 May 1916 and William's sacrifice is commemorated on the Portsmouth Naval Memorial.

References:
CWGC Casualty No 2875424
www.naval-history.

James S. ALLARDYCE

Service No: 241174. Rank: Pte. Regiment: 5th Bn. Gordon Highlanders.

Born in Peterhead in 1889, James was the son of John and Mary Allardyce of 22 St Peter St., Peterhead. He was also the brother of

Mary, Christine, Jessie, John, Eleanor and Edith Allardyce.

James enlisted in Peterhead and was killed in action on the 11 Apr 1917 near the Roclincourt Area. His sacrifice is listed on the Arras memorial which commemorates almost 35,000 servicemen from the United Kingdom, South Africa and New Zealand who died in the Arras sector between the spring of 1916 and 7 Aug 1918.

References:
CWGC Casualty No 738427

Alexander ALLISTON

Service No: 3523/ES. Rank: Engineman. Service: RNR - HM Yacht Iolaire.

Born on the 24 Nov 1856, Alexander was the husband of Sarah Clark Alliston. They had at least 3 children together: Margaret, William and Alexander Alliston.

Alexander died of illness aboard the hired yacht "Iolaire" on the 4 May 1916 aged 59. Alexander's death was not as a result of the Iolaire disaster of 1919 when The Iolaire sank carrying sailors who had fought in the First World War back to the Scottish island of Lewis. Alexander's sacrifice is commemorated on the Portsmouth Naval Memorial.

References:
CWGC Casualty No 327007
http://www.naval-history.net

Adam James ANDERSON

Service No: 38570. Rank: Pte. Regiment: 13th Bn. Royal Scots.

Adam was born in Peterhead and was the son of Adam James and Agnes Anderson of 1B James St., Peterhead and later of 65 Union Grove, Aberdeen. Adam was brother to Jeannie and Williamina Anderson. Before enlisting he was an apprentice watchmaker with Mr W.M. Milne, Rosemount Viaduct, Aberdeen.

Adam enlisted in Aberdeen but was killed in action on the 28 Mar 1918, aged 19 and he has no known grave. His sacrifice is commemorated on the Arras Memorial. This memorial commemorates almost 35,000 servicemen from the United Kingdom, South Africa and New Zealand who died in the Arras sector between the spring of 1916 and 7 Aug 1918.

References:
CWGC Casualty No 738609
Buchan Observer 21 May 1918, 24 Jun 1919

Alexander Finnie ANDERSON

Service No: 240765. Rank: Sgt. Regiment: 5th Bn. Gordon Highlanders.

Born in Peterhead in 1894, Alexander was the son of James and Mary Ann Anderson of 1 Roanheads, Peterhead. He was also the husband of Maggie Jane Smart (formerly Anderson) of 9 William Square, Footdee, Aberdeen. Alexander was a brother to James, Jemima, John (who also fell on the same day), Josephine, Hugh and Williamina Anderson.

Alexander enlisted in Peterhead and was killed in action on the 31 Jul 1917, aged 27. He died on the same day as his brother John Anderson during the same battle, namely the 3rd Battle of Ypres or Passchendaele. His body has never been found and so Alexander's sacrifice is commemorated on the Ypres (Menin Gate) Memorial.

References:
CWGC Casualty No 910107

Alexander Wright ANDERSON

Service No: 2704. Rank: Pte. Regiment: 5th Bn. Gordon Highlanders.

Alexander was born in Cruden on the 27 Jan 1896, the son of Ann Anderson of Blackhills, Cruden. He was also the grandson of Mrs Agnes Anderson of 17 Castle St., Peterhead. Before the war, Alexander worked for Mr J. Reid, contractor, Peterhead.

After enlisting in Peterhead, he was only 20 years old when he was originally listed as missing but later was classed as "killed in action" on the 26 Mar 1916. Alexander's sacrifice is recorded on the Arras Memorial which commemorates almost 35,000 servicemen from the United Kingdom, South Africa and New Zealand who died in the Arras sector between the spring of 1916 and 7 Aug 1918, and have no known grave.

References:
CWGC Casualty No 738613
Birth Certificate.

Hector ANDERSON

Service No: S/24599. Rank: Pte. Regiment: 9th Bn. Seaforth Highlanders.

Hector was the son of John & Helen (m/s Reid) Anderson of Alness, Ross-shire. His father was a labourer and had passed away by the time of Hector's death. Hector was a draper working at 2 Mackie Place, Peterhead.

Hector died of illness on the 8 Sep 1920 as a result of injuries sustained in the war. His brother–in-law Donald McKenzie of 18 Prince St., Peterhead was the informant.

References:
CWGC Casualty No 326976

John ANDERSON

Service No: 3085. Rank: Pte. Regiment: 5th Bn. Gordon Highlanders.
Service No: 240940. Rank: Pte. Regiment: 5th Bn. Gordon Highlanders.

Born in Peterhead in 1887, John was the son of James and Mary Ann Anderson of 1 Roanheads, Peterhead. He was a brother to James, Jemima, Josephine, Alexander (who fell on the same day), Hugh and Williamina Anderson. Prior to the war, John was living at 56 Baker St; Aberdeen.

It was on the 31 Jul 1917 during the 1st day of the Battle of Passchendaele, more correctly known as the 3rd Battle of Ypres, when John fell. His brother Alexander also fell on this day in the same battle. John is buried in the New Irish Farm Cemetery, St Jean-Les-Ypres.

References:
CWGC Casualty No 451917
Aberdeen City Roll of Honour
Buchan Observer.

William ANDERSON

Service No: A/20823. Rank: Pte. Regiment: 16th Bn. (Manitoba Regt) Canadian Infantry.

Born about 1891 in Peterhead, William was the son of James K. & Jessie M.M. Anderson of Peterhead. He was the brother of Mary, James, Helen M., Charles and Alexander Anderson of 77 Broad St. and later of 29 Maiden St., Peterhead.

William fell on the 1 Dec 15, aged 24. He served with the 16th Bn. Canadian Infantry which was also known as the "Canadian Scottish". William is buried at the La Plus Douve Farm Cemetery.

References:
CWGC Casualty No 444607
Canadian Great War Project

Murdoch McLeod ANGUS

Service No: 460225. Rank: Pte. Regiment 90th Bn. Canadian Infantry.
Service No: 154680. Rank: Spr. Regiment: 9th Bn. Canadian Railway Troop.

Murdoch was born in Peterhead on the 4 Jun 1884, the son of James Murrison and Isabella (m/s Cordiner) Angus of 33 Queen St., Peterhead. A cooper by trade, Murdoch was the brother of William A., Ann M., James M., John C., Jane R., Margaret and Isabella Angus.

Murdoch emigrated to Canada and enlisted on the 14 Jun 1915 at Winnipeg, Manitoba. Murdoch spent a great deal of time in the military hospitals near Etaples after being wounded by bomb shrapnel to the chest, neck, ear and back. He died of his wounds on the 16 Jun 1918 aged 34. He is buried in the Etaples Military Cemetery. Murdoch's brother-in-law George R. Henderson also fell during 1918.

References:
CWGC Casualty No 496892
Buchan Observer Article 18 Jun 1918
Canadian Great War Project

William ARTHUR*

Rank: Able Seaman. Service: Mercantile Marine – SS Hanna Larson.

Born in Peterhead in about 1855, William was the husband of Mary (m/s Aiken) Arthur of 76 Byethorne, South Shields.

Whilst on a passage to the Tyne to collect a cargo of coal, four shells were fired at the SS Hanna Larsen. The master stopped the engine but within 15 minutes ordered full speed ahead and attempted to get clear of the German submarine UC-39. After another round of shelling the master stopped the vessel and ordered the crew to abandon ship. The firing continued and four men were wounded whilst attempting to take to the lifeboats, one of whom, William Arthur later died on the 9 Feb 1917. William's sacrifice is recorded in the United Kingdom Book of Remembrance which commemorates all the United Kingdom casualties of the two World Wars who were not formerly recorded by the Commonwealth War Graves Commission.

References:
CWGC Casualty No 2979137

Alexander AULD

Service No: S/9563. Rank: Pte. Regiment: 1st Bn. Gordon Highlanders.

Alexander was residing at 20 Tolbooth Wynd, Peterhead when he died of influenza on the 7 Nov 1918 aged 30. He had previously served in the Gordon Highlanders during the early part of the war. Alexander's sacrifice is recorded on the Peterhead Memorial.

References:
CWGC Casualty No 326977

John BAIN

Service No: 21483/DA. Rank: Deckhand. Service: RNR - HMS Vivid.

Born in about 1893 in Aberdeenshire, John was the son of Alexander (occ farmer) and Jemima (m/s Charles) Bain of Rattrayhouse, Crimond, Aberdeenshire. He was also the husband of Margaret (m/s Ritchie aka Morrice) Bain of 16 Chapel St. Peterhead whom he married on the 15 May 1912. Prior to the war, John was a gamekeeper.

John sadly died of illness whilst in-service at HMS Vivid, the RN Base, Devonport, on the 16 Jul 1918. John's death is commemorated on the Peterhead Memorial.

References:
CWGC Casualty No 327008.
www.naval-history.net

Robert George BAIN

Service No: 202451. Rank: Pte. Regiment: 1st /5th Bn. Royal Scots Fusiliers.

Born in New Deer about 1877, Robert was the son of George and Agnes Greig (m/s Clark) Bain of 23 King St., Peterhead, and also the husband of Jane Low (m/s Cadger) Bain of 725 Gallowgate, Whitevale, Glasgow. They had five sons together, including George C. (b.1900) and James Smart (b.1906) Bain. Robert was employed by Messrs Shinnie, Aberdeen as a coachbuilder where he captained the firm's cricket team.

He emigrated to Canada in 1912 only to return in 1916 to join the Gordon Highlanders. Robert later transferred to the Royal Scots Fusiliers and died in Palestine on the 24 Oct 1917, aged 39. His death is honoured on the Dier El Belah War Cemetery Memorial which is now in Gaza, Palestine.

References:
CWGC Casualty No 645414
Aberdeen City Roll of Honour

George BAIRD

Service No: 240761. Rank: Sgt. Regiment: 1st Bn. Gordon Highlanders.

George was born in 1894 and was the second son of William and Isabella Davidson Baird of 2 Port Henry Rd., Peterhead. George was also brother to Barbara, Maggie Jane A. and John S. Baird who was killed on the 26 Oct 1917. George was a stone polisher with the Great North of Scotland Granite Co. Peterhead.

George enlisted in Peterhead and died of his wounds on the 11 May 1918, aged only 23. He died at the 26th General Hospital and is buried in the Etaples Military Cemetery. During the First World War, the area around Etaples was the scene of immense concentrations of Commonwealth hospitals and reinforcement camps.

References:
CWGC Casualty No 498710

John Stuart BAIRD

Service No: 240878. Rank: Cpl. Regiment: 2nd Bn. Gordon Highlanders.

John was born in Peterhead and was the youngest son of William and Isabella Davidson Baird of 2 Port Henry Rd., Peterhead. He was also brother to Barbara, Maggie Jane A. and George Baird. Prior to the war, John was a cooper with Messrs Sinclair & Buchan, fish curers, Peterhead.

In Nov 1917, John was reported as missing presumed a prisoner of war. In Sep 1918 his mother received official confirmation that he had been taken prisoner. However, John had actually been killed in action at the Battle of Passchendaele on the 26 Oct 1917. His body was never recovered and his sacrifice is honoured on the Tyne Cot Memorial. John's brother George would later die in 1918.

References:
CWGC Casualty No 846789

William George BAIRD

Service No: 2692. Rank: Pte. Regiment: Gordon Highlanders.
Service No: M/354029. Rank: Sgt. Regiment: Army Service Corps – MT.

William was born in Peterhead in 1894, the son of David and Jane (m/s Davidson) Baird of 8 North St., Peterhead. He was also a brother to Alfred, David (who served with the Colours as a Cpl.) and Thomas Baird.

William enlisted into the Gordon Highlanders before being transferred to the ASC. He was seriously wounded in the spring of 1917 and returned to England. William died of pneumonia on the 30 Oct 1918, aged 23, at the Balgowan VAD Hospital, Kent. He was buried in Peterhead on the 6 Nov 1918. William is honoured on the Peterhead War Memorial.

References:
CWGC Casualty No 326978

Douglas Innes BANNERMAN

Service No: S/20010. Rank: Pte. Regiment: 2nd Bn. Black Watch (Royal Highlanders).

Born and enlisted in Peterhead, Douglas was a twin son of the late Captain and Georgina Bannerman of 30 Marischal St. Peterhead. Douglas' father was a shipmaster and prior to the war, Douglas was employed as a clerk with Mr James Sutherland, Victoria Stables, Peterhead. He was brother to Mary Jane, Susan, Georgina, Archibald, Clarissa, Dorothy and Cecil Bannerman.

During the First World War, the liner Arcadian was requisitioned from the RMSP Co. and converted into a transport ship. On the 15 Apr 1917, the ship with a company of 1,335 troops and crew was proceeding from Salonika to Alexandria destined for Mesopotamia. Whilst in the southern Aegean, 26 miles N.E. of Milo, the troops having just completed boat-drill when a submarine approached unseen and discharged a torpedo which sank the vessel in six minutes. Fortunately the men's recent exercise at the boats imparted steadiness and confidence and 1,058 were rescued, either through their own efforts or by the escorting destroyer.

Douglas died that day, aged 21 and his death is commemorated on the Chatby Memorial in Alexandria, Egypt.

References:
CWGC Casualty No 1438347
1914-1918.invisionzone.com

Alexander G BARRON

Service No: 240718. Rank: Pte. Regiment: 4th Bn. Gordon Highlanders.

Alexander was born in Burghead, Banffshire the son of Margaret Barron. He was also the grandson of Mrs Adams of Roanheads and the nephew of Mrs. E. Milne, of 13 Seagate, Peterhead. Prior to the war Alexander was a farm servant within the district.

Alexander enlisted in Maud and was killed near the village of Thun-St. Martin on the 14 Oct 1918 and was initially buried there. Later his grave was moved to the Naves Communal Cemetery Extension.

References:
CWGC Casualty No 307713

John BEAGRIE

Service No: 1869. Rank: Pte. Regiment: 5th Bn. Gordon Highlanders.
Service No: 240324. Rank: Pte. Regiment: 1st /5th Bn. Gordon Highlanders.

John was born in Peterhead on the 27 Sep 1889, the son of Peter and Georgina Milne Beagrie, and the husband of Amelia (m/s Baird) Beagrie of 69 Broad St., Peterhead. They had a son together, George Thomson Beagrie (b.1917). At the outbreak of war John lived at 14 Wallace St. Peterhead.

John enlisted in Peterhead in 1914 into C Coy of the 5th Bn. Gordon Highlanders and later he served in D Coy of the 1st /5th Bn. He was injured in the Battle of Passchendaele (3rd Battle of Ypres) and later died of wounds on the 14 Aug 1917, aged 28. John is buried in the Mendinghem Military Cemetery. Mendinghem, like Dozinghem and Bandaghem, were the popular names given by the troops to groups of casualty clearing stations posted to the area of Poperinge, West-Vlaanderen during the First World War.

References:
CWGC Casualty No 436910

George BEATON

Service No: 10275. Rank: Sgt. Regiment: Gordon Highlanders. Attached to the West African Regiment WAFF.

George was born in Peterhead circa 1887 and was the husband of Mary B. Beaton, of 62, Bon-Accord St., Aberdeen. He enlisted into the Gordon Highlanders in Peterhead.

Attached to the West African Regiment, George died of malaria on the 7 Aug 1916 in Sierra Leone and his death is recorded on the Freetown (King Tom) Cemetery Memorial.

References:
CWGC Casualty No 419752
Aberdeen City Roll of Honour.

George BEATON

Service No: 5012/DA. Rank: Leading Deckhand. Service: RNR - HMS Pembroke.

Born in Burnhaven, Peterhead on the 22 Apr 1888, George was the son of Kenneth and Betsy (m/s Walker) Beaton and the brother of Sarah A., Christina W., Isabella W., Ellenora, Kenneth, Nellie, Robert and Alexander Beaton.

George passed away on the 31 Jan 1919 from illness at HMS Pembroke, Dorset.

References:
CWGC Casualty No 326980

Robert BENNETT

Service No: 2692. Rank: Pte. Regiment: Gordon Highlanders.
Service No: 3/5844. Rank: Pte. Regiment: 2nd Bn. Gordon Highlanders.

Born and enlisted in Peterhead, Robert was the son of Allington Frederick Morley and Ann (m/s Wood) Bennett of 23 Marischal St., Peterhead. He was brother to Frances M., Alexander, Maggie A., Harriet, Florence G. and John Bennett.

During the 1st Battle of Ypres in 1914, a small British Expeditionary Force succeeded in securing the town before the onset of winter, pushing the German forces back to the Passchendaele Ridge. Robert was killed in action on the 29 Oct 1914. Aged 24 years, his sacrifice is remembered on the Ypres (Menin Gate) Memorial which commemorates the thousands of soldiers who have no known grave.

References:
CWGC Casualty No 927480

Andrew BIRNIE

Service No: 21893. Rank: Pte. Regiment: Scottish Rifles.
Service No: 81200. Rank: Pte. Regiment: 16th Bn. Highland Light Infantry.

Other than having been born in Aidrie, little else is known about Andrew.

Initially joining the Scottish Rifles, Andrew was later posted to the HLI. He was killed on the 28 Nov 1917 and his sacrifice is honoured on the Tyne Cot Memorial which almost 35,000 officers and men whose graves are not known.

References:
CWGC Casualty No 845042

Alexander BIRNIE

Service No: S/14335. Rank: Pte. Regiment: 7th Bn. Queen's Own Cameron Highlanders.

The son of Mr and Mrs Alex Birnie of 72 Longate, Peterhead, Alexander was born in Peterhead and enlisted in Glasgow.

Alexander was killed on the 6 May 1916 aged 24 years whilst serving with C Coy of the 7th Bn. Queen's Own Cameron Highlanders. His sacrifice is honoured on the Loos Memorial which commemorates over 20,000 officers and men who have no known grave.

References:
CWGC Casualty No 727732

Edgar George William BISSET

Rank: 2Lt. Regiment: 5th Bn. Gordon Highlanders.
Rank: 2Lt. Regiment: 6 Sqn Royal Flying Corps.

Edgar was the son of James Davidson and Agnes Isabella (m/s Bruce) Bisset of Union Bank House, Peterhead. He was also brother of Norman and Walter Bisset.

Edgar was commissioned 2Lt. in the Gordon Highlanders, he was attached to the Royal Flying Corps. Edgar was killed in action on 7 Jan 1917. He "went up on a shoot" with a pilot, but had hardly started when a German machine dived on them and started firing before they knew they were attacked. Bisset immediately stood up in his seat and faced the German, reaching up for his gun, but fell back with a bullet through the head. The pilot managed to make a miraculous escape and landed as near as he dared behind the lines, and had Bisset removed to a hospital, but to no purpose as death must have been instantaneous. This was Bisset's last " shoot " to qualify him for his 'wings'. A fellow-officer, communicating the news to his father, said Bisset was an exceedingly popular member of "A" Flight of the squadron to which he was attached, and added: "He would be the very last to wish me to say anything to his credit, and I feel that it would be quite superfluous, as a life like his was so transparently beautiful and sincere that it needs no eulogies. He has left a gap in our mess which no new draft from England can possibly fill, but I thought you would like to know that he died as he lived — a British gentleman." Edgar was only twenty years of age.

References:
CWGC Casualty No 436954
(Royal Flying Corps) Officers' Book Page 242.
Aberdeen City Roll of Honour
Aberdeen University Roll of Service

James BOOTH MC*

Service No: 2625. Rank: Pte. Regiment: 4th Bn. Black Watch (Royal Highlanders).
Service No: 200404. Rank: LCpl. Regiment: 4th Bn. Black Watch (Royal Highlanders).
Rank: Lt. Regiment: 56th Bn. Machine Gun Corps.

A sometime resident of both Peterhead and Aberdeen, James arrived in France on the 22 Feb 1915 and following promotion to LCpl he was commissioned into the MGC on the 24 Mar 1917. James was killed on the 6 Nov 1918 and is buried in the Angreau Communal Cemetery where two plots in the communal cemetery contain the bodies of soldiers of the 56th (London) Division, who fell on 4-7 Nov 1918.

References:
CWGC Casualty No 481606

John BOOTH

Service No: 2405. Rank: Sgt. Regiment: Royal Newfoundland Regiment.

Born in Peterhead on the 21 Sep 1889, John was the third son of James (occ. cooper) and Jessie (m/s English) Booth of 43 Marischal St., Peterhead. He was the brother of James, William, George M., Charles, Janet and Robert Booth. John later emigrated to Canada and at the outbreak of war he joined the Royal Newfoundland Regiment.

On the first day of the Battle of the Somme, no unit suffered heavier losses than the Newfoundland Regiment which had gone into action 801 strong. The roll call the next day revealed that the final figures were 233 killed or dead of wounds, 386 wounded, and 91 missing. Every officer who went forward in the Newfoundland attack was either killed or wounded. John died at Monchy-Le-Preux on the 14 Apr 1917 Aged 27. His sacrifice is listed on the Beaumont-Hamel (Newfoundland) Memorial.

References:
CWGC Casualty No 722143
Aberdeen Roll of Honour: Vol V: Page 17
1901 Census: Peterhead: 232/1

William BREBNER

Service No: 3301S. Rank: Stoker. Service: RNR - HMS Invincible.

William (aka Billy) was the son of William and Alexandrina (m/s Winter) Brebner of 19 Longate, Peterhead. Born on the 13 Sep 1895, he was the brother of George, Donald McL. D.B., George, Alexander, Elizabeth D.B., Alexander W. and Helen Brebner.

On the 31 May 1916 during the Battle of Jutland, HMS Invincible was sunk where only six survivors were picked up by HMS Badger. Billy was aged 20 when he died aboard the Invincible and his loss is honoured on the Portsmouth Naval Memorial.

References:
CWGC Casualty No 2875863
wikipedia.org/wiki/HMS_Invincible(1907)

David BREMNER

Service No: 5042DA. Rank: Deckhand. Service: RNR - HMD Freuchny.

David was born in Peterhead on the 18 May 1876 the son of Daniel and Isabella Davidson Bremner of 21 North St. Peterhead.

The former Buckie boat – HMD Freuchny was mined and sank in the Adriatic off Brindisi on the 8 Jan 1916. His death is recorded on the Portsmouth Naval Memorial.

References:
CWGC Casualty No 2875864

William James BREMNER

Service No: 9134. Rank: Pte. Regiment: 1st Bn. King's Own Scottish Borderers.

William was born in Peterhead circa 1885 and was the husband of Chrissie Taylor Bremner of 28 James St. and later of 17 Queen St., Peterhead.

William was a professional soldier who in 1911, was serving in India with the 1st Bn. KOSB. This Bn. went on to fight at Gallipoli in 1915 before transferring to the Somme in

Mar 1916. Prior to the war, William had retired from the Army however, his service records indicate that he re-enlisted into the Army with the 2nd Bn. KOSB. He arrived in France on the 5 Dec 1914 and was killed during the Battle of the Somme on the 1 Jul 1916 aged 31. His death is honoured on the Thiepval Memorial.

References:
CWGC Casualty No 2875863

Allan John BROOKS

Service No: 266773. Rank: Pte. Regiment: 7th Bn. Gordon Highlanders.

Allan was born Peterhead in 1898 the son of William and Sarah Brooks and the brother of William, Isobel and Harold Brooks. The family lived at 1 Port Henry Road. and prior to that at 16 St Mary St., Peterhead. Allan worked as a joiner with Mr James Taylor, St Peter St., Peterhead before joining up.

Allan enlisted in Aberdeen and died on the 26 Mar 1918. His sacrifice is listed on the Arras Memorial which commemorates almost 35,000 servicemen from the United Kingdom, South Africa and New Zealand who died in the Arras sector between the spring of 1916 and 7 Aug 1918 and have no known grave.

References:
CWGC Casualty No 742293
1911 Census – 1 Port Henry Road.

William M.C. BROOKS

Service No: 3839. Rank: Pte. Regiment: 1st/5th Bn. Gordon Highlanders.

Born in 1896 in Peterhead, William was the son of Robert & Jessie Brooks of the 24 Albion St., Peterhead and later of the Invernettie Brickworks. His siblings include; Robert, John, George, Maggie and Allan Brooks.

William enlisted in Peterhead into his local Regiment, the Gordon Highlanders. On the 13 and 14 Nov 1916, the 51st Highland Division, including the Gordon Highlanders, the 63rd (Royal Naval), 39th and 19th (Western) Divisions finally succeeded in capturing Beaumont-Hamel, Beaucourt-sur-Ancre and St. Pierre-Divion. William was killed on the first day of this offensive aged 20 years old. He is buried in the Ancre British Cemetery, Beaumont-Hamel.

References:
CWGC Casualty No 2853322
Buchan Observer.

David Bisset BROWN

Service No: 1871. Rank: Sgt. Regiment: 5th Bn. Gordon Highlanders.

David was the third son of William (occ. cooper) and Isabella Brown of 47 Clarence St., Aberdeen and also the grandson of Charles Brown of 50 Longate, Peterhead. David had three brothers; William, Peter and Alexander. Prior to the war David was a cooper in the employment of Mr D. Milligan, fishcurer, Peterhead.

He enlisted into the Gordon Highlanders in Aberdeen and fell when, in Nov 1916 the 51st Highland Division captured the town of Beaumont-Hamel. Many of the fallen were buried in the Mailly Wood Cemetery. David fell on the 13 Nov 1916 aged 21.

References:
CWGC Casualty No 111265
ADJ 02 Dec 1916 City & Peterhead
Buchan Observer: 1914
Aberdeen City Roll of Honour

John BROWN

Service No: 142427. Rank: Chief Stoker. Service: HMS Pomone.

John died of illness, whilst on harbour service in Dartmouth on the 11 Nov 1918. He is buried in the Torquay Cemetery which now contains 136 burials from the First World War.

References:
CWGC Casualty No 350704

John Neddrie (Niddrie) BROWN

Service No: CH/236/S. Rank: Pte. Regiment: Royal Marine Light Infantry.

John was the son of William (occ. cooper) and Isabella Brown of 47 Clarence St., Aberdeen and the grandson of Charles Brown, of 50, Longate, Peterhead.

John served with RMLI and the 3rd Royal Marine Bn. He died of illness on the 6 Dec 1918 aged 31

and is buried at the Portianos Military Cemetery, Lemnos Greece.

References:
Note: Monument incorrectly inscribed as Pte JM Brown RMLI
CWGC Casualty No 626732

Alfred BRUCE

Service No: 1276TS. Rank: Trimmer. Service: RNR - HMT Nellie Nutten.

Alfred was the son of James and Isabella (m/s Gray) Bruce, of Peterhead and husband of Elizabeth Bruce of 44 Walker Rd., Torry, Aberdeen. He was also the brother of Isabella, Alexander J., Victor G. and John G. Bruce.

HMT Nellie Nutten was built in Aberdeen in 1901 and was sunk on the 11 Jul 1916 by gunfire from the U-boats; U-46, U-49, U-52 and U-69. The action occurred 100 miles off the Coast of Aberdeen whilst escorting a fishing fleet. HMT Era and HMT Onward were also sunk that day. The crew boarded the Dutch fishing lugger SCH197, which landed them in Scotland. One crew member was taken prisoner aboard U-52 and two crew members were killed, one of those being Alfred. Alfred's sacrifice is commemorated on the Portsmouth Naval Memorial.

Reference:
CWGC Casualty No 2875941
www.naval-history.net

George BRUCE

Service No: S/43299. Rank: Pte. Regiment: 1st Bn. Gordon Highlanders.

George was born and enlisted in Peterhead and was killed in action on the 11 Apr 1917 during the Arras Offensive of the Apr-May that year. He is commemorated on the Arras Memorial and he has no known grave.

References:
CWGC Casualty No 742640

James Smith BRUCE

Service No: 240281. Rank: Pte. Regiment: 12th Bn. Gordon Highlanders.

Born on the 10 Oct 1897, James was the son of William and Mary (m/s Macdonald) Bruce of Mains of Inverugie, Peterhead. James was the brother of John C., Robert W.B., Williamina M.M., Alexander, Emily A., Alfred and George Bruce.

James enlisted in Peterhead and was killed in action on the 24 Mar 1918. He was awarded the Territorial Force Medal 1914 – 1919 along with the Victory and British Medals. His sacrifice is listed upon the Arras memorial which holds the names of 35000 soldiers who died in the area between 1916 and 1918 and have no known grave.

References:
CWGC Casualty No 742644
The Aberdeen Roll of Honour Vol IV

Joseph Miller BRUCE

Service No: S/14010. Rank: Pte. Regiment: 1st Bn. Gordon Highlanders.

Joseph was born in Peterhead on the 20 Dec 1879, as Joseph Bruce Miller - the son of Jane Miller. Jane then married James Bruce in 1880 and from that date, Joseph was known as Joseph Miller Bruce. The family lived at 4 Port Henry Rd. Peterhead.

Having previously served in the South Africa campaign, Joseph joined a minesweeper when the Great War broke out. After four months minesweeping Joseph enlisted into the Gordon Highlanders in Aberdeen. He was injured at the Battle of the Somme and died of wounds on the 18 Aug 1916 at the Bronfay Farm Military Hospital. At the age of 36, he was buried at the nearby Bronfay Farm Military Cemetery, Bray-Sur-Somme.

References:
CWGC casualty No 535549
Birth Certificate

Peter BRUCE

Service No: 432897 Rank: Cpl. Regiment: 49th Bn. Canadian Infantry (Alberta Regiment).

Born about 1887, Peter was the son of George and Jessie D (m/s Reid) Bruce of 16 Gladstone Rd., Peterhead. He was also the brother of James, Christian, Andrew D., Alexander, Barbara and George Bruce. Prior to which he was a printer employed by the Buchan Observer.

Peter emigrated to Canada in 1906 and he enlisted in Edson, Canada on the 21 Jan 1915. Peter was killed in action on the 30 Oct 1917 and his death is commemorated on the Ypres (Menin Gate) Memorial. Before serving with the 49th Bn. CEF, Peter served with the Imperial Forces.

References:
CWGC Casualty No 922495
CEF 49th Bn. Nominal Roll 1915

Robert James BRUCE

Rank: Pte. Regiment: London Scottish.
Rank: 2Lt. Regiment: 6th Bn. South Staffordshire Regiment.

Robert was the son of Robert & Jessie Bruce of 4 St Peter St., Peterhead, and was also the brother of Jessie, Joan and Mary Bruce. He was educated at the Blackhills School and the Peterhead Academy. Prior to the war, Robert was employed by Mr J. D. Christie, chemist, Marischal St., Peterhead and later of Messrs Shirley & Co of London.

Robert initially joined the London Scottish and arrived in France in 1916. After being selected for a commission in his regiment Robert was gazetted into the South Staffordshire Regiment in Nov 1917. Robert died on the 2 Feb 1918, aged 21 and is buried in the Flesquieres Hill British Cemetery. His gravestone is adjacent to a beautiful red rose bush.

References:
CWGC Casualty No 336664
Buchan Observer Feb 1918

Alexander BUCHAN

Service No: 1311SA Rank: Mate. Service: RNR – HMD Lily Reaich.

Alexander was the eldest son of Alexander Buchan of 7 Union St. Peterhead. He had two serving brothers: Robert, a mate on a government vessel and James who was also injured.

Alexander joined the service in Feb 1915 and was lost on the 25 Feb 1916 when HMD Lily Reaich was lost as a result of a mine explosion in the Adriatic off Durazzo. Alexander's sacrifice is honoured on the Portsmouth Naval Memorial.

References:
CWGC Casualty No 2875953

Alexander BUCHAN*

Service No: 3/5845. Rank: Pte. Regiment: 2nd Bn. Gordon Highlanders.

Alexander was born in Peterhead and was the son of James and Mrs Buchan later of 186 St James Rd, Townhead, Glasgow.

After enlisting in Peterhead, he arrived in France on the 7 Nov 1914 but was then killed in action only four days later on the 11 Nov 14. His body was never recovered and Alexander's sacrifice is honoured on the Ypres (Menin Gate) Memorial.

References:
CWGC Casualty No 929713

Alexander BUCHAN

Service No: 2615/5. Rank: Pte. Regiment 5th Bn. Gordon Highlanders.
Service No: 240687. Rank: Sgt. Regiment: 1st/5th Bn. Gordon Highlanders.

Born and enlisted in Peterhead, Alexander was the son of Alexander Davidson Buchan and Isabella (m/s Daniel) Buchan of 15 St Peter St., Peterhead. He was also the elder brother of Thomas (who fought in and survived the war), Catherine Shearer, Katie, John Duguid, William Cruickshank and Mary Buchan. Prior to enlisting he was a farm servant.

Alexander first entered the French theatre on the 2 May 1915 and was awarded the 1915 Star. He fought for nearly two years gaining promotion to the rank Sgt. He was injured whilst fighting at the Roclincourt Area where he lost a leg. Alexander later died of his wounds on the 19 Apr 1917. Alexander is buried in the Etaples Military Cemetery.

References:
CWGC Casualty No 499508

Alexander D. BUCHAN

Service No: S/7942. Rank: Pte. Regiment: 1st Bn. Gordon Highlanders.

Alexander was the eldest son of Mr and Mrs Alexander D. Buchan of Roseberry Terrace, Wick, Caithness. He was born in Peterhead, and prior to the war was a salmon fisherman. Alexander was also the nephew of John Buchan of Messrs Sinclair & Buchan, fishcurer, Peterhead.

Alexander enlisted in 1914 and arrived in France on the 10 May 1915. He was wounded at the Battle of Loos in Sep 1915. After convalescence, Alexander was transferred to the 1st Bn. Gordon Highlanders and returned to the front. He was killed on the 13 Nov 1917, aged 20 and his sacrifice is commemorated on the Thiepval Memorial.

Alexander's WW1 Medal card indicates that he may have served in the 8th Bn. just prior to his death.

References:
Gordon Highlander's War Diary 1916
CWGC Casualty No 766105

Alick H. BUCHAN

Service No: 397TC. Rank: Deckhand.
Service: RNR – HMD Jean.

Born in Peterhead on the 8 Feb 1896, Alick was the son of Alexander "Ake" and Eliza Jean Buchan of 2 Hay Crescent, Peterhead. He was the brother of Joseph, James (who fell in 1918), Gladys Mary and Irene Agnes Buchan.

HMD Jean was part of a hundred-strong fleet of trawlers and drifters that had been refitted for antisubmarine and minesweeping roles. In their antisubmarine role these small ships were also used for operating the submarine nets and utilizing its cannon to shoot at submarines that had surfaced. Earlier in May 1917 the Jean had taken part in the Battle of Otranto where it had been badly damaged (shell through the boiler). She was later mined and sunk in the Aegean on the 17 Oct 1917. Alick's name appears on the Portsmouth Naval Memorial.

References:
CWGC Casualty No 3040733

Andrew A. BUCHAN

Service No: 2489. Rank: Cpl. Regiment: 5th Bn. Gordon Highlanders.

Andrew was married with a young family and lived at 5 New St. Peterhead. Before the war he worked as a draper in Fraserburgh.

Andrew enlisted in Peterhead and entered the French theatre on the 5 Dec 1915; where he was awarded the 1915 Star. He was killed in action on the 27 Jul 1916 and his sacrifice is recorded on the Thiepval Memorial. He has no known grave as does 72,000 other men who died during this battle and have no known burial place.

References:
CWGC Casualty No 766107

Benjamin BUCHAN

Rank: Engine Driver. Service: Royal Naval Reserve.

Born in 1893 in Peterhead, Benjamin was the son of Benjamin and Isabella (m/s Low) Buchan of 12 Maiden St. Peterhead. Benjamin died of influenza complicated by vascular disease on the 4 Jul 1918.

References:
Constitution St MIs
Death Certificate.

George Simpson BUCHAN

Service No: 4333TS. Rank: Trimmer. Service: RNR - HMT Gelsina.

George was the son of James Buchan of 14 Skelton St., Peterhead and also the husband of Ellenora Smith Buchan of 14 Wallace St., Peterhead.

HM Trawler Gelsina, whilst acting as a minesweeper was mined and sunk just off Aberdeen on the 25 Jun 1917. George perished during this tragedy with four others. Aged 35, his death is recorded on the Portsmouth Naval Memorial.

The peace-time operator of the Gelsina was a Walter M. Olney of Grimsby.

References:
www.naval-history.net
CWGC Casualty No 3040734

James BUCHAN

Service No: 2178. Rank: Pte. Regiment: Scottish Horse.
Service No: 5173. Rank: Pte. Regiment: Black Watch (Royal Highlanders).
Service No: S/40646. Rank: Pte. Regiment: Black Watch (Royal Highlanders).
Rank: 2Lt. Regiment: 15th Bn. The Loyal North Lancashire Regiment.

Born in Peterhead on the 6 Dec 1893, James was the son of Alexander "Ake" and Eliza Jean Buchan. He was the brother of Joseph, Alick (who drowned in 1917 with the sinking of HM Drifter Jean), Gladys Mary and Irene Agnes Buchan.

James enlisted as a Pte into the Scottish Horse and then served in the Black Watch (Royal Highlanders) before being commissioned into the 15th Bn. the Loyal North Lancs. James first entered the war in the Balkans on the 18 May 1915 and was

killed in action on the 22 Mar 1918 still only aged 25. His death is recorded on the Pozieres Memorial. This memorial commemorates over 14,000 casualties of the United Kingdom and 300 of the South African Forces who have no known grave.
James' medals were returned to the War Ministry in 1922 and were re-issued later that year. The reason given was simply "Commissioned". Correspondence on this matter was sent to Mrs A. Buchan of 2 Hay Crescent, Peterhead (Mother).

References:
CWGC Casualty No 1578062
WW1 Medal Card

James BUCHAN

Service No. K/33821. Rank: Stoker 1st Class. Service: RN – HMS Rob Roy.

Born in Peterhead, James was the son of James Buchan and the husband of Eliza W. Buchan of 58 Mary St., Falkirk.

James died of illness on the 16 Feb 1919 during the spanish influenza epidemic. He is buried in the Camelon Cemetery, Stirlingshire.

References:
CWGC Casualty No 2753715

John BUCHAN

Service No: 3050. Rank: Pte. Regiment: 5th Bn. Gordon Highlanders.

John enlisted in Peterhead in Feb 1915. Prior to the war John was a carter in the employment of Messrs James Reid & Sons.

Wounded on the 13 Nov 1916 during the action at Beaumont-Hamel, John died of his wounds on the 15 Nov 1916 aged 34 years. John was evacuated to the Casualty Clearing Stations at Puchevillers and is buried in the nearby British Cemetery.

Upon his death, his daughter of 77 Longate, Peterhead was advised of his death.

References:
CWGC Casualty No 510893

John BUCHAN

Service No: 1356TS. Rank: Trimmer. Service: RNR – HMD Unity III.

John was the son of Mrs Margaret Milne of 4 Port Henry Rd., Peterhead.

On the 10 Oct 1915 aged 19 years old, John drowned off the Unity III. The drifter was used for minesweeping or maintaining submarine nets.

References:
CWGC Casualty No 3033408

Joseph BUCHAN

Service No: 1659. Rank: Pte. Regiment: Royal Army Medical Corps.
Service No: 263149. Rank: Pte. Regiment: 17th Bn. Royal Sussex Regiment.

Joseph was the eldest son of Robert (occ. baker) and Annie Buchan of Skelton St., Peterhead. He was also brother to Maggie, Bessie, Annie, William J. and Robert Buchan.

Joseph joined up in 1914 and first entered the war in Egypt on the 31 Mar 1915 with the RAMC. He later joined the KOSB and then the Royal Sussex Regiment. Twice wounded he died of further wounds on the 23 Aug 1918. He is buried in the Cabaret- Rouge British Cemetery, Souchez near Calais.

References:
CWGC Casualty No 585112

Thomas BUCHAN

Service No: 467040. Rank: Pte. Regiment: 13th Bn. Canadian Infantry (Quebec Regiment).

Thomas was born on the 29 Feb 1880 in Peterhead and was the son of David "Aul Herring Davy" and Jessie (m/s West) Buchan of Buchanhaven, Peterhead. He was also the husband of Christina Buchan of 29 High St., Buchanhaven, Peterhead. Thomas and Christina gave up their greengrocer business to emigrate to Canada. Thomas' siblings included: David "Herring Davy", Joseph, Betsy Ann, Mary, Jessie, Jeanie, Agnes and Harry J. Buchan.

Thomas enlisted on the 23 Jul 1915 in Calgary into the 13th Bn. Canadian Infantry (Quebec Regiment). He died of his wounds less than a year later on the 19 Apr 1916, aged 36. He is buried in the Chester Farm Cemetery near West-Vlaanderen in Belgium.

References:
CWGC casualty No 445831
Attestation Paper
http://www.collectionscanada.gc.ca

William BUCHAN

Service No: 2565DA. Rank: Deckhand.
Service: RNR - HMT Strathrannoch.

William was born on the 6 Aug 1882 and was the husband of Elizabeth Buchan of 34 Hay Crescent, Peterhead.

On the 6 Apr 1917, HMT Strathrannoch, a hired trawler and minesweeper was mined and sunk in the North Sea. William aged 32, perished with 12 other men. His sacrifice is commemorated on the Portsmouth Naval Memorial.

References:
CWGC Casualty No 3040736
www.naval-history.net

William BUCHAN

Service No: 4975TS. Rank: Trimmer.
Service: HMS Magnet and HMT Rose II.

William was the son of James Murdoch Buchan and the husband of Maggie Buchan of 5 Kintore Place, Aberdeen.

HMT Rose II a hired trawler and minesweeper was mined and sunk in the North Channel on the 23 Apr 1917 and all souls were lost, William was 33 years old. His sacrifice is commemorated on the Portsmouth Naval Memorial.

Reference:
CWGC Casualty No 3040737
www.naval-history.net

Alexander BURNETT MM*

Service No: 859378. Rank: Sgt. Regiment: 43rd Bn. Canadian Infantry.

Born in Aberdeenshire on the 16 Jul 1884, Alexander was married to Jessie Burnett of 872 Pine St, Winnipeg, Manitoba.

A one-time resident of Peterhead, Alexander enlisted on the 24 Nov 1915 in Winnipeg. He was killed in action on the 1 Oct 1918. His sacrifice is honoured on the Vimy Memorial. On the opening day of the Battle of Arras, 9 Apr 1917, the four Divisions of the Canadian Corps, fighting side by side for the first time, scored a huge tactical victory in the capture of the 60 metre high Vimy Ridge.

References:
CWGC Casualty No 1565890
The War Book of Turriff & 12 Miles Round: Page 235

James Fyvie BURNETT

Service No: S/13649. Rank: Pte. Regiment: 1st Bn. Gordon Highlanders.

Born in Peterhead, James was the son of John Burnett and Jessie (m/s Thomson) Burnett of 24 Prince St., Peterhead. James was a brother to Jeanie, Jane, Elizabeth, Robina, John, Ivan, Alexander, William and Mary Burnett. Prior to the war James worked as a hairdresser in Marischal St., Peterhead.

James enlisted into the Gordon Highlanders in late 1915, arriving in France in early 1916. He was injured during the Battle of the Somme and died of wounds on the 23 Aug 1916, aged 28. James is buried in the La Neuville British Cemetery, Corbie.

References:
CWGC Casualty No 66618

William John Bruce BURNETT

Service No: 138113. Rank: Pte. Regiment: Machine Gun Corps.

Born on the 4 Apr 1899 in Peterhead, William was the son of Sarah Hay Burnett, who in 1916 married Patrick Geddes of 4 Port Henry Road, Peterhead.

William enlisted in Aberdeen into the MGC and was serving with the 63rd Bde. Machine Gun Corps. R.N. Division, when he died of his wounds on 28 Sep 1918, aged 19 years. William is buried in the Sunken Road Cemetery, Boisleux-St Marc.

Reference:
CWGC Casualty No 284855

James Paterson BUTTERS

Service No: 1312/SA. Rank: Second Hand. Service: RNR – HM Yacht Nairn.

James was the son of James and Agnes (m/s Paterson) Butters of St Monance, Fifeshire and the husband of Barbara Butters of 5 James St., Peterhead. James was the brother to David, Julia and Joseph Butters.

Whilst aboard HM Yacht Nairn James died of illness on the 28 Oct 1918 and he is buried in the Peterhead Constitution Street Cemetery.

References:
CWGC Casualty No 326983

George Angus CARLE

Service No: S/43315. Rank: Pte. Regiment: 1st Bn. Gordon Highlanders.

Born in about 1892 in Peterhead, George was the youngest son of Gordon and Mary Carle of Bloomfield Cottage, South Rd., Peterhead. He had a number of brothers and sisters including; William, Mary Magdaline, Christian and Charles Brichar Carle.

George was killed in action on the 14 Jun 1917 and his death is commemorated on the Arras Memorial. This memorial honours almost 35,000 servicemen from the United Kingdom, South Africa and New Zealand who died in the Arras sector and have no known grave.

References:
CWGC Casualty No 743667

John Hendry CARDNO

Service No: 3199/B. Rank: Seaman. Service: HMS Sirius.

John was born in Peterhead in 1883 and was the son of David Hawthorne and Margaret (m/s Geddes) Cardno of 9 James St., Peterhead. He was also the husband of Mary Jane (m/s Parry) Cardno of 12 Love Lane, Peterhead whom he married in 1907.

John died of illness on the 25 Nov 1914 whilst serving aboard HMS Sirius, an old light battle cruiser. He is buried at St Mary's Cemetery, Shotley near Ipswich, Suffolk.

References:
CWGC Casualty No 397792
Marriage Certificate.

William Leslie CARNEGIE

Service No: 16. Rank: Pte. Regiment: 8th Coy Australian Machine Gun Corps.

Born in Peterhead, William was the son of Robert and Alexandrina Carnegie, of Sunny View, Cairntrodlie, Peterhead. He was educated at Peterhead Academy and became a joiner in the employment of Mr James Tailor, builder, Peterhead.

William served for 3 years in the 5th Bn. Gordon Highlanders before emigrating to Australia in about 1912 where he settled in Albury, NSW. On the 19 Jul 1915 William enlisted into the Australian Imperial Force at Liverpool, NSW and served as a driver in the 30th Bn. AIF.

On the 9 Nov 1915 William embarked on HMAT Beltana bound for Suez. He arrived on the 11 Dec 1915 and was transferred to the 8th Australian Machine Gun Company. Serving at Tel-el-Kebar, he was demoted to the rank of Pte. Six months later, William embarked at Alexandria bound for France aboard the MV Tunisian. He arrived in Marseilles on the 26 Jun 1916 and was killed in action on the 20 Jul 1916 aged 25. William was buried at the ANZAC Cemetery, Sailly-Sur-La-Lys.

References:
CWGC Casualty No 187400
Australian Archives

John CARR

Service No: S/7540. Rank: Pte. Regiment: Gordon Highlanders.
Service No: 302811. Rank: Pte. Regiment: 7th Bn. Royal Scots.
Service No: 28766. Rank: Pte. Regiment: Royal Scots.

Born in Dundee around 1885, John was the son of Alexander and Bridget (m/s Chalmers) Carr. In 1915, whilst posted to Peterhead, John met and married Mary Eliza Simpson of the Old Ropeworks, Peterhead. John and Mary became the parents of at least two sons.

John fought at Gallipoli from 11 Aug 1915 before being killed in action in Flanders on the 23 Aug 1918. His sacrifice is honoured on the Vis-En-Artois Memorial which bears the names of over 9,000 men who fell in Picardy and Artois, between the Somme and Loos, and who have no known grave.

References:
CWGC Casualty No 1740815
Marriage Certificate.

William R. CASSIE

Service No: S/8338. Rank: Pte. Regiment: 2nd Bn. Gordon Highlanders.

Born in Longside, William enlisted into the Gordon Highlanders in London.

He went to France on 1 May 1915 and died on the 25 Sep 1915. He was awarded the 1914-15 Star along with the British War and Victory Medals. His sacrifice is honoured on the Loos Memorial which commemorates over 20,000 officers and men who have no known grave, who fell in the area from the River Lys to Grenay.

References:
CWGC Casualty No 729429

James CHALMERS

Service No: 6431. Rank: Pte. Regiment: 1st/5th Bn Gordon Highlanders.
Service No: 292570. Rank: LCpl. Regiment: 1st/5th Bn. Gordon Highlanders.

James (aka Jim) was born in 1898 in Peterhead and was the eldest son of QMS James Chalmers of the Gordon Highlanders and Mrs Chalmers of The Cottages, HM Convict Prison, Peterhead. Prior to the outbreak of hostilities, James was in the employment of Mr Charles Bruce, Chapel St., Peterhead.

James enlisted in Aberdeen in Jan 1916 and was killed during the Battle of Buzancy on the 28 Jul 1918. He is laid to rest at the Raperie British Cemetery, Villemontoire.

References:
CWGC Casualty No 297675
Buchan Observer Article 6 Aug 1918

John Barron CHALMERS

Service No: S/40061. Rank: LCpl. Regiment: 2nd Bn. Gordon Highlanders.

Son of Alexander and Isabella Chalmers of 63 Kirk St., Peterhead, John was the brother to Mary J., Lizzie, George and Alexander Chalmers.

John enlisted in Aberdeen and was killed on the 26 Oct 1917 aged 24. He is buried in the Hooge Crater Cemetery.

References:
CWGC Casualty No 457664

Andrew M. CHEYNE

Service No: 13243. Rank: Pte. Regiment: 15th Bn. Highland Light Infantry.

Born in Aberdeen, Andrew was the son of Mrs. J. Forsyth of 12 Back St., Peterhead. As a carriage driver in Glasgow, he enlisted into the HLI.

Andrew first entered the war in France on the 23 Nov 1915, but died of his wounds on the 17 Dec 1917 at the Mendingham Field Hospital and is buried in the nearby Mendinghem Military Cemetery. Mendinghem, like Dozinghem and Bandagehm, were the popular names given by the troops to the group of casualty clearing stations.

Reference:
CWGC Casualty No 437137

Alfred CHISHOLM*

Service No: 9369. Rank: Pte. Regiment: 1st/5th Bn. Kings Own Scottish Borderers. Service No: 201728. Rank: Pte. Regiment: 1st/5th Bn. Kings Own Scottish Borderers.

Born in Peterhead, Alfred was the youngest son of Alexander and Susan (m/s Carle) Chisholm of 38 Cassilliss Rd., Maybole, Ayrshire.

Whilst serving with the Egyptian Expeditionary Force in Palestine, Alfred died of his wounds on the 16 Dec 1917. His death is recorded on the Jerusalem Memorial which commemorates the 3,300 Commonwealth servicemen who died during the First World War in operations in Egypt or Palestine and who have no known grave.

References:
CWGC Casualty No 1644690

Roderick CHISHOLM

Service No: 11396. Rank: LCpl. Regiment: 2nd Bn. Royal Scots.

Born in Inverness, Roderick was the son of Roderick Chisholm a prison officer at Peterhead Prison. Prior to joining the Royal Scots he worked at the Buchan Observer newspaper in Peterhead where he was remembered as an amiable and kindly lad.

On the 11 Aug 1914, Roderick was one of the first to be sent to France with the BEF earning himself the 1914 Star. He fell barely a month later on the 13 Sep 1914, aged only 20 years old. His sacrifice is detailed on the La Ferte-Sous-Jouarre Memorial. This memorial commemorates nearly 4,000 officers and men of the British Expeditionary Force who died in Aug, Sep and the early part of Oct 1914 and who have no known grave.

References:
CWGC Casualty No 878099
Buchan Observer 20 Oct 14

Alexander J. CHRISTIE*

Service No: 202375. Rank: Pte. Regiment: 2nd Bn. Gordon Highlanders.

Born in Peterhead and a resident of Downiehills, Peterhead, Alexander was killed in action on the 2 Apr 1917 during the Battle of Arras and the location of his grave is not known. Andrew's sacrifice is recorded on the Arras Memorial which commemorates almost 35,000 servicemen from the United Kingdom, South Africa and New Zealand who died in the Arras sector between the spring of 1916 and 7 Aug 1918.

References:
CWGC Casualty No 744363
1919 Peterhead Roll of Honour.

Alexander CLARK MC

Rank: Lt (Quartermaster). Regiment: 9th Bn. Seaforth Highlanders.

Alexander was the husband of Martha J. Clark, of Sandison's Buildings, High St., Alness, Ross-shire and the son of Alexander Clark, railwayman, of 84 Queen St., Peterhead.

Alexander was a profession soldier who had served for 27 years in the British Army. Prior to the war he was the drill instructor at the Alness Barracks. He had served in Sudan, South Africa, and India. During the Greek/Turkish War he raised a party of occupation on Crete. In the Sudan, Alexander fought at Atbara, Omdurman and was highly decorated during the relief of Khartoum. In India, Alexander fought in the Frontier battles. He was awarded the Military Cross for bravery before he died of wounds on the 13 Apr 1918 aged 46 and is buried in the Haringhe (Bandaghem) Military Cemetery.

References:
CWGC Casualty No 93616
Buchan Observer Article 30 Apr 1918

David CLARK

Service No: 3/6714. Rank: Pte. Regiment: 1st Bn. Gordon Highlanders.

Born at Sandyford, Lanarkshire in 1879, David was the son of William and Elizabeth (aka Jeannie),(m/s Cheyne) Clark of

Aberdeen. David married Alexandrina Mabel Hepburn on the 28 Oct 1914 in Aberdeen whilst on special leave from the 3rd Gordon Highlanders. David and Alexandrina lived at 26 Balmoor Terrace, Peterhead.

David enlisted in Aberdeen on the 31 Aug 1914 and arrived in France on the 3 Aug 1915 then on the strength of the 1st Bn. He was killed in action only 11 days later on the 14 Aug 1915. David is buried in the Chester Farm Cemetery which was the name given to a farm about 1 Km south of Blauwepoort Farm, on the road from Zillebeke to Voormezeele.

References:
CWGC Casualty No 445850
Marriage Certificate
Service Record

George William CLUBB*

Service No: 2960. Rank: Pte. Regiment: 1st/4th Bn. Gordon Highlanders.

Born in Aberdeen on the 16 Mar 1895, George was the son of William (Police Sgt) and Mary (m/s Godsman) Clubb of 34 Thistle St., Aberdeen. George was also the grandson of Mrs Clubb of Coplandhill, Peterhead. He was the brother of James G., Elizabeth B., Alexander F. and Jane May Clubb.

George enlisted in Aberdeen and arrived in France on the 26 Mar 1915. He died of his wounds on the 11 Sep 1916 aged only 21 years. George is buried in the Cite Bonjean Military Cemetery, Armentieres which was used by field ambulances and fighting units until Apr 1918. The cemetery now contains 2,132 Commonwealth burials of the First World War.

References:
CWGC Casualty No 275975

James CLYNE MM*

Service No: 2619. Rank: Pte. Regiment: 5th Bn. Gordon Highlanders.
Service No: 240690. Rank: LCpl. Regiment: 5th Bn. Gordon Highlanders.

Born around 1896 in Peterhead, James was the 2nd son of David and Jane J. (m/s Watson) Clyne of Auchtygall, Peterhead. He was the brother of Mary, David, Amelia, Jane and William Clyne.

James enlisted in Peterhead and after training in England he left for France on the 2 May 1915. James was killed in action on the

17 May 1917 and his body was never found. His sacrifice is recorded on the Arras Memorial which commemorates almost 35,000 servicemen from the United Kingdom, South Africa and New Zealand who died in the Arras sector and have no known grave.

References:
CWGC Casualty No 744883
1901 Census

James COCKBURN

Service No: S/31914. Rank: Pte. Regiment: 7th Bn. Queen's Own Cameron Highlanders.

Born in Peterhead, James was the son of James and Mary Cockburn of Roselyn Calt, Balmoor Terrace, Peterhead. He was also the brother of Mary B.M. Cockburn.

James enlisted in Aberdeen and at the time of his death was attached to the Lovat Scouts. He fell on the 28 Mar 1918, aged 19 years old. James was amongst the 35,000 allied servicemen who died in the Arras Sector between the spring of 1916 and the 7 Aug 1918 who have no known grave.

References:
CWGC Casualty No 744932

Arthur Hamilton COLLYER

Service No: 2661. Rank: Pte. Regiment: 1st/5th Bn. Gordon Highlanders.
Rank: 2Lt. Regiment: 5th Bn. Gordon Highlanders (Territorial Force).

Born in 1892, Arthur was the son of Arthur Hamilton and Anna Bella (m/s Gray) Collyer, of Dollar. He was also the younger brother of Gertrude, Elizabeth and Sylvia Collyer.

Arthur went to France on the 3 May 1915 where he was promoted to LCpl. He was then commissioned into the 5th Bn. Gordon Highlanders (TF) on the 16 Jul 1916. Arthur was seriously wounded at Athies which was captured by the 9th (Scottish) Division on the 9 Apr 1917. Arthur later died of his wounds on the 23 Apr 1917 aged 25, and is buried in the Athies Communal Cemetery Extension.

His medals were forwarded to his mother in 1922 who was then living at 6 Church St, Rhyl, North Wales.

References:
CWGC Casualty No 256844

James COOK

Service No: 6451DA. Rank: Deckhand.
Service: HMT Clifton.

The son of John and Alexina Cook of
Pulteneytown, Wick, James was also the
husband of Mary Mitchell Cook of 28 Maiden
St. Peterhead and later of A4, Boddam. He
left a widow and a family of six.

On the 18 Feb 1917, HMT Clifton was
sweeping at the entrance to Cork harbour in
Ireland when there was a massive explosion
and the ship sank in seconds. She had struck
one of the very mines she was trying to
clear, and with no watertight compartments
and cemented bulkheads she would have
sunk very quickly. James lost his life that day
aged 34. His name can be found on the
Portsmouth Naval Memorial.

References:
CWGC Casualty No 3040817

John COOPER

Service No: 6/4014. Rank: Pte. Regiment:
2nd Bn. Canterbury Regiment, NZEF.

John was born in Peterhead, the son of
Robert Cooper of South Balmoor, Peterhead.
He was one of three brothers who fought in
the war. John had emigrated to New Zealand
in 1909 where he became a farm manager.

John was killed on the 21 Sep 1916 but his
death was not reported until the 8 Oct 1916.
His death is commemorated on the
Caterpillar Valley (New Zealand) Memorial.
This memorial commemorates more than
1,200 officers and men of the New Zealand
Division who died in the battles of the
Somme in 1916, and whose graves are not
known.

John's brother William Cooper, served with
the NZEF and despite being wounded in 1917
he survived the war.

References:
CWGC Casualty No 1463050
Buchan Observer 1916

Alexander CORDINER

Service No: 3178C. Rank: Deckhand.
Service: RNR – HMS Bulwark.

Born in Peterhead in 1886 and married to
Margaret Barbara Jane Stephen. Alexander
was the father of David Stephen, Jeanie
Buchan and George Smith McGee Cordiner.

On the 26 Nov 1914, HMS Bulwark was
moored at No.17 Buoy, Kethole Reach off
Sheerness in the River Medway, loading
ammunition from supply boats alongside.
Without warning she blew up at 0753 with
"an appalling explosion... when the smoke
cleared she had entirely disappeared".
Sabotage was originally suspected. That day
792 lives were lost - 50 officers, 738 ratings
and 4 canteen staff. Alexander was one of a
number of Peterhead men killed that day. His
death is honoured on the Portsmouth Naval
Memorial.

References:
CWGC No Casualty No 2870897
www.naval-history.net

David CORDINER

Service No: 5155DA. Rank: Deckhand.
Service: RNR - HMD Lily Reaich.

David was born in Boddam on the 21 Apr
1892, the son of Alexander and Isabella
Cordiner, later of 67 St. Peter St., Peterhead
and the brother of Alexander Cordiner (1885
– 1923).

Having joined the service in Mar 1915, David
was lost when the Lily Reaich, a hired net
drifter was mined and sank in the Adriatic off
Durazzo on the 25 Feb 1916. David was one
of a crew of ten that perished that day. He
was aged 23 years and his death is
commemorated on the Portsmouth Naval
Memorial.

References:
CWGC Casualty No 2876284

Thomas CORDINER*

Service No: S/43072. Rank: LCpl. Regiment:
2nd Bn. Gordon Highlanders.

Born in Peterhead in 1897, Thomas was the
eldest son of John and Margaret (m/s
Gordon) Cordiner of Dens, Peterhead. He
was also the brother of Margaret, George and
Helen Jane Lind Cordiner.

As a Territorial, he volunteered at the
outbreak of war in 1914. He went to France
in the summer of 1915 but was then
seriously wounded. In early 1917 he
returned to the front and was killed on the 7
Oct 1917. His sacrifice is recorded on the
Tyne Cot Memorial which bears the names of
almost 35,000 officers and men whose
graves are not known.

Thomas was awarded the Territorial Force

War Medal in addition to the Victory and British War Medals.

References:
CWGC Casualty No 841352

John George COWAP

Service No: 4642/TS. Rank: Trimmer. Service: RNR - HMS Whitehill.

John was serving aboard HMS Whitehill, a hired drifter when he died of illness on the 7 Mar 1919. His death is honoured on the Peterhead Memorial.

Reference:
CWGC Casualty No 326984

James COWE

Rank: Engineer. Service: RNR.

James was born in Peterhead in 1888 the son of David and Helen (m/s Noble) Cowe. He was the brother of Ellen (b.1881), William (b.1881) and Charles (b.1891) Cowe. As his father had been previously married to Jessie Strachan - he was also half-brother to Andrew (b.1860), David (b.1862), John (b.1864) and Barbara (b.1866) Cowe.

James was married to Jessie Ann Bruce when he died of illness on the 21 Dec 1919 at 4 Great Stuart St. Peterhead.

Peter COWIE*

Service No: 3322. Rank: Pte. Regiment: 1st/5th Bn. Gordon Highlanders.

Peter was the 5th son of Robert Cowie (better known as Fowlie) of Blackhills, Peterhead and then of 17 St. Andrew St., Peterhead.

Peter enlisted in Peterhead and was killed by a mine explosion on the 26 Mar 1916 aged only 17 years. His body was one of the very few recovered that day. Peter is buried in the Maroeuil British Cemetery which was begun by the 51st Highland Division when the Commonwealth Forces took over the Arras front in Mar 1916. Almost half of the graves are those of Highland Territorials.

References:
CWGC Casualty No 120715
Buchan Observer 11 Apr 1916

James CRAIB

Service No: 2583 (originally 2583/5). Rank: LCpl. Regiment: 5th Bn. Gordon Highlanders.

James was the son of Mrs Milne, Meldrum Bldgs, New Byth and the husband of Mrs Craib of 4 St Peter St., Peterhead. He left two children and his occupation was listed as a carter in the employ of Mr James Reid, carting contractor.

James enlisted in Peterhead into the Gordon Highlanders during Nov 1914. He arrived in France on the 2 May 1915 and was killed six weeks later on the 17 Jun 1915 aged only 22. He died at Festubert and his sacrifice is commemorated on the Le Touret Memorial. The Memorial in Le Touret Military Cemetery, Richebourg-l'Avoue, is one of those memorials that were erected by the Commonwealth War Graves Commission to record the names of the officers and men who fell in the Great War and whose graves are not known.

References:
The War Book of Turriff & 12 Miles Round: Page 180
CWGC Casualty No 1559566
Buchan Observer: Photo

Robert CRAIG

Service No: S/18121. Rank: Pte. Regiment 1st Bn. Gordon Highlanders.

The son of Robert and Helen (m/s Main) Craig, Robert was also the husband of Mary (m/s MacPherson) Craig of 24 Maiden St., Peterhead. They had three children together and lived at 86 High St., Stonehaven. He was brother to Isabella, William, George, Jessie and Mary Craig. For the ten years prior to the war, Robert worked for Mr James Reid, carting contractor, Peterhead.

Robert was killed in action on the 28 Nov 1917, aged 32 and is buried in the Ecoust Military Cemetery, Ecoust-St. Mein. This military cemetery was begun in Apr 1917 and used by fighting units until Mar 1918.

References:
CWGC Casualty No 316877

Robert CRAIG

Service No: S/43403. Rank: Pte. Regiment: 1st /5th Bn. Gordon Highlanders.

The son of James and Jessie Craig of 30 Balvernie St., Dufftown, Banffshire, Robert was also a native of Mortlach, Banffshire.

Robert was killed during the Battle of Buzancy on 28 Jul 1918, aged 20. He is buried at the Buzancy Military Cemetery. Robert was awarded the Territorial Force Medal which was awarded to former members of the Territorial Force who served prior to the 30 Sep 1914.

References:
CWGC Casualty No 274811

Alexander Park CRUICKSHANK

Service No: 3533. Rank: Pte. Regiment: 5th Bn. Gordon Highlanders.

Born about 1897 in Peterhead, Alexander (aka Sandy) was the youngest son of Mary Cruickshank of 2 Manse Terrace, Peterhead. Prior to the war, he was engaged as a stone polisher with the Great North of Scotland Granite Company.

Alexander joined the Colours in the summer of 1915. Whilst serving with the Gordon Highlanders he was killed on the 13 Nov 1916 when the 51st Highland Division suffered heavy losses during the capture of Beaumont-Hamel. Aged only 19, Alexander is buried in the Mailly Wood Cemetery Mailly-Maillet.

References:
CWGC Casualty No 111318

James CRUICKSHANK

Service No: 5/20000. Rank: Rifleman. Regiment: 1st Bn. Royal Irish Rifles.

Born in Peterhead, James was the son of John and Margaret Jane Cruickshank of 2 Brickfield Cottages, Londonderry and the brother of William John Cruickshank of 6 Baronet Street, Londonderry. In civilian life James was a cooper in the employment of Messrs, Ballintine, Strand Road, Londonderry.

James joined up in Aug 1917 in Londonderry, N.Ireland. He had been at the front for only a month when he was killed in action on the 7 May 1918, aged 18. James is buried in the Bard Cemetery in Belgium.

References:
CWGC Casualty No 439894

Robert CRUICKSHANK

Service No: S/24008. Rank: Pte. Regiment: 7th Bn. Seaforth Highlanders.

Robert was born in Peterhead; lived in Ellon and enlisted in Aberdeen.

Formerly a member of the Territorial Reserve Bn. (Irish Reserve), Robert enlisted into the Seaforth Highlanders. He died during the attack on the village of Kemmel and the adjoining hill, Mont Kemmel. This was the scene of fierce fighting in the latter half of Apr 1918, in which both Commonwealth and French forces were engaged. Robert died on the 19 Apr 1918 and is buried in the Klein-Vierstraat British Cemetery.

References:
CWGC Casualty No 455353
Buchan Observer Article 6 Aug 1918

Stephen CURRIE

Service No: 2957/5. Rank: Pte. Regiment: 5th Bn. Gordon Highlanders.
Service No: 240873. Rank: Pte. Regiment: 5th Bn. Gordon Highlanders.

Born and enlisted in Peterhead, Stephen was the son of James and Isabella (m/s Jaffrey) Currie of Rora, near Peterhead and then of 179, Hardgate, Aberdeen. He was the younger brother of Williamina, Jessie Ann, James J., Sarah Kennedy, Isabella and Elizabeth Currie.

Stephen arrived in France on the 21 Aug 1915 and was awarded the 1914-15 Star. He was killed in action at Ypres on the 30 Sep 1917 (or on a date thereafter), aged 21. Stephen's sacrifice is commemorated on the Tyne Cot Memorial which bears the names of almost 35,000 officers and men whose graves are not known.

References:
CWGC Casualty No 842149
Buchan Observer Article Jul 1918

John Smith DALGARNO

Service No: L/7286. Rank: Bdr. Regiment: A Bty Royal Field Artillery, 174th Bde.

Born in Peterhead and enlisted in Aberdeen, John was the son of Alexander and Lydia Joyner Dalgarno of 6 Weaver's Lane, Peterhead. He was also the brother of Flora Dalgarno.

John was killed on the 10 Jun 1917, aged 22, and he is buried at the New Military Cemetery, Vlamertinghe (now Vlamertinge).

References:
CWGC Casualty No 142186

Alexander James McKenzie DAVIDSON

Service No: 2703/C. Rank: Seaman. Service: RNR - HMS Bulwark.

Alexander was born Alexander James McKenzie Grieg on the 5 Nov 1884 in Crooked Lane, Peterhead. He was the son of Elizabeth Grieg who later married William Davidson, of Peterhead. In 1905, Alexander married Alice Davidson of Ugie St., Buchanhaven, Peterhead.

On the 26 Nov 1914, HMS Bulwark was moored at No.17 Buoy Kethole Reach off Sheerness in the River Medway. Whilst loading ammunition she blew up without warning at 0753.

Aged 29, Alexander was one of a number of Peterhead men killed that day. His death is listed on the Portsmouth Naval Memorial.

References:
CWGC Casualty No 2870962
Birth Certificate
Marriage Certificate

Alexander DAVIDSON

Service No: 3/3553. Rank: Pte. Regiment: 1st Bn. Gordon Highlanders.

Born in Peterhead, Alexander was the son of George and Helen Davidson of 4 Windmill St., Peterhead. Alexander's brother William Davidson was killed in Mar 1918.

He enlisted in Aberdeen and arrived in France on the 3 Jan 1915 earning himself the 1914-15 Star. Alexander fell during the major offensive of the 13 Nov 1916 at Beaumont-Hamel. His sacrifice is recorded on the Thiepval memorial which commemorates 72,000 casualties of the Somme who have

no known grave.

References:
CWGC Casualty No 755640

Arthur James DAVIDSON

Service No: 14709. Rank: Pte. Regiment: 14th (Fife and Forfar Yeo.) Bn. Black Watch (Royal Highlanders).

Born in Peterhead, Arthur was the son of Patrick and Jemima Shewan Davidson. Arthur enlisted into the Black Watch (Royal Highlanders) in Aberdeen.

Arthur died of his wounds on the 30 Dec 1917 aged 25, in Egypt and is now buried in the Ramleh War Cemetery, Israel. The cemetery was begun by the medical units, but some graves were brought in later from the battlefields and from Latron, Sarona and Wilhema Military Cemeteries.

References:
CWGC Casualty No 652206
Aberdeen City Roll of Honour: North Constitution St

Bailie Patrick DAVIDSON

Service No: GS/74828. Rank: Pte. Regiment: 11th Bn. Royal Fusiliers.

Born in Peterhead in 1899, Baillie was the youngest son of Mrs Lockhart of 9 Crown St., Aberdeen, and the grandson of Mrs Webster of Merchant St. Peterhead.

Baillie joined the Colours in Nov 1917 when he was only 18 years old. He had three brothers who were also serving their country; Frank in the Gordon Highlanders, Alexander in the RFA and Douglas who sailed aboard a minesweeper.

Other sources state that Bailie served with the former 41st Territorial Rerserve Bn (Service No 15471). Little is known of Bailie's service record other than he was killed on the 30th Aug 1918 and is buried in the Combles Communal Cemetery Extension.

References:
CWGC Casualty No 591701
Aberdeen City Roll of Honour: 9 Crown St;

Douglas DAVIDSON

Service No: 2899/ST. Rank: Trimmer. Service: RNR – HMS Halcyon.

According to the list of naval casualties,

Douglas was born on 29 Feb 1887 (no such date) in Peterhead and is recorded as having a sister; Mrs B. Willox of 41 Windmill St, Peterhead.

Douglas accidently drowned off Lowestoft whilst serving aboard HMS Halcyon on the 13 Mar 1917, aged 31 years. The Halcyon was an ex-torpedo gunboat and the Senior Naval Officer North Sea Fisheries boat. Douglas is buried in Peterhead.

References:
CWGC Casualty No 327012
Buchan Observer

George P.W. DAVIDSON

Service No: 9971. Rank: Pte. Regiment: 1st Bn. Gordon Highlanders.

Born in Peterhead and enlisted in Aberdeen, George was the son of David Davidson of 6 Backgate, Peterhead. Prior to enlistment, he was in the employment of Messrs A. Brown & Co., Broad St. Peterhead.

George entered theatre on the 13 Aug 1914, making him one of the first soldiers to join the BEF in France. He became a prisoner of war and George died, still a POW on the 27 Oct 1918 aged 30. He is buried at the Niederzwehren Cemetery in Germany. The cemetery was begun by the Germans in 1915 for the burial of prisoners of war.

Following the War, the UK War Department engaged in correspondence with a Miss L. Mair, Burnside, Cruden by Hatton, Aberdeenshire about the disposal of George's medals.

References:
CWGC Casualty No 903205
Buchan Observer Article 7 May 1918

James Collie DAVIDSON*

Service No: 4825. Rank: Pte. Regiment: Argyll and Sutherland Highlanders.
Service No: 326535. Rank: Pte. Regiment: Argyll and Sutherland Highlanders.
Service No: 235116. Rank: Pte. Regiment: 8th Bn. Seaforth Highlanders.

James was the son of Mr and Mrs John Davidson of 28 Arlington St., Glasgow and was formerly from Peterhead.

James fell on the 31 Jul 1917 aged 21 and has no known grave. His sacrifice is recorded on the Ypres (Menin Gate) Memorial which records tens of thousands of soldiers who fell in Flanders who have no known grave.

References:
CWGC Casualty No 1609170

James Masson DAVIDSON

Service No: 2528/5. Rank: Pte. Regiment: 5th Bn. Gordon Highlanders.
Service No: 240637. Rank: Pte. Regiment: 1st / 5th Bn. Gordon Highlanders.

James born in Peterhead in 1897 and was the eldest son of Mr James and Margaret Allan (m/s Masson) Davidson of 2 Tanfield Place, Peterhead. He was brother to Bella, Barbara, George, Allan, Ann Elizabeth, John Duke and Gladys Masson Davidson.

James lied about his age and was underage when he enlisted into the Gordon Highlanders. He arrived in France on the 2 May 1915 earning himself the 1914-15 Star. After being wounded, James was sent home to Peterhead to convalesce. His mother Maggie, threatened to go to the authorities to report him for being underage. James said he would never speak to her again if she did. After returning to the front he was again wounded, this time during the High Wood offensive of the 30/31 Jul 1917. He died of a gunshot wound on the 1 Aug 1917 at the 61st Casualty Clearing Station. James is buried at the Dozinghem Military Cemetery near Westvleteren, Belgium.

Three years after the war, his mother received a letter from James which had been written sometime during 1916 or 1917 and was not delivered. In the letter, James describes himself as being in the "Pink" and suggests that he may soon be moving up to the front.

References:
CWGC Casualty No 620377
Mr Jim Davidson (nephew) supplied additional material

James S. DAVIDSON

Rank: Able Seaman. Service: Mercantile Marine SS Ballogie.

The son of John and Sophia Davidson of 102

Great Western Rd., Aberdeen, James was born at Peterhead.

The SS Ballogie was carrying slag from Middlesbrough to Dunkirk when she was torpedoed without warning on the 9 Nov 1917 off the North Yorkshire coast. An enormous explosion destroyed the ship with the result of thirteen of the nineteen crew being killed including James, aged only 18. His sacrifice is recorded on the Tower Hill Memorial, London. The First World War section of the Tower Hill Memorial commemorates almost 12,000 Mercantile Marine casualties who have no grave but the sea.

The SS Ballogie was owned by J. & A. Davidson of Aberdeen and the Master was also killed on that day.

References:
CWGC Casualty No 2978248

Russell Watt DAVIDSON

Service No: 2528/5. Rank LSgt, Regiment: 5th Bn. Gordon Highlanders.
Service No: 240064. Rank: Sgt. Regiment: Gordon Highlanders attached to the 1st/2nd Bn. Kings African Rifles.

Born in Peterhead at 15 Chapel St., Russell was the eldest son of David and Williamina Salmon (m/s Watt) Davidson later of 6 Backgate, Peterhead and then of 73 Queen St., Peterhead. Russell had at least one sister and one brother; Williamina Salmon Watt Davidson and George Davidson.

Russell enlisted in Peterhead and arrived in France on the 2 May 1915 subsequently being awarded the 1914-15 Star. After being detached to the Kings African Rifles, James died on the 1 Oct 1917 aged 23, in East Africa. He is now buried in the Dar-es-Salaam War Cemetery in Tanzania.

Russell's Brother George was taken prisoner and survived the war to become an air-raid warden in Peterhead during the next war.

References:
CWGC Casualty No 898060

Thomas James DAVIDSON

Service No: S/43279. Rank: Cpl. Regiment: 1st Bn. Gordon Highlanders.

Thomas was the youngest son of Thomas (occ cooper) and Ann (m/s Lamond) Davidson of 26 North St., Peterhead. He had a brother and a sister; named Alexander and

Barbara Jane Davidson.

Thomas died of his wounds on the 28 Sep 1917, aged 22 at the Dozinghem Military Hospital and is buried nearby in the Dozinghem Military Cemetery.

References:
CWGC Casualty No 620379

William DAVIDSON

Service No: 2532. Rank: Pte. Regiment: 5th Bn. Gordon Highlanders.

Born and enlisted in Peterhead, William was the son of George and Annie Davidson of 6½ North St., Peterhead. He was also married to Christine (m/s Clark) Davidson and they had two children. By trade, William was a slater in the employment of Mr Greig, slater, Peterhead. William was also the brother of Andrew, George, Maggie, Janet and Annie Davidson.

William arrived in France in Aug 1915 after joining up the previous November. On the 30 Jul 1916, William having been promoted to Cpl, volunteered to assist to carry the wounded from the battlefield. While engaged in this work a shell burst nearby killing him. Aged 27, the location of his grave is unknown and his sacrifice is commemorated on the Thiepval Memorial.

William's wife Christine was to die on the 6 Jul 1917 in Peterhead, aged 28.

References:

CWGC Casualty No 755689
Aberdeen City Roll of Honour: 71 King St; Peterhead

William DAVIDSON

Service No: 2419/ES. Rank: Engineman.
Service: RNR – HMS Nairn

The only surviving son of Mrs Davidson of 44 Kirk St., Peterhead, William was the husband of Jemima Davidson of 25 St Andrew St., Peterhead.

William was an engineer aboard the drifter "Guide Me" when he died of influenza on the 12 Dec 1918 at 25 St Andrew St., aged 39. He was buried in Peterhead Cemetery.

References:
CWGC Casualty No 326985

William Buchan DAVIDSON

Service No: 2580. Rank: LCpl. Regiment: 5th Bn. Gordon Highlanders.

William, known locally as William Marshall, was the son of Mrs Bella Willcox, of 4, Windmill St., Peterhead.

William died at Gadle Braes, Peterhead on the 11 Jul 1915 and is buried in Peterhead Cemetery.

References:
CWGC Casualty No 327013

William J. DAVIDSON DCM

Service No: 6499. Rank: CSM. Regiment: 2nd Bn. Royal Scottish Fusiliers.

Husband of Annie Davidson of 16 Chestnut Row, Aberdeen, William was born in Peterhead and he enlisted in Aberdeen.

William was killed in action on the 17 May 1915 and his sacrifice is honoured on the Le Touret Memorial which commemorates over 13,400 British soldiers who were killed in this sector of the Western Front from the beginning of Oct 1914 to the eve of the Battle of Loos in late Sep 1915 and who have no known grave.

References:
CWGC Casualty No 1559844
Aberdeen City Roll of Honour

William Lamb DAVIDSON

Service No: 240773. Rank: Pte. Regiment: 7th Bn. Gordon Highlanders.

Born and enlisted in Peterhead, William was the second son of George and Helen Davidson of 4 Windmill St., Peterhead. Before the war he was a book keeper at the Peterhead Gut Factory.

William was killed in action on the 26 Mar 1918 and has no known grave. His brother Alexander had been killed eighteen months earlier at Beaumont-Hamel on the 13 Nov 1916.

William's sacrifice is honoured on the Arras Memorial which commemorates almost 35,000 servicemen from the United Kingdom, South Africa and New Zealand who died between the spring of 1916 and the 7 Aug 1918

References:
CWGC Casualty No 746747

William DICK*

Service No: 7552. Rank: Pte. Regiment: 11th Bn. Royal Fusiliers.

Born around 1881, William was the eldest son of John Dick late of Peterhead. He was also the husband of Mrs M.J. Dick of 148 Maygrove Rd. West Hampstead, London.

Educated at Peterhead Academy, William enlisted into the Middlesex Regiment at the outbreak of war. Following the re-organisation of the London Brigade, William found himself serving in the 11th Bn. Royal Fusiliers.

William arrived in France on the 26 Jul 1915 but died of his wounds at the Orpington Military Hospital in Kent on the 3 Oct 1916. He is buried in the Orpington (All Saints) Churchyard Extension.

References:
Buchan Observer 10 Oct 1916
CWGC Casualty No 367948

Cecil Barron DICKIE

Service No: 7036. Rank: Driver: Regiment 1st Bn. HB RFA (Reserve).
Rank: 2Lt. Regiment: Black Watch (Royal Highlanders).
Rank: Lt. Service: 107 Sqn Royal Flying Corps.

Cecil was the son of John Barron and Christina (m/s Bruce) Dickie of 51 Queen St., Peterhead. He was also the brother of Ella Agnes and John Alec Dickie and also the half-brother of John A. Dickie.

Cecil joined the 1st Bn HB RFA (Reserve) as a driver, aged 17. When he reached 18 years old he was commissioned into the Black Watch (Royal Highlanders) and arrived in France on the 22 Aug 1916. Later Cecil joined the Royal Flying Corps and was killed in action on the 18 Jul 1918 aged a mere 20 years.

Cecil's sacrifice is commemorated on both the Arras Memorial as a Black Watch (Royal Highlanders) soldier and the Arras Flying Services Memorial.

References:
CWGC Casualty No 747303
Buchan Observer 21 Jul 1918

Isaac DICKSON

Service No: S/17425. Rank: Cpl. Regiment: 1st Bn. Gordon Highlanders.

Born in Fife and enlisted in Inverness, Isaac was the nephew of Mrs Buchan of 17 Gladstone Rd., Peterhead. Prior to joining up he was in the employment of J.B. Dickie & Co, Alexandra Sawmills, Peterhead.

Issac fell on the 4 May 1918 and is commemorated on the Loos Memorial. This memorial commemorates over 20,000 officers and men who have no known grave.

References:
CWGC Casualty No 2941209
Buchan Observer 28 May 1918

Robert Morrison William DOUGLAS

Rank: Pte. Regiment: RAMC.
Rank: 2Lt. Regiment: 5th Bn. Gordon Highlanders.

Born in Old Deer, Robert was the third son of Alexander and Margaret Douglas of Victoria Cottage, Boddam and later of 2 St Mary St., Peterhead. He was the brother of Alexander, William, Gertrude, Frederick and Helena Douglas. Robert was employed by Mr Charles Bruce, ironmongers of Peterhead.

In Sep 1914, aged 20, Robert enlisted into the RAMC. He served at Gallipoli before being transferred to the Gordon Highlanders. Robert was commissioned in Mar 1917 and was wounded later that year. Having returned to the front in Feb 1918, Robert was killed in action on the 29 Mar 1918, aged 24 years.

Having no known grave, Robert's sacrifice is commemorated on the Pozieres Memorial.

References:
CWGC Casualty No 1580093
Buchan Observer 19 Apr 1918

Alexander DUELL

Service No: 452. Rank: Pte. Regiment: 2nd Bn. Gordon Highlanders.

Born in Kirkwall, Orkney Islands on the 10 Dec 1891, Alexander was the son of William & Annie (m/s Rendall) Duell of The Square, Burnhaven, Peterhead.

The 1911 Census shows that William and Annie had at least eight children: William, James, Ester, John (who also fell),

Alexander, George, Joan and Alfred.

A professional soldier, Alexander was serving with the 2nd Bn. Gordon Highlanders. At the outbreak of war he accompanied his regiment from Egypt to France, arriving in theatre on the 7 Oct 1914, earning the 1914 Star. Alexander died of his wounds at La Bassee in the 33rd Casualty Clearing Station on the 17 May 1915. His grave is in the Bethune Town Cemetery.

His father, William also served in the regular army before being discharged in 1915 to work as a printer at the Admiralty Works, Peterhead.

Alexander's younger brother John also fell in the conflict.

References:
CWGC Casualty No 62741
Peterhead War Memorial Project
Gordon Highlanders Website
Buchan Observer 18 Jan 1916 Photo.

John DUELL

Service No: 27174. Rank: Pte. Regiment: 17th Bn. Royal Scots (Lothian Regiment).

Born in Peterhead on the 15 May 1896 and standing only 5ft 1¾ inches tall, John was the son of William & Annie (m/s Rendall) Duell of 1 High Street, Burnhaven, Peterhead. Prior to the war, John worked as a farm labourer. John enlisted in Aberdeen on the 28 Jul 15.

John was the brother to William, James, Esther, John, Alexander (who also fell), George, Joan and Alfred Duell.

John's military records are available at the National Archives in London. His conduct sheet paints a picture of an unhappy soldier. The following offences occurred whilst waiting to go to France:

1 Oct 15 Absent from Route March 3 Days FP

26 Oct 15 Failing to get out of bed 2 Days CB
30 Nov 15 Absent from Parade 5 Days CB
4 Dec 15 Absent from Defaulters 5 Days CB
6 Dec 15 Drunk Admonished
9 Dec 15 Refused to obey orders 10 Days FP
27 Dec 15 Absent from 9:30pm till arrested
6pm 29 Dec 15 - 14 Days FP and 3 days loss
of pay

John died of his wounds in Flanders on the 8
Mar 1916 almost exactly a year after his
brother Alexander died of his wounds. His
grave is in the St Vaast Post Military
Cemetery, Richebourge Richebourg-L'avoue.

References:
CWGC Casualty No 569991
Buchan Observer 18 Jan 1916 Page 6. & 21
Mar 1916 Photo.

William Hadden DUFF

Service No: 640/TS(PO). Rank: Trimmer.
Service: RNR – HMS Zaria.

Born in circa 1875, William was the son of
William (occ mason) and Sophia (m/s
Hadden) Duff and was also the husband of
Ruth Bannerman. At the time of his death,
William and Ruth lived at 55 Gerrard St.,
Aberdeen. Listed as a fireman aboard the
minesweeper HMS Zaria, William died in Wick
Harbour on the 29 Oct 1915. Unusually the
manner of his death is not entered on his
death certificate. William is buried in Wick
Cemetery.

References:
CWGC Casualty No 667091
W.H. Duff Death Certificate 043/00 0154

James Alexander DUFFUS*

Service No: 1674. Rank: Pte. Regiment: 5th
Bn. Gordon Highlanders.
Service No: S43069. Rank: Pte. Regiment:
2nd Bn. Gordon Highlanders.

James was born in 1899 in Peterhead, the
son of Charlotte Duffus (later Webster) of
Blackhills, Peterhead.

James joined the 5th Bn. Gordon Highlanders
on the 3 Nov 1913 aged only 14 years old.
However, James' attestation papers states he
was 17 years old. James volunteered for
active service on the 17 Jun 1914 and he
arrived in France on the 30 Jun 1916. He was
then posted to the 2nd Bn. Gordon
Highlanders on the 28 Aug 1916 before being
listed as "missing" nine days later on the 6
Sep 1916. His medals, including the
Territorial Force War Medal were received by

his mother, now Mrs Webster of Stoneyhill,
Cruden, Port Errol, Aberdeenshire.

James' is buried in the Delville-Wood
Cemetery which was made after the
Armistice, when graves were brought in from
small cemeteries, isolated sites, and from the
battlefields.

References:
CWGC Casualty No 549224

James DUGUID

Service No: S/3648. Rank: Pte. Regiment: 1st
Bn. Gordon Highlanders.

James was born in Peterhead in 1888, the
son of John Laing and Janet (Jessie) (m/s
Alexander) Duguid of 23 Windmill St. He was
a brother to Janet A., Elizabeth, John,
Charles A., Isabella, Joseph W., Robert L.
(who also fell), Elspet M., George, Barbara,
Charles A., Joseph, Mary A., Williamina T.,
and Annie W. Duguid. He was formerly a
cooper in the employment of Messrs G. & J.
Donaldson, fishcurers, Peterhead.

Enlisted in Aberdeen, John entered the
French theatre on the 3 Jan 1915. After
being recommended several times for gallant
conduct in the field he was killed in action on
the 20 Feb 1917, aged 29 years of age. His
grave is located in the Faubourg D'amiens
Cemetery, Arras.

References:
CWGC Casualty No 283974

Robert L. DUGUID

Service No: 399/TS. Rank: Stoker. Service:
HMD Ada.

Robert was born on the 13 Oct 1889 the son
of John and Janet (m/s Alexander) Duguid.
Robert was the brother of Janet A., Elizabeth,
John, Charles A., Isabella, Joseph W., James
(who also fell), Elspet M., George, Barbara,
Charles A., Joseph, Mary A., Williamina T.
and Annie W. Duguid.

According to his death certificate, Robert, a
stoker aboard HMD Ada drowned off Kyle of
Lochalsh on the 18 Mar 1917.

References:
Death Certificate
Buchan Observer 1919 Roll of Honour

George William DUNBAR

Service No: 555. Rank: Pte. Regiment: Gordon Highlanders.
Service No: 290010. Rank: Pte. Regiment: 6th Bn. Gordon Highlanders.

Born in Peterhead on the 26 Oct 1896, George was the son of George and Jane (m/s Allardyce) Dunbar of 48 Spital, Aberdeen. He was also the grandson of Mr William Allardyce, shoemaker, Peterhead.
George's brother; Norman James Dunbar also fell in 1918.

George enlisted into the Gordon Highlanders at Banchory and died in France on the 16 Apr 1918, aged 21 years. He is buried in Vieille-Chapelle New Military Cemetery, Lacouture. This cemetery was used by local fighting Units and field ambulances.

References:
CWGC Casualty No 280268
Aberdeen City Roll of Honour: Hopewell Cottage, Banchory

Norman James DUNBAR

Rank: Pte. Regiment: Gordon Highlanders.

Service No: 117055. Rank: Cpl. Regiment: Machine Gun Corps.

Born in Peterhead on the 16 May 1898, Norman was the youngest son of George Buchan & Jane Clark (nee Allardyce) Dunbar of 48 Spital, Aberdeen. He was also the grandson of Mr William Allardyce, shoemaker, Peterhead. Norman was also the brother of George Dunbar who also fell in 1918.

Norman enlisted in Banchory into the Gordon Highlanders and later transferred to the Machine Gun Corps.

Norman was educated at Fraserburgh and Banchory. He was killed in action on the 19 Jul 1918, aged 20 years, and is buried in Meteren Military Cemetery.

References:
CWGC Casualty No 257660
Aberdeen City Roll of Honour: Hopewell Cottage, Banchory.

Alexander Robertson DUNCAN

Service No: 2872S. Rank: Stoker. Service: RNR - HMS Hawke.

Residing in Love Lane, Peterhead, Alexander

was the sole carer for his widowed mother. He also had a sister, Mrs Elsie Thomson of 5 Kintore Place, Aberdeen.

Alexander was about to celebrate his 24th birthday when he was lost. His mother had already despatched a present for his birthday. He did not appear on the list of survivors from HMS Hawke, an old cruiser, torpedoed and sunk by U-9 in the North Sea on the 15 Oct 1914.

References:
CWGC Casualty No 2871027
Buchan Observer 20 Oct 1914

William Charles DUNCAN

Service No: 2747/5. Rank: Pte. Regiment: 5th Bn. Gordon Highlanders.
Service No: 240767. Rank: Pte. Regiment: 5th Bn. Gordon Highlanders.

William was born in Peterhead on the 12 Jul 1886, the son of Elspet Duncan and the husband of Fanny (m/s Stephenson) Duncan of 5 Roanheads, Peterhead. A carter by trade, he was in the employment of Messrs James Reid and Sons. William was one of the first men to enlist in 1914.

Aged 31, William was killed in action at Pilkem Ridge on the 31 Jul 1917 during the 3rd Battle of Ypres, commonly known as the Battle of Passchendaele. He is buried in the New Irish Farm Cemetery, West-Vlaanderen.

References:
CWGC Casualty No 452258
Peoples Journal 25 Aug 1917
Buchan Observer 28 Aug 1917

Henry Fitzgerald DYKER

Service No: 2299. Rank: Pte. Regiment: 2nd/5th Bn. Gordon Highlanders (1st Reserve).

Henry was born at Forgue on the 10 Apr 1895. He was the son of Charles and Eliza Dyker (m/s Paterson), of Sauchen Bush, Buckie. He was a single man and an apprentice gardener at Fyvie Castle.

Henry died of scarlet fever on the 3 Feb 1915 in the Burgh Hospital, Peterhead whilst billeted at 56 Prince St., Peterhead. Records suggest that Henry caught scarlet fever whilst at the Bedford depot and he is buried in the Buckie New Cemetery.

References:
CGWC Casualty No 666924
Death Certificate 232/01 0034
The War Book of Turriff & 12 Miles Round
Page 284

James EDWARDS

Service No: 3/7522. Rank: Rifleman.
Regiment: 6th Bn. Royal Irish Rifles.

Born in Taris Roose, Glasgow, James enlisted in Glasgow but was a resident of Peterhead.

James went to France on the 23 Sep 1915 but died in Mesopotamia on the 6 Jul 1918. He is buried in the Baghdad (North Gate) War Cemetery. The North Gate Cemetery was begun in Apr 1917 and has been greatly enlarged since the end of the First World War by graves brought in from other burial grounds in Baghdad and northern Iraq.

References:
CWGC Casualty No 633315

Morris (Maurice) Webster ELRICK

Service No: Deal/12589(S). Rank: Pte.
Regiments: Royal Marine Labour Corps.

Morris was born in Peterhead on the 22 Mar 1872, the son of John and Christina (m/s Gordon) Elrick of Broad St. Peterhead.

He served at the Dunkerque Depot of the Royal Marine Labour Corps where he died of disease on the 2 Feb 1918. His sacrifice is commemorated at the Aberdeen (Trinity) Cemetery.

References:
CWGC Casualty No 326645
Marine Register 145/MR 0105
Birth Certificate

John Charles ESSLEMONT

Service No: 3196/C. Rank: Seaman. Service:
RNR – HMS Lama.

Born on the 29 Jan 1876 in Peterhead, John was the son of Thomas Marr and Jane Agnes (m/s McGregor) Esslemont of 164 Crown St., Aberdeen. He died as a result of an accident on the 7 Jul 1916 aboard HMS Lama, an armed boarding steamer.

He was originally buried in Sewri Cemetery, Bombay and re-interred in the Kirkee Cemetery in 1960. His sacrifice is commemorated on the Kirkee 1914-1918 Memorial. This memorial commemorates more than 1,800 servicemen and women who died in India during the First World War and who are buried in civil and cantonment cemeteries in India and Pakistan where their graves can no longer be properly maintained.

References:
CWGC Casualty No 1499023

John R. EWEN

Service No: 2820/5. Rank: Pte. Regiment:
5th Bn. Gordon Highlanders.
Service No: 240803. Rank: Pte. Regiment:
1st/5th Bn. Gordon Highlanders.

John was born in Strichen and enlisted in Peterhead. He sailed for France on the 5 Dec 1915 and was killed on the 16 Apr 1917 during the Maroeuil Wood, Fampoux Area engagement. John is buried at the St. Nicolas British Cemetery.

References:
CWGC Casualty No 50925

George Patton FALCONER

Service No: 4931. Rank: Pte. Regiment:
ASC.
Service No: S/9675. Rank: Pte. Regiment:
9th Bn. Northumberland Fusiliers.
Service No: 36721. Rank: Pte. Regiment: 9th Bn. Northumberland Fusiliers.

George was born in Peterhead and was the fourth son of Peter and Jane Falconer of 31 St Peter St., Peterhead. He was also the brother of William, Barbara, Christina, Charles, Helen, Jane and Isabella Falconer. Before the commencement of hostilities, George was employed by Mr John Wilson, baker, Ellis St., Peterhead.

George enlisted in Peterhead and in Apr 1918 was severely injured when he was gassed and medically evacuated to a field hospital. On returning to the front, George died of further wounds on the 25 Oct 1918. George was fatally injured at either the the Battle of the Selle or the Battle of Valenciennes. He is buried in the Awoingt British cemetery which was used by the nearby clearing stations.

A Pension, based on the Attestation Record was claimed for 36721 George P Falconer of the 9th Northumberland Fusiliers.

References:
CWGC Casualty No 536478
Medal Record Card and Service Pension

George FERGUSON

Service No: 2543. Rank: Pte. Regiment: 1st /5th Bn. Gordon Highlanders.
Service No: 240645. Rank: Pte. Regiment: 1st /5th Bn. Gordon Highlanders.

Born in Peterhead, George was the son of George and Mary Dyce Ferguson, of The Cottages, HM Prison, Peterhead.

He enlisted in Peterhead and was killed in action on the 23 Jun 1917, aged 20. George is buried in the Vlamertinghe New Military Cemetery.

References:
CWGC Casualty No 142311
Medal Record Card

Peter FERGUSON

Service No: S/17617. Rank: Pte. Regiment: Gordon Highlanders.
Service No: 138456. Rank: Pte. Regiment: 50th Bn Machine Gun Corps (Infantry).

Born in Mount Foot, Perth, Peter enlisted in Aberdeen and lived in Peterhead. He was the son of John Ferguson, of HM Prison, Peterhead and the husband of Jeannie Florence May (Flora) Uccellotti (formerly Ferguson), of Downiehills, Peterhead and later of 41 St Mary St., Peterhead. Prior to the war, Peter worked as a fireman on the North British Railway.

Peter was killed in action on the 31 Aug 1918 as part of the Advance to Victory campaign. He was still only 20 years old when he died. Peter's sacrifice is commemorated on the Vis-En-Artois Memorial which bears the names of over 9,000 men who fell in the period from the 8 Aug 1918 to the date of the Armistice.

References:
CWGC Casualty No 1742328

Robert William FERGUSON

Rank: Capt. Regiment: 5th Bn Gordon Highlanders.

Robert was born in Peterhead on the 20 Oct 1887 and was the son of Alexander Ferguson of 62 Queen St., Peterhead. An accomplished painter, he was educated at Peterhead Academy. Robert entered Aberdeen University in 1905 and graduated with an M.A. with honours in Mathematics in 1909 and also a further B.Sc., in 1910. He was a keen student of nature and took a special

course of Botany at Oxford University. He gathered valuable material concerning the Flora of Banffshire with a view to its publication. Robert proved himself a very successful teacher, doing good work at Aberlour, Nairn and Sharpe's Institute, Perth. Robert was well-liked Boy Scouts leader.

In Apr 1915, he enlisted in his old College Company, the 4th Bn. Gordon Highlanders and was later commissioned in the 5th Bn. and thereafter was appointed the Musketry Officer. Robert went through his training at Aberdeen, Peterhead and Ripon and then crossed to France in 1916. He took part in the early Somme Battles and was killed in action at Beaumont-Hamel on the 13 Nov 1916. He is buried at Hawthorn Ridge Cemetery No.2 Auchonvillers.

References:
CWGC Casualty No 613323
Aberdeen University Roll of Honour
Buchan Observer 21 Nov 1916

Alexander Canning FINNIE

Service No: 45101. Rank: Spr. Regiment: 3rd Field Coy, Canadian Engineers.

Alexander was born at 4 Stirling Villiage, Boddam on the 20 Dec 1886, the son of Mrs Isabella Chalmers (m/s Carle) Finnie, a domestic servant. He was also the husband of Christian Carle, of Bloomfield Cottage, South Rd, Peterhead (the daughter of Gordon and Mary Carle). Alexander emigrated to Canada where he undertook a number of jobs including a farmer, a baker and a railroad conductor.

He joined the Canadian Engineers on the 23 Sep 1914, at Valcartier in Canada and fought for three years before being killed in action near Passchendaele on the 30 Oct 1917. Alexander is buried at the Vlamertinghe New Military Cemetery. Alexander appears on the Peterhead Memorial and on the nearby Boddam Memorial.

References:
CWGC Casualty No 142317
Birth Certificate 1886, 232/02 0002
Marriage Certificate 1917 232/01 0085
Attestation Paper

Adam Kinghorn FLORENCE

Service No: 185663. Rank: Pte. Regiment Machine Gun Corps.

Adam was born in 1891 in Peterhead, the son of Alexander Allan and Margaret Clark (m/s Kinghorn) Florence. A butcher by trade he was mobilised into the Reserve Brigade on the 9 Feb 1916 aged 24 years old.

Posted to the Machine Gun Corps on the 2 Jul 1918, Adam never made it to France. He was given a Class Z Demobilisation on the 4 Feb 1919 due to ill health. Adam died of tuberculosis on 13 Jul 1920 at 2 Shiprow, Peterhead. Adam does not appear in the Commonwealth War Grave Commission records and the only record of his sacrifice is on the Peterhead War Memorial.

References:
Short Service Attestation Record
Death Certificate, 1920 232/01 0148

William Keith FORBES

Service No: 571. Rank: Pte. Regiment: 5th Bn. Gordon Highlanders.
Service No: 240044. Rank: Pte. Regiment: 5th Bn. Gordon Highlanders.

William was born in Peterhead in 1875, the son of John and Mary (m/s Keith) Forbes and the husband of Isabella Thompson of 6 Charlotte St., Peterhead. Prior to the war, William was employed by Messrs Singer of Peterhead.

He enlisted into the 5th Bn. Gordon Highlanders in Peterhead and entered the French theatre on the 2 May 1915. William was killed in action on the 21 Mar 1918. His sacrifice can be found on the Pozieres Memorial.

He was awarded the 1915 Star, Victory and British Medals which were later returned to the War Department. By 1930, his widow Isabella Forbes had moved to Niagara Falls Ontario, Canada. The medals were disposed of on the 13 Apr 1933. Their son, also named William Keith Forbes crossed into Canada from the USA many times between 1931 and 1937 at Niagara.

References:
CWGC Casualty No 1580971
Medal Record Card
Marriage Certificate 1896, 232/01 0024

Alexander FORMAN

Service No: 2533. Rank: Pte. Regiment: 1st/5th Bn. Gordon Highlanders.

Born in Peterhead, Alexander was the eldest son of Alexander and Jane Forman, of 31 Broad St., Peterhead. Prior to the commencement of hostilities he was employed as a cooper.

Alexander enlisted into the B Coy of the 5th Bn. Gordon Highlanders in Peterhead in Nov 1914. He sailed for France on the 21 Aug 1915 and was killed by a sniper at Cardonette on the 18 Mar 1916 aged 21. Alexander is buried in the Ecoivres Military Cemetery, Mont-St. Eloi.

References:
CWGC Casualty No 65234

George John FORREST*

Service No: 3205. Rank: Pte. Regiment: 5th Bn. Gordon Highlanders.
Service No: 240975. Rank: Pte. Regiment: 1st/5th Bn. Gordon Highlanders.

Born at Slains, Aberdeenshire in 1896, George was the son of William Gibb and Elspet (Elsie) (m/s Smith) Forrest of 24 Tolbooth Wynd, Peterhead.

George died of his wounds during the Arras offensive on the 27 May 1917. He is buried in the Haute-Avesnes British Cemetery which the 51st Highland Division started in Jul 1916 and it continued to be used by field ambulances of the divisions holding this part of the line.

Duplicate Medal Cards exist for George. One state that George's medals were never collected and were later destroyed. The other card, states that the medals were sent to Mr R. Smith, step-grandfather, Woodside, Blackhills, Peterhead.

References:
CWGC Casualty No 79841

John Robertson FOWLER

Rank: 3rd Engineer. Service: Mercantile Marine - SS Saint Ronald.

Born in 1883 in the parish of St Nicholas, Aberdeen, John was the son of Andrew and Elizabeth Fowler and the husband of Mary Webster M. (m/s Anderson) Fowler.

John was serving aboard the SS Saint Ronald

when it was sunk by the U-Boat U-82 on the 19 Sep 1917, 95 miles NNW from Tory Island. The ship was part of convoy HH21 from Chesapeake Bay, USA. John's death is commemorated on the Tower Hill Memorial in London.

References:
CWGC Casualty No 2886743
Marriage Certificate 1914
Birth Certificate 1883

Alexander FRASER*

Service No: 32448. Rank: Pte. Regiment: 15th Bn. Highland Light Infantry.

Born in Peterhead, Alexander was the son of James Fraser a former dyer at the Kirkburn Mill, Peterhead. Originally residing at 44 Windmill St., Peterhead, the family moved to 20 St Andrew's Place, Lanark. Alexander was educated at the Peterhead Academy.

Alexander was killed in action on the 15 Aug 1917. His grave has not been discovered and Alexander's sacrifice is honoured on the Nieuport Memorial which commemorates 566 Commonwealth officers and men who were killed in Allied operations on the Belgian coast and have no known grave.

References:
CWGC Casualty 1640652

George Alexander FRASER

Service No: 1784. Rank: LCpl. Regiment: 1st/5th Bn. Gordon Highlanders.

George was born in Old Deer, Aberdeenshire in 1897 the son of Lewis and Christine Fraser, of Easterton, Peterhead.

He enlisted in Peterhead and arrived in France on the 5 Dec 1915 earning the 1915 Star. George was killed in action at Cardonette on the 26 Mar 1916 aged 18 years. George is buried at the Maroeuil British Cemetery which was begun by the 51st Highland Division when Commonwealth forces took over the Arras front in Mar 1916.

References:
CWGC Casualty No 120775
Medal Card

John FRASER

Service No: 3609. Rank: Pte. Regiment: 5th Bn. Gordon Highlanders.

John was the fifth son of Colin and Sophia

Jaffray Fraser of Glasgow. He was also the brother-in-law of Arthur Blow of 19 York St. Peterhead.

He enlisted into Gordon Highlanders in Peterhead and was killed on the 13 Nov 1916 aged 21, at Beaumont-Hamel where the Gordon Highlanders suffered heavy casualties. John is buried in the Mailly Wood Cemetery which the 51st Highland Division utilised following the capture of Beaumont-Hamel.

References:
CWGC Casualty No 111386
Buchan Observer 28 Nov 1916

John FULTON (FOULTON)

Service No: 3313S. Rank: Stoker. Service: RNR – HMS Invincible.

Born on the 4 Mar 1890, John was the son of John Fulton and Mary Ann Buchan Fulton of Peterhead and the husband of Margaret B. Anderson Fulton of 24, Maiden St., and later of 3 Crooked Lane, Peterhead.

John was lost, aged 27, when HMS Invincible was sunk on the 31 May 1916. After the Battle of Jutland the Royal Navy tried to push home its advantage by deploying its battle cruisers. Sadly the Invincible, part of the 3rd Battle Cruiser Squadron was lost.

References:
CWGC Casualty No 2876883
www.Naval-net

Alexander GAMMACK*

Service No: S/40067. Rank: Pte. Regiment: 2nd Bn. Gordon Highlanders.

Born on the 29 Sep 1886 at Rathen, Aberdeenshire, Alexander was the son of Mary Gammack. He married Mary Coull Sim in 1910 in St Fergus and they had one daughter together named Margaret Isabella Gammack. She was born on the 28 Mar 1916 and they all lived at Balmoor Cottage, Peterhead. Prior to the war, Alexander had been a farm servant in the district.

Alexander fell on the 2 Apr 1917 and has no known resting place. His sacrifice is honoured on the Arras Memorial which commemorates almost 35,000 servicemen from the United Kingdom, South Africa and New Zealand who died in the Arras sector between the spring of 1916 and 7 Aug 1918.

References:
CWGC Casualty No 1557959

John Albert GARDEN

Service No: 3084. Rank: Pte. Regiment: 5th Bn. Gordon Highlanders.
Service No: 240939. Rank: Pte. Regiment: 5th Bn. Gordon Highlanders.

John was born in Peterhead in 1897, the son of John and Isabella (m/s McKay) Garden. He was also the grandson of Mrs Garden of 18 James St. and later of 21 Merchant St. Peterhead. Before the war his occupation was a butcher.

John enlisted into the Gordon Highlanders in Aberdeen and sailed for France on the 4 Dec 1915. Twice wounded, once with a gunshot wound to the head, he was killed in action on the 3 Dec 1917. His sacrifice is recorded on the Cambrai Memorial which commemorates more than 7,000 servicemen of the United Kingdom and South Africa who died in the Battle of Cambrai in Nov and Dec 1917 and whose graves are not known.

References:
CWGC Casualty No 1753072
Birth Certificate 1897, 232/01 0497
Buchan Observer 25 Dec 1917

James Daniel Milne GAVIN

Service No: 22127. Rank: Pte. Regiment: 7th Bn. Canadian Infantry (British Columbia Regiment).

Born in Cruden near Peterhead on the 14 Jun 1895, James was the son of Francis (aka Frank) and Margaret Gavin.

After emigrating to Canada and residing at 390, Ottawa Avenue, East Kildonan, Winnipeg; James enlisted into the CEF at Valcartier, Quebec on 23 Sep 1914. James had previously served with the 100th Winnipeg Grenadiers despite being only 5ft 5½ in tall.

James was killed during the 2nd Battle of Ypres on the 24 Apr 1915. Initially,he was reported as missing in action and then later declared dead on that date. Burial records indicate James died during at attack near St. Julien. Aged only 19 years old, his name appears on the Ypres (Menin Gate) Memorial.

References:
CWGC Casualty No 1592393
Aberdeen City Roll of Honour, City and CEF Attestation Form

David Kelly GEARY

Service No: S/23131. Rank: Pte. Regiment: 8th Bn. Black Watch (Royal Highlanders).

David was born in Peterhead about 1899 and was the fourth son of Alexander and Isabella Moir (m/s Kelly) Geary of 22 Chapel St., Peterhead. He had at least seven brothers and sisters including; Alexander, Catherine, Isabella, George, William, Mary and Margaret Geary. Prior to the war, David was the chauffeur to Dr Gillespie of Peterhead.

Having previously served in the 38th Territorial Reserve Bn., David enlisted into the Black Watch (Royal Highlanders) in Aberdeen. He was killed in action on the 24 Mar 1918 during the period of crisis in Mar and Apr 1918 when the Allied Fifth Army was driven back by overwhelming numbers across the former Somme battlefields. At the time of his death, David was only 19 years old. His resting place remains unknown and he is commemorated on the Pozieres Memorial.

References:
CWGC Casualty No 1581314

Alexander GEDDES

Service No: 2008C. Rank: Seaman. Service: RNR – HMS Bulwark

Born in Sep 1876, Alexander was the son of James and Margaret Geddes. He was also the brother of Mrs Jemima Moore of 2 Seagate, Peterhead.

On the 26 Nov 1914 HMS Bulwark was totally destroyed whilst moored at No.17 Buoy, Kethole Reach off Sheerness in the River Medway, Kent. Alexander was one of a number of Peterhead men that were killed that day. Alexander was aged 39 years and his death is listed on the Portsmouth Naval Memorial.

References:
CWGC Casualty No 2871172

Andrew Donald McKenzie GEDDES

Service No: 241253. Rank: Pte. Regiment: 1st /6th Bn. Gordon Highlanders.

Born at 7 Union St., Peterhead, Andrew was the son of Andrew and Jane (m/s Benzie) Geddes of 12 Errol St., Peterhead. Prior to the war, he worked at the Admiralty Works, Peterhead.

Andrew enlisted into the Gordon Highlanders in Peterhead. At the age of 29, Andrew died of his wounds on the 5 Aug 1917. He passed away in one of the clearing hospitals near the Pas-de-Calais. He is buried in the Etaples Military Cemetery.

References:
CWGC Casualty No 501361
Birth Certificate 1888, 232/01 0202

James GEDDES

Service No: 5019/DA. Rank: Deck Hand.
Service: RNR – HMS Nairn.

James was the son of Peter Copland and Catherine (m/s Insch) Geddes and also the husband of Rosalie E. Geddes of 34 North St., Peterhead.

James died in Back St, Peterhead on the 9 Dec 1918 aged 26, whilst serving with the armed steam ship HMS Nairn. He is buried in Peterhead Cemetery.

Rosalie, his wife passed away early that month in Love Lane, Peterhead aged 22.

References:
CWGC Casualty No 326986

James GEDDES

Service No: 144080. Rank: Pte. Regiment: 73rd Bn. Canadian Infantry.

James was born in 1896, the son of William Geddes of Back St. Peterhead. He emigrated to Canada in 1913.

James enlisted into the 73rd Bn. Canadian Infantry and was reported missing on the 1 Mar 1917. He is buried in the Cabaret-Rouge British Cemetery, Souchez. This cemetery has a particularly close connection with the Canadian Infantry as hundreds of Canadians who were killed at the Battle of Vimy Ridge in Apr 1917 were ultimately laid to rest here.

References:
CWGC Casualty No 585749
Buchan Observer

John GEDDES

Service No: 16621DA. Rank: Deck Hand.
Service: RNR - HMS Louvain.

John was born on the 28 Aug 1892 in Aberdeen and was the son of Georgina Geddes of 89 Roanheads, Peterhead.

John was killed in action when HMS Louvain was sunk by the submarine UC-22 in the Mediterranean on the 20 Jan 1918. He was aged 26 and his body was never recovered. His sacrifice is remembered on the Portsmouth Naval Memorial.

An account of the incident follows: "On 21 Jan 1918, HMS Louvain an armed boarding Steamer (formally the SS Dresden) was torpedoed by a German U-boat SM *UC-22* in the Aegean Sea with the loss of seven officers and 217 men. The submarine sighted an escorted steamer and decided to lay mines in front of her while at the same time positioning herself for a torpedo attack. A minute after getting her 10th mine out, *UC-22* began her torpedo attack. The single shot was fired at a range of 600 meters and a hit was scored. The submarine was quite near a destroyer when she fired her torpedo and she was soon counter-attacked. Due to the very high number of casualties and the presence of a destroyer close by, it must be assumed that the Louvain sank very quickly."

References:
CWGC Casualty No 3039761
UK Commonwealth War Graves 1914-1918

Robert GEDDES

Service No: 240623. Rank: Pte. Regiment: 5th Bn. Gordon Highlanders.

Robert was born in 1899 in Peterhead and was the son of James and Barbara Geddes of 23 Marischal St., Peterhead. His siblings included; John, James, Annabella, Alex, Sarah, Helen and Barbara Geddes.

Robert enlisted in Peterhead and was killed in action on the 28 Jul 1918 at the Battle of Buzancy.

Robert has no known grave and so is commemorated on the Soissons Memorial which commemorates almost 4,000 officers and men of the United Kingdom forces who died during the Battles of the Aisne and the Marne in 1918 and have no known grave.

References:
CWGC Casualty No 1758238

William GEDDES*

Service No: 438057. Rank: Pte. Regiment: 3rd Bn. Canadian Infantry.

Born in Cullen on the 4 Apr 1884, William was the son of Elizabeth Geddes of Cullen. A sometime resident of Peterhead, William emigrated to Canada where he enlisted in Port Arthur, Ontario.

He died of his wounds on the 11 Jul 1917 and is buried in the La Targette British Cemetery, Neuville-St. Vaast which was formerly known as Aux-Rietz Military Cemetery.

References:
CWGC Casualty No 530796

William James Strachan GIBB

Service No: 105585. Rank: Gnr. Regiment: Royal Garrison Artillery.

William was born in Peterhead on the 4 Jan 1880, the son of Alexander and Elizabeth (m/s Strachan) Gibb. He married Ellen Dorothy Harriet Fisher in 1907 in London. At the outbreak of the war, William was living in Dulwich with his wife and two children.

William enlisted on the 26 Jul 1916 and served with the 213 Bty and the 281 Bty, RGA. He was posted to France on the 30 Dec 1916 only to be medically evacuated on the 29 Nov 1917. William was discharged on 17 Jan 1918 and was awarded the Silver War Badge which was awarded to all military personnel who were discharged for injury or sickness. William died at 51 Broad St, Peterhead on the 24 Jun 1920 as a result of tuberculosis. William's sacrifice is not currently listed with the CWGC.

References:
Service Record and Medical Card

Alfred H. GIBSON
(Middle name is probably "Haggerston")

Service No: TS 641. Rank: Trimmer. Service: RNR – HMT Pitstruan.

Alfred was born in 1880, the son of Alfred Haggerston and Catherine (m/s Bain) Gibson. He married Elsie Gibson of Stuartfield (both had Gibson as their surname). At the time of his marriage, Alfred lived in St Peter St., Peterhead and his occupation is listed as a carter. They later moved to 64 Longacre Street, Aberdeen.

HMT Pitstruan had been requisitioned by the Admiralty when was destroyed by a mine explosion off Noss Head, Wick on the 13 Apr 1917. Alfred died that day and his name appears on the Portsmouth Naval Memorial.

References:
CWGC Casualty No 3040989
Marriage Certificate

John GILES

Service No: 4224. Rank: Pte. Regiment: Highland Light Infantry.
Service No: 48518. Rank: Pte. Regiment: 1st/4th Bn. Royal Scots Fusiliers.

John was born in South Leith in 1898 and enlisted in Leith, Edinburgh. He was the only son of David Giles, compositor, Edinburgh, and the nephew of Adam Giles of Tanfield House, Peterhead.

John went to France on the 23 Dec 1915 and was killed in action on the 1 Sep 1918. John is buried in the Queant Road Cemetery, Buissy. Buissy was reached by the Third Army on 2 Sep 1918, after the storming of the Drocourt-Queant line.

References:
CWGC Casualty No 313531

James GORDON

Service No: 2118. Rank: Pte. Regiment: 5th Bn. Gordon Highlanders.
Service No: 240431. Rank: Pte. Regiment: 5th Bn. Gordon Highlanders.

Born in circa 1892 in Peterhead, James was the son of Mrs. Mary Gordon of 4 Threadneedle St., Peterhead.

James enlisted in Peterhead in B Coy of the Gordon Highlanders in 1914 and arrived in France on the 5 May 1915 earning the 1915 Star. Having already been wounded in Apr 1916, James was killed on the 18 Apr 1917 during the major Arras offensive of Apr-May 1917. His body was never found and his death is commemorated on the Arras Memorial which commemorates almost 35,000 servicemen from the United Kingdom, South Africa and New Zealand who died in the Arras sector and whose bodies were never found.

References:
CWGC Casualty No 636731
Buchan Observer 1914.

John Fraser GORDON*

Service No: 687458. Rank: Pte. Regiment: 47th Bn. Canadian Infantry.

Born at Muirsford, Ross and Cromarty on 16 Nov 1888, John was the son of Mr and Mrs

Alexander Gordon of Inverlochy, Fort William. He was the husband of Mrs Isabella Cumming, of 31, Union St., Keith, Banffshire, whom he married in 1917. John was also the nephew of Mr and Mrs James Gordon of the Glenugie Distillery, Peterhead. Prior to the war, John had emigrated to Canada and was an accountant at the Bank of Montreal, Kamloops, BC.

Before joining the Canadian Infantry, John had served 4½ years with Gordon Highlanders. John was killed in action at Canal du Nord during the capture of Bourlon Wood on the 28 Sep 1918. He is buried in the Quarry Wood Cemetery, Sains-Les-Marquion which was made by the 102nd Canadian Battalion in Oct 1918 and there are now over 250, 1914-18 war casualties buried in this cemetery.

References:
CWGC Casualty No 596125

William GORDON

Service No: 2837. Rank: Sgt. Regiment: 4th Regt. South African Infantry attached to the MGC.

 William was born in 1878 in Peterhead, the son of Alexander and Jane (Jean) Sangster Gordon of Stuartfield, formerly of Peterhead. He married Helen A. (m/s Blain) Gordon on the 3 Apr 1912 in Ganteng, South Africa. They had two children; Reginald (b.1913) and Helena (b.1915). Helen later returned to Scotland and lived at 31 Bruntsfield Avenue, Edinburgh.

Described by a local newspaper as the cleverest detective in Johannesburg, William joined the 4th Regiment of the South African Infantry known as the "South African Scottish". This regiment was formed from immigrant Scots living in Cape Town and the Transvaal. William saw service during the South African and South West African Campaigns, he then transferred to the European Expeditionary Force. William fought at Senussi in Egypt before arriving in France. He was killed in the first few days of the Battle of the Somme on the 5 Jul 1916 aged 38.

William is buried in the Peronne Road Cemetery, Maricourt which was first used at the Battle of the Somme in 1916.

References:
CWGC Casualty No 310946

William GORDON

Service No: 5176. Rank: A/Cpl. Regiment: Gordon Highlanders.
Service No: 201978. Rank: Cpl. Regiment: 4th Bn. Gordon Highlanders.

Born in Peterhead on the 4 Jun 1888, William was the son of William and Robina (m/s McLeod) Gordon. He was also the husband of Mrs H. Duncan (formerly Gordon) of 328 Rosedale Avenue, Winnipeg, Canada. William was employed by Messrs. Sinclair and Buchan, fishcurers of Peterhead. He enlisted into the Gordon Highlanders in Aberdeen.

William died of his wounds on the 21 Mar 1918 and is buried in the Grevillers British Cemetery near to the Pas de Calais.

References:
CWGC Casualty No 290127

William GRAHAM

Service No: 1156. Rank: Piper. Regiment: 5th Bn. Gordon Highlanders.

Born in Peterhead, William was the son of William Graham, prison officer, Peterhead and the step-son of Christina Graham.

William enlisted in Peterhead into his local regiment the 5th Bn. Gordon Highlanders. He was sent to France on the 2 May 1915 and died a month later on the 3 Jun 1915. William is interred in Pont-Du-Hem Military Cemetery, La Gorgue. This Cemetery was begun, in an apple-orchard, in Jul 1915, and used until Apr 1918, by fighting units and Field Ambulances.

References:
CWGC Casualty No 596876
The Pipes of War: page 128

Albert John GUTHRIE

Rank: Lt. Regiment: 5th Bn. Gordon Highlanders.

Albert was the son of the Rev. William G. Guthrie and Maria Ann P. Guthrie, of Manse of Glass, Aberdeenshire, and was born in Coull, Aberdeenshire, circa 1891.

Commissioned on the 24 Nov 1914, he was sent to France on the 29 Jul 1915 earning the 1915 Star. Albert was killed in action whilst leading his platoon against German trenches on the 30 Jul 1916. This day the Gordon Highlanders suffered a huge number of casualties. He was aged 25 years at the time and his body was never recovered. Albert's sacrifice is recorded on the Thiepval Memorial, which commemorates those lost on the 1 Jul 1916 advance.

References:
CWGC Casualty No 788113

John HENDERSON

Service No: S/13992. Rank: Pte. Regiment: 3rd Bn. Gordon Highlanders.

John was born on the 3 Jun 1895 in Portknockie, Banff, the only son of James John and Jemima Gordon (m/s Trail) Henderson of 56 King St., Peterhead. Before enlisting into the Gordon Highlanders, John worked at the Burgh Surveyors.

Initially listed as missing, John was killed in action at Delville Wood on the 18 Jul 1916 aged only 21 years old. His body was never found and his name is inscribed on the Thiepval Memorial which commemorates the massive losses incurred in the major offensives of Jul 1916.

References:
CWGC Casualty No 791184
Mowat Public Family Tree

John HENDERSON

Service No: 3611. Rank: Pte. Regiment: 3rd/5th Bn. Gordon Highlanders.
Service No: S/40251. Rank: Pte. Regiment: 2nd Bn. Gordon Highlanders.

Born in Peterhead circa 1888, John was the son of Mr and Mrs John Henderson of 14 Ugie St., Peterhead. He was also a brother to George, Charlotte, Jeannie and Diana Henderson.

John enlisted on the 14 Dec 1915 into the 3rd /5th Bn. Gordon Highlanders and was posted to France on the 20 Aug 1916. A qualified bomb thrower, John was posted to the 2nd Bn. Gordon Highlanders on the 10 Sep 1916. John was injured on the 2 Jan 1917 whilst on fatigue duty. After recovering from those injuries he was killed in action on the 12 Jul 1917. John is buried in the Ecoust Military Cemetery, Ecoust-St. Mein.

References:
CWGC Casualty No 316894
Service Record

John HEPBURN

Service No: 141614. Rank: Sapper. Regiment: 9th Field Coy, Royal Engineers.

John was born circa 1890 in Peterhead. He was the eldest son of John Hepburn of 14 Constitution St., Peterhead and was employed by his father as a mason.

John enlisted in Nov 1915 into the Royal Engineers in Aberdeen. He was killed in action on the 17 Oct 1916 and his body was never found. His name is inscribed on the Thiepval Memorial which commemorates the massive losses incurred in the major offensives of Jul 1916.

References:
CWGC Casualty No 791317

James John HEPBURN

Service No: 6276. Rank: Pte. Regiment: 7th Bn. Australian Infantry, A.I.F.

Born on the 8 Feb 1892 in Peterhead, James was the son of Isabella Hepburn at 40B Kirk St., Peterhead. James' occupation is listed as a seaman.

He joined the Australian Imperial Force on the 24 May 1916 in Melbourne, NSW aged 23 years. By then both his parents are deceased and James lists his next-of-kin as his Aunt Barbara Craig of 59 Kirk St., Peterhead who later moved to 5B Weavers Lane, Peterhead.

James set sail for England on HMAT Euripides arriving in Plymouth a month later. It appears that he was hospitalised for a total of 84 days with an infectious disease! Which would now be described as a social disease. He sailed for France, via Folkestone, Kent on the 10 Apr 1917 only to be killed by a shell explosion on the 4 Oct 1917. James' sacrifice is listed on the Ypres (Menin Gate) Memorial. The Menin Gate is one of four memorials to the missing in Belgian Flanders.

References:
CWGC Casualty No 924165
Birth Certificate 232/01 0074
National Australian Archives – Service Records
Red Cross Report pages 1- 17

Cecil Arthur Dickson HILL

Service No: 1740. Rank: Pte. Regiment: Royal Army Medical Corps.
Service No: 241440. Rank: LCpl. Regiment: 1st/5th Bn. Gordon Highlanders.

Born in Peterhead in 1893, Cecil was the youngest son of John Robert Trail Hill, M.A., (Sherriff officer) and Mary Anne Wyndham Wilson Hill of 23 Queen St., Peterhead.

Cecil enlisted in Aberdeen and entered the war in the Balkans on the 16 Mar 1915 as a Pte in the RAMC. After Gallipoli, he was transferred to the Gordon Highlanders and was posted to France. Cecil, now aged 25 died of his wounds on the 21 Aug 1918 at the 11 Stationary Hospital. Earlier he had been reported as dangerously wounded. Cecil is interred in the St. Sever Cemetery Extension, Rouen.

References:
CWGC Casualty No 518319
Buchan Observer Article 6 Aug 1918

Alexander Robertson HORNE*

Service No: 4940. Rank: Pte. Regiment: 5th Bn. Gordon Highlanders.

Born on the 22 Jun 1887 in Aberdeen, Alexander was the eldest son of Alexander R. and Annie (m/s Lyall) Horne of Cruden and later of 180 Crown St., Aberdeen. Alexander was the brother to Joseph L., Annie E., Eliza J., Stephen A., Margaret W. and Helen B. Horne.

Educated at Robert Gordon's College and then Aberdeen University, Alexander spent over 5 years as an assistant master at Peterhead Academy. He enlisted into the Gordon Highlanders and was sent to France. In Dec 1916, Alexander was wounded and returned to England. He died of his wounds at Dunston Military Hospital on the 25 Jan 1917 and is buried in the Aberdeen (Allenvale) Cemetery.

References:
CWGC Casualty No 326360
Aberdeen University Roll of Honour

George Clarkson HUNTER

Service No: 2555/ST. Rank: Trimmer. Regiment: RNR – HMT Beluga.

Born at Hetton-le-Hole, Co. Durham on the 13 Jul 1879, George was the son of Edmund and Margaret Anne Hunter and the husband of Jemima Ann Hunter of 35 High St., Timaru, New Zealand. Later his wife Jemima would come to reside at 65 Queen St., Peterhead.

George died from disease on the 15 Feb 1919 whilst serving aboard HMT Beluga. He is buried in Peterhead Cemetery.

References:
CWGC Casualty No 326987

James HUNTER

Service No: 1739. Rank: Pte. Regiment: Royal Army Medical Corps.
Service No: 241398. Rank: Sgt. Regiment 1st/6th Bn. Gordon Highlanders.

Born in 1893 in Peterhead, James was the son of Isaac and Elizabeth Hunter of 39 Maiden St. Peterhead. He was also the brother of Isaac, Elizabeth and Charlotte Hunter. His father, Isaac was born in Ireland and was employed in the insurance industry.

James enlisted in Aberdeen into the RAMC, and was sent to the Balkans on the 16 Mar 1915. He transferred to the 1st/6th Bn. Gordon Highlanders where he saw action in Flanders. James was killed in action on the 26 Aug 1918 and is buried in the Brown's Copse Cemetery, Roeux, The Germans re-entered the village of Roeux at the end of Mar 1918, and it was finally retaken by the 51st Highland Division by the following August.

References:
CWGC Casualty No 567813

William James HUTCHISON

Service No: 711: Rank: Pte. Regiment: 4th Bn. Australian Infantry AIF.

Born in Peterhead in 12 Dec 1876, William was the son of William (occ draper) and Anne (m/s Cassie) Hutchison of 27 Cairntrodlie, Peterhead, later of 1 Thistle St., Peterhead. He emigrated to Australia in 1911 and was employed as a station hand.

William enlisted in Sydney, NSW and sailed for the Dardanelles in the Balkans. He was wounded at Gallipoli and evacuated to Egypt. He was admitted to the Ghezireh Hospital in Cairo for treatment and he died of typhoid in the same hospital on the 20 Jun 1915, aged 38. William is buried in the Cairo War Memorial Cemetery.

References:
CWGC Casualty No 112897
Australian Archives

Thomas HUTTON

Service No: 2719/5. Rank: Pte. Regiment: 1st/ 5th Bn. Gordon Highlanders.
Service No: 240749. Rank: Pte. Regiment: 8th/10th Bn. Gordon Highlanders.

Thomas was born in 1892 in Peterhead, the third son of Thomas (occ sailmaker) and Mary J. Hutton of 14 Harbour St., Peterhead,

Thomas enlisted into the 1st/5th Bn. Gordon Highlanders in Peterhead and was sent to France on the 2 May 1915. Later, he was posted to the 8th/10th Bn. Gordon Highlanders. Thomas was killed in action on the 24 Aug 1917 during the 3rd Battle of Ypres, aged only 24 years old. Thomas' body has not been found and his sacrifice is commemorated on the Tyne Cot Memorial.

References:
CWGC Casualty No 1632895

Thomas HUTTON

Service No: 3188. Rank: Pte. Regiment: 1st/5th Bn. Gordon Highlanders.

Thomas was born on the 15 Sep 1897 at 12 Castle St., Peterhead and was the son of William Strachan Hutton and Margaret (m/s Buchan) Hutton later of 136 Walker Rd., Torry, Aberdeen. He was also the grandson of Mrs T. Hutton of 14 Castle St., Peterhead. Prior to the war, Thomas was an apprentice carpenter in the employment of Messrs Irvin and Sons, ship-builders, Peterhead.

Thomas enlisted into the Gordon Highlanders in Aberdeen and was posted to France on the 5 Dec 1915. He was killed in action on the 13 Nov 1916, aged 19; during the Beaumont-Hamel offensive in which the Gordon Highlanders suffered heavy losses. Thomas is buried in the Auchonvillers Military Cemetery.

References:
CWGC Casualty No 71944
Aberdeen City Roll of Honour: 30 Nov 1916
Buchan Observer 28 Nov 1916

James IMLACH

Service No: 3491/ES. Rank: Engineman.
Service: RNR – HMS Iolaire.

James was born in Portessie, Banffshire on the 29 Nov 1891 the son of Mrs Martin Buchan of 8 Great Stuart St., Peterhead. He died of illness aboard HMS Iolaire on the 31 Jul 1918 and is buried in Peterhead Cemetery.

HMS Iolaire, meaning Eagle in Gaelic, was an Admiralty yacht which sank on the 1 Jan 1919 was one of the worst peacetime maritime disasters in United Kingdom waters. At least 205 perished of the 280 aboard.

References:
CWGC Casualty No 326988

Alexander James INNES

Service No: R-258865. Rank: Pte. Regiment: Royal Army Service Corps.
Service No: 29646. Rank: Pte. Regiment: 1st Bn. Prince Albert's (Somerset Light Infantry).

Born in Peterhead in 1898, Alexander was the son of Elizabeth A. Webster of 10 Albion St., Peterhead. Prior to the war, Alexander worked for Messrs James Reid & Sons, carting contractors, Peterhead.

He enlisted into the Royal Army Service Corps in Aberdeen. After transferring to the 1st Bn. SLI, Alexander died of his wounds on the 24 Jun 1918 aged 21 and is interred in the Lapugnoy Military Cemetery.

References:
CWGC Casualty No 54284
Buchan Observer Article 9 Jul 1918

Thomas William IRVIN

Rank: Lt. Regiment: 5th Bn. Gordon Highlanders

Thomas was born in 1884, the fourth son of Alderman Richard & Ann (m/s Driver) Irvin of North Shields, Northumberland and also the husband of Christiana Leech (m/s Watkinson) Irvin of West Rd., Peterhead. They had two children together; Charles and Catherine. He came to Peterhead in 1910 to take up the local management of his father's drifter business.

47

Commissioned into the 5th Bn. Gordon Highlanders in 1915, Thomas left for France on the 4 Feb 1916 but died of wounds on the 20 May 1916, Age 32. Thomas is buried in St Hilaire Cemetery, Frevent.

References:
CWGC Casualty No 527974

John Watt JACK

Service No: 5410. Rank: Pte. Regiment: 13th Bn. Scottish Horse.
Service No: 315639. Rank: Pte. Regiment: Black Watch (Royal Highlanders).

Born in Peterhead on the 5 Jan 1894, John was the eldest son of William and Jessie Watt of St. John's Wood, Inverugie, Peterhead. In civilian life he was a naval architect in Glasgow.

At the outbreak of the war, John enlisted in Edinburgh into the 13th Scottish Horse. He was later posted to the Black Watch (Royal Highlanders). By Aug 1915, He had seen action at Gallipoli and Salonika before being posted to France. He was killed in action on the 4 Oct 1918 aged 25. John is buried in the Unicorn Cemetery, Vend'huile.

References:
CWGC Casualty No 177569

Malcolm Chalmers JACK

Service No: 1825. Rank: Pte. Regiment: 1st Highland Field Ambulance Reserve, Royal Army Medical Corps.
Service No: 301279. Rank: Pte. Regiment: Royal Army Medical Corps.

Malcolm was born in Peterhead in 1894 the son of John and Mary (m/s Murray) Jack, of Linksview, Peterhead and later of Dales House, near Peterhead. He was also the brother to Murray

Munro and William James Jack. The family emigrated to Canada in 1921.

Malcolm enlisted in Aberdeen on the 10 Nov 1914 into the 1st HFA aged 19 years old and standing only 5'4" tall. A short history of his military career follows which is taken from his Service Record:

3 May 1915 - Embarked for France (Le Havre) to join the BEF.
2 Aug 1915 - Joins up with the BEF.
23 Jun 1916 - Wounded in action, Gunshot wound to right foot - Returned to England.
Jun 1917 - Returns to France.
16 Oct 1917 - Gassed and returned to England (actually the Edinburgh War Hospital in Scotland).
Mar 1918 - Returned to Active Service and sent to Egypt.
Apr 1918 - Re-joins the BEF in France.
May 1918 - Joins the 2nd /1st Field Ambulance.
6 Jun 1918 - Died of pneumonia at the 26th General Hospital at Etaples aged 24.

Malcolm is buried in the Etaples Military Cemetery; the area around Etaples was the scene of immense concentrations of Commonwealth reinforcement camps and hospitals.

References:
CWGC Casualty No 502580
Buchan Observer Article 11 Jun 1918
Service Record

Robert Lawrence Munro JACK

Service No: 3191. Rank: Pte. Regiment: 5th Bn. Gordon Highlanders.
Rank: 2Lt. Regiment: 1st/5th Bn. Gordon Highlanders.
Rank: 2Lt. Regiment: Royal Flying Corps.

Born circa 1885, Robert was the son of Peter and Elizabeth A.S. (m/s Sinclair) Jack. He had a number of brothers and sisters including Ernest, William, Elizabeth and Avina Jack. There had another brother named Harold or Henry. Prior to the war, Robert was an employee of John B. Dickie, Alexandra Sawmills of Peterhead.

Robert joined the Gordon Highlanders as a Pte and quickly gained promotion to Sgt. He was then commissioned 2Lt on the 18 Dec 1915. Robert went to France on the 2 Jul 1916 only to later transfer to 16 Sqn Royal Flying Corps. He died of his wounds on the 26 Feb 1917 and is buried in the Aubigny Communal Cemetery Extension. From Mar 1916 to the Armistice, Aubigny was held by

Commonwealth troops and burials were made in the Extension until Sep 1918.

References:
CWGC Casualty No 52402

William JACK

Service No: 1910. Rank: Pte. Regiment: 1st/5th Bn. Gordon Highlanders.
William was the son of Alexander Murno and Amelia (m/s McIntosh) Jack formerly McGregor. A cabinet maker by trade, he lived at 3 Merchant St., Peterhead.

William enlisted into C Coy of the Gordon Highlanders and was sent to France on the 5 Dec 1915. By Jun 1916, he had been hospitalised in France and was medically discharged on the 9 Dec 1916. William died on the 24 Jan 1922, aged 27 in the Royal Mental Hospital Aberdeen of injuries sustained in the war. William's death certificate lists his normal residence as 3 Merchant St., Peterhead. His sacrifice is recorded on the Peterhead Memorial.

References:
Death Certificate 1922

Alexander Milne JAFFRAY MM

Service No: 1829. Rank: Pte. Regiment: 5th Bn. Gordon Highlanders.

Alexander was born in Peterhead in 1896, the son of Alexander and Mrs Jaffray of The Brae, Peterhead. He was also the nephew of Provost Leask and William Jaffrey. Alexander lived at 6 Harbour St., Peterhead and prior to the war he was in the employment of Messrs A. Brown & Co. warehousemen, Broad St. Peterhead.

Alexander enlisted into C Coy of the 5th Bn. Gordon Highlanders and was posted to France on the 2 May 1915. He was killed in action on the 25 Jul 1917 by an exploding shell. He had volunteered to go into the trenches with a young fellow newly arrived, when a shell passed between the two, fatally wounding Alexander. Previously he had been awarded the Military Medal for all his good work whilst on active service. Alexander's sacrifice is recorded on the Thiepval Memorial.

References:
CWGC Casualty No 795434
Buchan Observer 1 Aug 1916

William Butters JAMIESON

Service No: S/14056. Rank: Pte. Regiment: 8th/10th Bn. Gordon Highlanders

Born on the 1 Sep 1895, William was the son of Mary Butters (later Mrs Cooper) of 13 Seagate, Peterhead. By decree of court, his father was named as Alexander Forbes Jamieson. Prior to the outbreak of war, William was in the employment of John B. Dickie, Windmill St., Peterhead. William enlisted in Peterhead and was killed on the 1 Aug 1917 during the 3rd Battle of Ypres and his sacrifice is listed on the Ypres (Menin Gate) Memorial. The Third Battle of Ypres was an offensive mounted by Commonwealth forces to divert German attention from a weakened French front further south. The campaign finally came to a close in November with the capture of Passchendaele.

The CWGC incorrectly lists William's middle name as 'Butler'

References:
CWGC Casualty No 1616101

John Mutch JOHNSTONE*

John's details appeared on the 1919 Peterhead Roll of Honour as a former resident of Peterhead and served at HMS Drake. He fell during 1917.

Alexander Macdonald KEITH

Service No: 10630. Rank: Sgt. Regiment: 2nd Bn Gordon Highlanders.

Born in 1890 in St Giles, Edinburgh, Alexander was the son of Angus Keith and Annie Smith (m/s McDonald) Keith, of Ropework Cottages, South Rd., Peterhead, later of Bloomfield Cottage, South Rd., Peterhead.

Alexander joined the Army in 1908 a year after his father's death and served in England, Egypt and India.

Alexander arrived in France on 7 Oct 1914 and was promoted to Sgt on the 17 May 1915. He was killed in action on the 18 Jun 1915, aged 25. His name is inscribed on the Le Touret Memorial which commemorates over 13,400 British soldiers who were killed in this sector of the Western Front from the beginning of Oct 1914 to the eve of the Battle of Loos in late Sep 1915 and who have no known grave.

References:
CWGC Casualty No 855664
Service Record

James Rennie KEITH

Service No: S/43286. Rank: Sgt. Regiment: 1st Bn. Gordon highlanders.

James was born in Peterhead, the son of Robert and Annie Keith of 22 Constitution St., Peterhead. Prior to the war, James was an apprentice engineer in the employment of Messrs Milne and Robb, Windmill St., Peterhead.

James enlisted in Peterhead into the Gordon Highlanders and was wounded in 1917 where he was recommended for gallantry in the field. On recovering, he was returned to the front only to die of further wounds on the 6 May 1918, aged only 21 years. James is buried in the Lapugnoy Military Cemetery. The dead were brought to this cemetery from casualty clearing stations, chiefly the 18th and the 23rd at Lapugnoy and Dozinghem.

Though listed as a Cpl on the Peterhead Memorial, his medal card states that James held the rank of Sgt when he died.

References:
CWGC Casualty No 54324

James F. KELMAN

Service No: S/23037. Rank: Pte. Regiment: 6th/7th Bn. Gordon Highlanders.

James' name was added to the Peterhead Memorial at a later date. Very little is known of James F. Kelman other than the military records show that he was born in Peterhead and enlisted in Truro.

James died of his wounds on the 13 Oct 1918 and is buried in the Avesnes-Le-Sec Communal Cemetery Extension. The extension was made by the 51st Highland Division in Nov 1918. At the Armistice, it contained 100 burials dating from the period 12-26 Oct 1918, 46 of which were Seaforth Highlanders and 41 Gordon Highlanders.

References:
CWGC Casualty No 192031

William John KELLY*

Rank: 2Lt. Regiment: 6th Bn. Gordon Highlanders.

William was the son of Lt. Col. W. J. Kelly

and Mrs A. Kelly, of Abbotswell Villa, Kincorth, Bridge-of-Dee, Aberdeen.

William was killed in action on the 25 Sep 1915 aged only 23 years. His sacrifice is honoured on the Loos Memorial which commemorates over 20,000 officers and men who have no known grave.

References:
CWGC Casualty No 733390

James LAIRD

Service No: T4/057071. Rank: Driver. Regiment: Royal Army Service Corps.

James was the son of James and Mary Laird of Waterside, Peterhead and the husband of Eliza C. M. Laird of Craigour Rd., Torphins, Aberdeenshire.

Enlisted in to 238th MT Coy., Royal Army Service Corps, James died of his wounds on the 20 Dec 1918 aged 27 in Greece. There is a high probability that James may have died of influenza. James is interred in the Bralo British Cemetery in Greece. Towards the end of 1917, the Salonika lines of communication were diverted through Bralo, Itea and Taranto because of German submarine activity in the Mediterranean. The 49th Stationary Hospital was gradually transferred to Bralo and the rest camps were established at Bralo and Itea. The cemetery was begun in Oct 1917 and used until Apr 1919. A large proportion of the burials are due to the influenza epidemic of 1918.

References:
CWGC Casualty 342252

Alfred LAMB*

Service No: 6654. Rank: Tpr. Regiment: Scottish Horse.
Service No: 6120. Rank: Pte. Regiment: Black Watch (Royal Highlanders).
Service No: 268051. Rank: Pte. Regiment: 6th Bn. Black Watch (Royal Highlanders).

Born in Aberdeen in 1883, Alfred was the husband of Mary Lamb, North Mayfair, Saskatoon, Saskatchewan.

A sometime resident of Peterhead, Alfred fell on the 2 Apr 1917 aged 34. He is buried in the Aubigny Communal Cemetery Extension which was used from Mar 1916 to the Armistice.

References:
CWGC Casualty No 52553

William LAWRENCE

Service No: 8873. Rank: Pte. Regiment: 1st Bn. Gordon Highlanders.

Born in Peterhead around 1886, William was one of six children born to James and Mary Thomson Lawrence of 9 Ship Row, Keith Inch, Peterhead. He was also the husband of Joan (m/s Cooper) Lawrence of 9 Oglivie Terrace, Leven, Fife. They had one child together named Joan who was born in Wemyss.

William Joined the Army in 1903 in Aberdeen, he served in Ireland before transferring to the Reserve. William was mobilised on the 5 Aug 1914 for service with the BEF. He was killed in action on the 27 Aug 1914 aged 28. William's sacrifice is recorded on the La Ferte-Sous-Jouarre Memorial which commemorates the 3,740 officers and men of the British Expeditionary Force (BEF) who fell at the battles of Mons, Le Cateau, the Marne and the Aisne and have no known grave.

Joan, his wife received a 15 shillings a week widow's pension.

References:
CWGC Casualty No 879449
Service Record

Alexander LEASK

Service No: 240726. Rank: Pte. Regiment: 1st Bn. Gordon Highlanders.

Alexander was born at 4 Skelton Street, Peterhead on the 6 Sep 1897, the son of Alexander Milne Leask and Miss Nellie Buchan Strachan. Nellie later married George Murray in 1900 and they lived at 30 Hay Crescent, Peterhead.

Enlisted in Peterhead, Alexander joined the 1st Bn. Gordon Highlanders and was killed in action on the 24 Mar 1918 aged 21 years old. His body has never been recovered and his sacrifice is commemorated on the Arras Memorial which commemorates almost 35,000 servicemen from the United Kingdom, South Africa and New Zealand who died in the Arras sector and have no known grave.

References:
CWGC Casualty No 782673
Birth Certificate

David Houston LEONARD

Service No: S/43649. Rank: Pte. Regiment: 1st Bn. Gordon Highlanders.

Born in Dundee the son of George and Margaret (m/s Maxwell) Leonard, David was a resident of Peterhead when he enlisted into the 1st Bn. Gordon Highlanders.

Whilst serving in France, David was taken seriously ill and returned to the UK. David died at the Red Cross Hospital in Bellahouston, Glasgow, of acute lymphatic leukaemia on the 19 Feb 1917 aged 18. His usual residence is listed as 5 Tanfield Place Peterhead. David is buried in the Glasgow Western Necropolis which contains 355 First World War burials.

David was the younger brother of John Maxwell Leonard who fell in 1915.

References:
CWGC Casualty No 666224
Death Certificate 644/18 0066

John Maxwell LEONARD

Service No: 3/6223. Rank: Pte. Regiment: 1st Bn. Gordon Highlanders.

Born in Dundee, John was the second son of George and Margaret (m/s Maxwell) Leonard of 5 Tanfield Place, Peterhead. In peacetime John's occupation was a carter in the employ of James Sutherland, contractor, Peterhead.

John enlisted into the Gordon Highlanders and arrived in France in Nov 1914. Whilst at the front he received a gunshot wound to the head. He later died of his wounds at the Fulham Military Hospital, Hammersmith, London on the 26 Aug 1915 aged 19. He is buried in Kensal Green (All Souls') Cemetery, London.

John was the elder brother of David who died of illness in 1917.

References:
CWGC casualty No 2905811

51

Alexander Milne LESLIE*

Service No: 2361. Rank: CSM. Regiment: 1st/4th Bn. Gordon Highlanders.

Alexander was the son of Mr and Mrs Robert Birnie Leslie of 19 Duthie Place, Aberdeen. Both his parents were former residents of Peterhead and his uncle was Provost Leask. At the time of his death, Alexander had recently married Annie McAdam of 196 Union Grove, Aberdeen. He served his apprenticeship with Messrs Burnett and Reid, advocates, Aberdeen before moving to London.

Before the war Alexander served with the Territorial Reserve and once hostilities commenced he returned to Aberdeen to re-enlist. Alexander arrived in France on the 4 Dec 1915. He was killed by a trench mortar on the 30 May 1916 and is buried in the Louez Military Cemetery, Duisans which was begun by French troops and taken over by the 51st Highland Division as a "front-line cemetery" in Mar 1916.

References:
CWGC Casualty No 29497
Buchan Observer 1916

Peter LIGERTWOOD*

Service No: PO/14301. Rank: Sgt. Regiment: Royal Marines Light Infantry.
Rank: Capt. Regiment: Royal Marines Light Infantry.

Born in Cruden, Aberdeenshire on the 14 Nov 1887, Peter was the son of Peter and Mary Ligertwood (both native of Peterhead). He was also married to Sarah Annall, of 16 Blake Rd., Gosport, Hants whom he married on the 29 Dec 1910. Peter was brother to Annie, William, Jane and Frederick Ligertwood.

Peter enlisted in Aberdeen on the 22 Jan 1906 and was promoted to Sgt on the 20 Sep 1914. He was commissioned Lieutenant RM on the 18 Jan 1916. He joined the BEF on the 27 Apr 1917 where he served with the 1st RM Bn. Peter spent two months in hospital (17 May 1917 - 5 Jul 1917) before re-joining the 2nd RM Bn. He died of further wounds on the 26 Oct 1917 and was "Mentioned in Despatches" on the 7 Nov 1917.

Peter is believed to be buried in the Poelcapelle British Cemetery which was made after the Armistice when graves were brought in from the surrounding battlefields. There are now 7,479 Commonwealth servicemen of the First World War buried or commemorated in the Peolcappelle British Cemetery. 6,230 of the burials are unidentified but special memorials commemorate casualties known or believed to be buried among them.

References:
CWGC Casualty No 491765

John Thomson LOUDON

Service No: 203351. Rank: Pte. Regiment: Gordon Highlanders.
Service No: 116999. Rank: LCpl. Regiment: 9th Bn. Machine Gun Corps (Infantry).

Born in Peterhead in 1893, John was the son of Mrs Mary Loudon of 108 Queen St., Peterhead. Prior to the war John was employed by Mr John Pyper, warehouseman, Broad Place, Peterhead.

John enlisted into the Gordon Highlanders before being posted to the MGC. John died of his wounds on the 1 Oct 1918 aged 25, and his sacrifice is recorded on the Tyne Cot Memorial which now bears the names of almost 35,000 officers and men whose graves are not known.

References:
CWGC Casualty No 833196

John Wallace LOW

Service No: 54284. Rank: Gunner. Regiment: 26th Siege Bty. Royal Garrison Artillery.

Born in Fraserburgh in 1895, John was the son of Robert and Isabella Low of 15 St Peter St., Peterhead, later of Blackhouse. He was part of a large family with three brothers and five sisters. They were George, James (serving with the Scots Guards), William, Helen, Robina, Isabella, Catherine and Christina Low.

James enlisted in Aberdeen on the 1 Dec 1914 and sadly died of tubercular meningitis on the 14 Apr 1915 aged 17. He never made it to France and died at Lydd Hospital in Kent. John is buried in the Lydd (All Saints) Churchyard.

References:
CWGC Casualty No 369457
Service Record

George Alfred LOWE

Service No: 10995. Rank: Pte. Regiment: 6th Bn. Gordon Highlanders.

Born in New Deer, George was the son of William and Elizabeth Lowe of 2 Braeheads, Banff.

George enlisted in Keith and was sent to France on the 10 Nov 14 earning the 1914 Star. Unfortunately he was killed in action only 70 days later on the 19 Jan 1915 aged 22 years.

George is buried in the Rue-Du-Bacquerot (13th London) Graveyard, Laventie. This graveyard was begun by the 1st Royal Irish Rifles in Nov 1914 and was closed in Jul 1916.

References:
CWGC Casualty No 597982

James Philip LUNDIUS

Rank: Sgt. Regiment: RAMC.
Rank: Lt. Regiment: 1st/5th Bn. Gordon Highlanders.

Of Swedish descent, James was born in Peterhead around 1892 and was the son of Oskar and Mary Lundius of 19 Marishall St., Peterhead. Oskar Lundius was born in Helsingborg, Sweden.

Formerly a Sgt in 2nd Field Ambulance RAMC, James was commissioned into the Gordon Highlanders on the 9 Apr 1915 and arrived in France a year later on the 10 Apr 1916. James was at the front for just over a month when he was killed in action on the 28 May 1916 aged 24 years. James is buried in the Maroeuil British Cemetery. This cemetery was begun by the 51st Highland Division when Commonwealth forces took over the Arras front in Mar 1916. Almost half of the graves are those of Highland territorials.

James' parents received a sympathy letter from the King and Queen.

References:
CWGC Casualty No 120893
Oskar Lundius' Master's Certificate

Stephen LYNCH

Service No: SS/117350. Rank: Stoker 1st Class. Service: RN – HMS Queen Mary.

Stephen was born on the 8 Sep 1891 at 7 Crooked Lane, Peterhead, the son of Sarah Lynch and later the stepson of Alexander Niddrie. He was unmarried and worked as a cooper/fish worker in Peterhead. Stephen was also the half-brother of Sarah Lynch later of Sinclair Rd, Torry, Aberdeen.

Stephen joined the 3rd Bn. Gordon Highlanders at the outbreak of hostilities and was wounded three times in France. He was medically discharged from the army due to injuries sustained in action. Stephen then joined the Navy in Aug 1915 and served aboard HMS Revenge. He transferred to HMS Queen Mary a month before it was lost at the Battle of Jutland on the 31 May 1916.

References:
CWGC Casualty No 3037214
Buchan Observer 1916

James Robert MACKAY (McKAY)

Service No: 3241. Rank: Pte. Regiment: 1st/5th Bn. Gordon Highlanders.

James was the son of Peter and Isabella (m/s Gordon) McKay and was born on the 11 Apr 1897 at Braehead, Auchindom, Mortlach, later residents of 60 Longate, Peterhead. James worked as a farm worker in the Cruden area.

James was killed in action on the 30 Jul 1916 aged 19 years. On the 1 Jul 1916, supported by a French attack to the south, thirteen divisions of Commonwealth forces launched an offensive on a line from north of Gommecourt to Maricourt. Losses were catastrophic and James' sacrifice is recorded on the Thiepval Memorial, the memorial to the missing of the Somme, which bears the names of more than 72,000 officers and men of the United Kingdom and South African forces who died on the Somme and have no known grave.

References:
CWGC Casualty No 803121
Birth Certificate

Douglas Robertson MACKIE

Service No: 255439. Rank: Pnr. Regiment: 18th Div. Signal Coy. Royal Engineers.

Douglas was born in Oldmeldrum, Aberdeenshire in 1897, the son of Adam Mackie, a station master, later resident of Peterhead. Douglas worked as a clerk in Peterhead office of the Great Northern Scottish Railway.

Enlisted in Peterhead, Douglas was killed in action on the 25 Mar 1918, when the Allied Fifth Army was driven back by overwhelming numbers across the former Somme battlefields in Mar/Apr 1918. Douglas' name is inscribed on the Pozieres Memorial. This Memorial commemorates over 14,000 casualties of the United Kingdom who have no known grave.

References:
CWGC Casualty No 1584877
Buchan Observer Article 9 Apr 1918

Francis James MACKIE

Service: M2/051736. Rank: Pte. Regiment: Royal Army Service Corps.
Rank: 2Lt. Regiment: 19th Bn. The King's (Liverpool Regiment).

Born in Fraserburgh in 1890, Francis (aka Frank) was the youngest son of Robert and Jean (Jane) Mackie of 44 Queen Street, Peterhead. In 1901, he was resident of Orkney and just prior to the war, Francis' occupation was an engineer.

Originally he joined the Royal Army Service Corps and entered the French and Flanders theatre on the 30 Apr 1915. He was commissioned as 2Lt into The King's (Liverpool) Regiment on 26 Jun 1916. Having already been wounded, Francis was killed in action on the 29 May 1917, aged 28. He is buried in the Vlamertinghe New Military Cemetery which was used by fighting units and field ambulances until Jun 1917.

References:
CWGC Casualty No 138486
1901 Scotland Census

Peter Copland MACKIE

Service No: 1396. Rank: Pte. Regiment: 5th Bn. Gordon Highlanders.
Service No: 240111. Rank: Sgt. Regiment: 5th Bn. Gordon Highlanders.

Peter was born in Peterhead and was the son of James and Georgina Mackie of Tanfield Place, Peterhead, Peter enlisted into the Gordon Highlanders soon after the outbreak of war.

He arrived in France on the 2 May 1915 and was injured almost immediately when he was wounded in the left ear and the right shoulder and wrist. Peter was wounded a further three times on the 26 Mar 1916; the 28 Apr 1916 and the 31 Jul 1916 before being killed in action on the 17 May 1917. His sacrifice is recorded on the Arras Memorial.

References:
CWGC Casualty No 3077802
1911 Census for Peterhead

William MACKINTOSH*

Service No: 859109. Rank: Piper. Regiment: 43rd Bn. Canadian Infantry.

Born on the 21 Feb 1884 and brought up by his mother Jean Mackintosh at Graystone Farm near Peterhead. William emigrated to Canada in 1903 and worked for the Electric Car Service in Winnipeg.

William enlisted in Winnipeg and was killed in action on the 11 Apr 1918. He is buried at La Targette British Cemetery, Neuville-St. Vaast

References:
CWGC Casualty No 530960
Canadian Great War Project
Buchan Observer 1918

David Ross MACPHERSON (McPherson)

Service No: S/2477. Rank: Engineman.
Service: RNR - HMD J.A.C.

David was born in 1891 in Cullen, Banffshire the son of George and Mary Ross McPherson and the husband of Janet McPherson of 32 James St., Peterhead.

David died from disease on the 5 Feb 1919 aged 28, whilst serving aboard the minesweeper HMD J.A.C. He is buried in Haidar Pasha Cemetery, Turkey. During the First World War the cemetery was used by the Turks for the burial of Commonwealth prisoners of war and after the Armistice, when Istanbul was occupied, further burials were made, mainly from No.82 General Hospital. In addition, 119 graves were brought in from other smaller cemeteries.

References:
CWGC Casualty No 427998

Robert MACPHERSON (McPherson)

Service No: 1622/TS(PO). Rank: Trimmer.
Service: RNR – HMT Ashton.

Born in 1897, Robert was the son of John
and Helen (m/s Copland) McPherson. He
was a fisherman and his usual residency was
19 Windmill St, Peterhead.

Robert died of natural causes, a combination
of sudden heart failure and pneumonia at 21
Hadden Street, Aberdeen on the 20 Oct 1916
aged 29. He was serving with the Royal
Naval Reserve at the time of his death.
Robert is buried in Peterhead Cemetery.

References:
CWGC Casualty No 326990
Death Certificate.

Robert James Bruce MAIR

Service No: 35749. Rank: Pte. Regiment: 5th
Bn. Highland Light Infantry.

Born in 1891, in Peterhead, Robert was the
son of John and Christian Bruce Mair of
Peterhead. Robert was the youngest brother
of Christina, Joseph, Elizabeth, Helen, Ann
and John Mair. Prior to the war, Robert was
employed in his father's fishcuring business.

Enlisted into the HLI in Aberdeen, Robert
died of his wounds on the 26 Aug 1918 aged
27 years. He is buried in the St Hilaire
Cemetery Extension. The great majority of
the burials in the cemetery were carried out
from the many local military hospitals.

References:
CWGC Casualty No 528277

Joseph MARR*

Service No: 159. Rank: Pte. Regiment: 2nd
Bn. Gordon Highlanders.

Born around 1892 in New Pitsligo,
Aberdeenshire, Joseph was the son of Capt.
Joseph and Jane (m/s Duncan) Marr of 34
Gilbert St. Bucksburn, Aberdeen. Joseph was
the brother of Annie, Jeannie and David
Mather Marr and the half-brother of William
and Jessie Bella Marr. Prior to the Great War
Joseph's father, a professional soldier was a
Sgt in the Territorial Battalion of the Gordon
Highlanders based in Peterhead.

Joseph enlisted in Strichen and arrived in
France on the 7 Oct 1914. He was killed at
the Battle of Ypres on the 29 Oct 1914 and
his sacrifice is honoured on the Ypres (Menin

Gate) Memorial which now bears the names
of more than 54,000 officers and men whose
graves are not known.

References:
CWGC Casualty No 929713

William MARR

Service No: 1290/ES. Rank: Engineman.
Service: RNR - HMS Thalia.

Born on the 4 Jun 1883 at 82 Longate,
Peterhead, William was the son of William
Davidson Marr and Margaret Robertson (m/s
Sutherland) Marr. He was married to Jessie
P. Marr of 7 James St., Peterhead.

Whilst aboard HMS Thalia, a base ship,
William died from disease on the 21 Nov
1918, aged 37 and is buried in Peterhead
Cemetery.

References:
CWGC Casualty No 326992
Maritime Return 1918
Birth Certificate

Andrew Stephen MASSON

Service No: 2617. Rank: Seaman. Service:
RNR – HMD Industry (PD.378).
Service No: S/24482. Rank: Pte. Regiment:
Seaforth Highlanders.
Service No: 138283. Rank: Pte. Regiment:
Royal Army Medical Corps.

Born on the 21 Jan 1891 in Peterhead,
Andrew was the youngest son of William
Masson, a fishcurer, and Helen (m/s
Strachan) Masson of 130 Queen St.,
Peterhead. He was also a brother to William
(he also fell) and Elizabeth Ann Masson.
Andrew was married to Jeannie West Masson
and had two children; Elizabeth (b.1913) and
Thomas Buchan (b.1916) Masson and they
all lived at 15 Skelton St., Peterhead.

Andrew originally joined the RNR in late 1916
before transferring to the Seaforth
Highlanders. Having sustained 60% disability
with valvular disease of the heart (a common
term for being gassed) he was transferred to
the Royal Army Medical Corps in London
where he completed the war in a training
establishment.

Andrew was killed in a motor cycle accident
on the 7 May 1921 on the road near Station
Farm, Longhaven, Cruden.

References:
Service Record

William MASSON MM

Service No: 1785. Rank: Pte. Regiment: 1st Res Highland Field Ambulance.

Service No: 301258. Rank: Pte. Regiment: 89th Field Ambulance, Royal Army Medical Corps.

Born in 1891 in Peterhead and residing at Bethany House, Peterhead, William was the son of William Masson, a fishcurer, and Helen (m/s Strachan) Masson of 130 Queen St., Peterhead. He was also brother to Andrew Stephen Masson and Elizabeth Ann Masson.

William enlisted into the 1st Bn. HFA on the 19 Sep 1914 in Aberdeen and was posted to Egypt. In Apr 1916 William departed Suez for Marseilles to join the BEF in France. On the 23 Jul 1917 he was awarded the Military Medal for bravery. William died of his wounds which he received in action on the 6 Oct 1917 aged 28. These wounds included gunshot wounds to the head, left buttock and forearm.

William is buried in the Boulogne Eastern Cemetery, Boulogne which was one of the three base ports most extensively used by the Commonwealth armies on the Western Front throughout the First World War.

References:
CWGC Casualty No 47993
London Gazette 18 (Jul) Sep 1917

Robertson MATHEW*

Born in Peterhead on the 27 Jun 1895 at 38 James St., Peterhead, Robertson (aka Robin) was the son of John Scroggie and Catherine (Kate) Ann (m/s Brown) Mathew. By 1901 the family was living in Grangemouth, Stirlingshire. Robertson had up to 14 brothers and sisters including; James, Brown[1], Margaret S.B., John S., Charlotte, John, Catherine, Agnes W.B., Alexander, Colin B. and Charlie B. Mathew.

Robertson was a Sick Birth Attendant and died aboard HMS Stonecrop (aka the Q Ship Glenfoyle). She was torpedoed in the North

Atlantic on the 18 Sep 1917, the day after she sank the U-88. The commander of the U-88 was Walther Schwieg, infamous as being the U-boat Commander who sank the RMS Lusitania.

References:
Buchan Observer Oct 1917

William Davidson MATTHEW

Service No: 351430. Rank: Pte. Regiment: 1st/6th Bn. Black Watch (Royal Highlanders).

Born in Peterhead in 1890, William was the son of William (occ mason) and Jessie Matthew of 7 Thistle St., Peterhead. He enlisted into the Black Watch (Royal Highlanders) in Aberdeen.

William died of his wounds on the 9 Aug 1918 in the 1st Australian General Hospital, Rouen and is buried in the St Sever Cemetery Extension, Rouen. Almost all of the hospitals at Rouen remained there for the whole of the war.

References:
CWGC Casualty No 519502

John MAY

Service No: 29563. Rank: Pte. Regiment: 79th Bn. Territorial Reserve.
Service No: 55923. Rank: Pte. Regiment: 3rd Bn. Highland Light Infantry.
Service No: 41363. Rank: LCpl. Regiment: 1st Bn. Royal Scots Fusiliers.

Born in Peterhead in 1898, John was the son of John Whyte May and Isabella Jaffray (m/s Smith) May of 45 Landale Rd., Peterhead. A joiner by trade he had two brothers, George and Robert and also two sisters, Eliza and Phyllis. Prior to the war, he was employed by his father as a house carpenter.

John enlisted into the 79th Territorial Reserve Bn. on the 15 Feb 1917 and completed training in Montrose. He joined the Scottish Division in France on the 28 Mar 1918, where he was promoted to LCpl. 15 days later, on the 12 Apr 1918 John was posted "missing, presumed dead" aged 19 years. His body has never been found and his sacrifice is honoured on the Ploegsteert Memorial, This memorial commemorates more than 11,000 servicemen of the United Kingdom and South African forces who died in this sector and have no known grave.

---

[1] Brown is the correct if rather unusual forename

References:
CWGC Casualty No 870319
Service Record

Alexander McCLURE

Service No: A/6845. Rank: Pte. Regiment: 2nd Bn. Royal Scots Fusiliers.

Alexander was born in Peterhead about 1893 and was the son of Mr and Mrs Thomas McClure, of the Officers' Quarters, HM Convict Prison and later of 13 Kirk St., Peterhead.

He enlisted in Glasgow and was sent to France on the 6 Oct 1914 earning the 1914 star. Alexander was captured by the Germans and spent the rest of the war as a prisoner of war. He died at the Cassel prisoner of war camp on the 22 Oct 1918 aged 25 and is buried in the Niederzwehren Cemetery in Germany. This cemetery was begun by the Germans in 1915 for the burial of prisoners of war who died at the local camp.

References:
CWGC Casualty No 903848

Joseph Robertson MCCOMBIE*

Service No: 4659. Rank: Pte. Regiment: 5th Bn. Seaforth Highlanders.

Born in Peterhead in 1880, Joseph was the son of Joseph and Margaret (m/s Robertson) McCombie of Peterhead and was also the brother of Eliza Helen McCombie. Joseph was married to Maggie Jane (m/s Fotheringham) McCombie, of 145, Victoria Rd., Kilburn, London whom he married in 1913 in Kent.

Joseph was killed on the 13 Nov 1916 during the attack on Beaumont-Hamel and is buried in the Beaumont-Hamel British Cemetery. This highly fortified town was attacked and reached on 1 Jul 1916, but it could not be held. It was attacked again, and this time was taken, on 13 Nov 1916.

References:
CWGC Casualty No 180758

Bruce McDONALD

Service No: S/43308. Rank: Sgt. Regiment: 1st Bn. Gordon Highlanders.

Born in Peterhead, Bruce was the foster son of Mr & Mrs Donald McDonald of the Officers' Quarters, Peterhead Prison and later of "Ormidale", West Carn Rd., Barnhill,

Broughty Ferry, Forfarshire. He was formerly in the employ of Messrs Brown & Co, drapers, Broad St. Peterhead.

Bruce enlisted into the Gordon Highlanders in Peterhead. He was killed by a sniper when rushing the German lines on the 13 Nov 1916 aged 20. He has no known grave and his name is inscribed on the Thiepval Memorial. This memorial is to the missing of the Somme and bears the names of more than 72,000 officers and men of the United Kingdom and South African forces who died in the Somme sector.

References:
CWGC Casualty No 802465
Buchan Observer Nov/Dec 1916

Donald McDONALD

Service No: 19102. Rank: LCpl. Regiment: 13th Bn. Royal Irish Rifles.

Donald was born in Peterhead on the 7 Aug 1891, the son of Peter and Janet Webster McDonald of 43½ Marischal St., Peterhead. Donald's father's occupation was a sea captain who originated from the Isle of Uist. Donald was from a large family, he was one of ten children.

Donald enlisted into the Irish Rifles in Newry, N. Ireland and arrived in France on the 6 Oct 1915. He was killed in action on the 21 Mar 1916 aged 25 years. Donald is buried in the Mesnil Ridge Cemetery, Mesnil-Martinsart, This cemetery was made by Field Ambulances and fighting units (mainly of the 29th and 36th (Ulster) Divisions) between Aug 1915 and Aug 1916.

References:
CWGC Casualty No 613531
Ireland, Casualties of WW1

William McDONALD

Service No: 1373. Rank: Pte. Regiment: 1st/5th Bn. Gordon Highlanders.

Born in the parish of Tyrie near Peterhead, William was the son of Mrs Jane McDonald of 14 Wallace St., Peterhead.

William enlisted in New Deer and was sent to France on the 2 May 1915. He was killed in action on the 15 Nov 1916 during the attack on Beaumont-Hamel. William is interred in the Y Ravine Cemetery, Beaumont-Hamel.

References:
CWGC Casualty No 2742943

James McGEE

Service No: 2986. Rank: Pte. Regiment: 5th Bn. Gordon Highlanders.
Service No: 292186. Rank: Pte. Regiment: 6th Bn. Gordon Highlanders.

Born in Peterhead, James was the son of Mrs. Margaret McGee of 58 Roanheads, Peterhead.

Having enlisted in Peterhead, originally into the 5th Bn. Gordon Highlanders, James was killed on the 23 Apr 1917 aged 20 years. James' body was never found and his sacrifice is commemorated on the Arras Memorial which remembers almost 35,000 servicemen from the United Kingdom, South Africa and New Zealand.

References:
CWGC Casualty No 3077477

James Cyness McGEE (McGHEE)

Service No: S/14774. Rank: Pte. Regiment: 9th Bn. Gordon Highlanders.

James was born in 1881 in Crimond, the son of Mrs Rogers of Millbrec Cottage, Mintlaw, Aberdeenshire.

James enlisted in Old Deer and was killed in action at Passchendaele on the 22 Aug 1917. His sacrifice is commemorated on the Tyne Cot Memorial.

References:
CWGC Casualty No 833803

John McGEE (McGHEE or McGHIE)

Service No: 3361. Rank: Pte. Regiment: 5th Bn. Gordon Highlanders.

John was the son of Mr and Mrs Peter McGhee of 38 Windmill St., Peterhead. He was born in Old Deer in 1897 and was also the brother of Alexander and Maggie McGhee. Before the war, John was employed as a farm servant in the Rora district.

Just after the commencement of hostilities, John enlisted into the Gordon Highlanders. He died of his wounds near Courcelette on the 29 Nov 1916. John is buried in the Adanac Military Cemetery, Miraumont. The Adanac Military Cemetery (the name was formed by reversing the name "Canada") was made after the Armistice when graves were brought in from the Canadian battlefields around Courcelette and small cemeteries surrounding Miraumont.

References:
CWGC Casualty No 183605

Leslie McGREGOR

Service No: 9480/DA. Rank: Deckhand. Service: RNR – HMS Mikasa.

Born on the 15 May 1896 in Peterhead, Leslie was the son of William Henry McGregor of The Row, Kimundy, Longside, Aberdeenshire.

Leslie died in Aberdeen of illness on the 2 Jul 1916, aged 22 and is buried in the Peterhead Cemetery.

References:
CWGC Casualty No 327019

James William McHATTIE*

Service No: 1331. Rank: Pte. Regiment: London Regiment.
Rank: Lt. Regiment: 3rd/5th Bn. York and Lancaster Regiment.
Rank: Lt. Regiment: 20 Sqn Royal Air Force.

Born in 1893 in Enfield, Middlesex, James was the son of James and Maggie (m/s Gillespie) McHattie, former residents of Peterhead and later of 34 Main Avenue, Bush Hill Park, Enfield, Middlesex.

James enlisted into the London Regiment as a Pte and served with the BEF from the 15 Sep 1914. On the 20 Dec 1915 James was commissioned into the Yorks and Lancs Regiment. Later he was attached to the Royal Air Force. James was killed on the 25 Apr 1918 and is buried in the Longuenesse (St. Omer) Souvenir Cemetery. St. Omer was the General Headquarters of the British Expeditionary Force from Oct 1914 to Mar 1916. The Commonwealth section of the cemetery contains 2,874 Commonwealth burials of the First World War (6 remain unidentified).

References:
CWGC Casualty 22150

Thomas McINTOSH

Service No: S/43335. Rank: Pte. Regiment: 1st Bn. Gordon Highlanders.

Born in Peterhead on the 10 Feb 1897,

Thomas was the son of Robert and Isabella Hutchison (m/s Allardyce) McIntosh of 38 Windmill St., Peterhead. Thomas was also the brother of Jessie Ann Allardyce, William John, Robert, Austin, Norman, Sarah Allardyce and John McIntosh.

Thomas enlisted into the Gordon Highlanders and was killed on the 17 Jun 1917. His body was never recovered and his name is annotated on the Arras Memorial which commemorates almost 35,000 servicemen from the United Kingdom, South Africa and New Zealand who died in the Arras sector and have no known grave.

References:
CWGC Casualty No 3077629

Donald McIVER

Service No: 1612C. Rank: Stoker. Service: RNR - HMS Newmarket.

Born in 1869 in Aultbea, Rosshire, Donald was the husband of Jane McIver of 82 Longate, Peterhead.

Donald died with the loss of HMS Newmarket on the 17 Jul 1917. HMS Newmarket, was a steamer built in 1907 by Earle's S.B. & Eng. Co., Ltd. Hull. In Oct 1914 she was requisitioned by the Royal Navy for use as a minesweeper. On the 17 Jul 1917, the German submarine UC-38 torpedoed and sank her south of Ikaria Island in the Aegean Sea (37°17'N, 26°15'E). The loss of life was heavy and there were only three survivors from a crew of 73. Donald was 48 years old and his loss is recorded upon the Portsmouth Naval Memorial.

References:
CWGC Casualty No 3041276
Great War Forum – HMS Newmarket

Adam Sutherland McKAY (MACKAY)

Service No: S/19578. Rank: Pte. Regiment: Gordon Highlanders.
Service No: S/41424. Rank: Pte. Regiment: 1st/7th Bn. Black Watch (Royal Highlanders).

Born in Peterhead in 1900, Adam was the youngest son of John and Catherine Mackay, of 84 Queen St. and later of 18 Kirk St., Peterhead. He was brother to David Douglas, Margaret Helen., Kathrine Livingstone and Robert MacKay. Adam was an apprentice with Mr G. Robertson, motor and cycle agent, Peterhead.

Adam enlisted into the Gordon Highlanders in Aberdeen only a few weeks before his brother Robert was killed. Adam later transferred to the Black Watch (Royal Highlanders). He was killed on the 9 Apr 1918, aged 18 and his death is honoured on the Loos Memorial which commemorates over 20,000 officers and men who have no known grave.

References:
CWGC Casualty No 735158
Buchan Observer Article 28 May 1918

Robert John McKAY (MACKAY)

Service No: 1909. Rank: Pte. Regiment: Royal Army Medical Corps
Service No: 301340. Rank: Pte. Regiment: Royal Army Medical Corps.

Born around 1888 in Edinburgh, Robert was the eldest son of John and Catherine MacKay, of 84 Queen St. and later of 18 Kirk St., Peterhead. He was also the brother to David Douglas, Margaret Helen and Kathrine Livingstone and Adam MacKay. Robert was employed by Mr William Gibson of Peterhead before going to work in Canada.

Having returned to Scotland, he enlisted in Aberdeen into the Royal Army Medical Corps. Robert arrived in France to serve with the BEF on the 16 Mar 1915. He later transferred to the 2nd / 1st HFA and was killed on the 16 May 1917 as the result of a shell explosion. Aged 29, Robert is buried in the St. Nicolas British Cemetery. From Mar 1916 to the Armistice, the village of St. Nicolas was occupied by Commonwealth forces and for much of that time it was within the range of German artillery fire.

References:
CWGC Casualty No 51041
Service Record

George McKECHNIE

Service No: 2862. Rank: Pte. Regiment: Gordon Highlanders.
Service No: 240819. Rank: Pte. Regiment: Gordon Highlanders.
Service No: 337138. Rank: Pte. Regiment: Labour Corps.
Service No: 403108. Rank: Spr. Regiment: Royal Engineers.
Service No: WR/305578. Rank: Spr. Regiment: Inland Waterways and Docks, Royal Engineers.

George was born in 1885 in Peterhead into a very large family - being one of thirteen children. His parents were William Neil and

Margaret (m/s Thoirs) McKechnie. George was married to Maggie (m/s Hendry) McKechnie of St. Fergus. He was brother to Maggie, William, Anne, Mary, Neil, Jane, Isabella, Alexander, John, Lizzie, Thomas and Jessie McKechnie all of whom were born in Peterhead between 1859 and 1887.

George enlisted into the Gordon Highlanders in Peterhead but due to disability he transferred to the Labour Corps. Later in the war, George transferred to the Royal Engineers. He drowned at Sandwich, Kent on the 4 Mar 1918 aged 33 and is buried at St. Fergus Old Churchyard.

References:
CWGC Casualty No 327041

Andrew McKENZIE

Service No: 3109. Rank: Pte. Regiment: 2nd/5th Bn. Gordon Highlanders.

Andrew was the son of Andrew and Elspet (m/s Hepburn) McKenzie of Copland Hill, Peterhead, later of Blackhouse, Peterhead.

Andrew joined the Gordon Highlanders on the 9 Apr 1915 and was released for harvest work later that autumn. On the 30 Jul 1916, Andrew was discharged from the Army being no longer fit for Army service. His medical records indicate that he has contracted tuberculosis and was released to the Peterhead Sanatorium. Andrew died on the 15 Mar 1917 aged 32 and is buried with his brother James in Constitution Street Cemetery, Peterhead, who also died from tuberculosis. (See below). Andrew's details are currently missing from the Commonwealth War Graves Commission records.

References:
Service Pension Record
Constitution Street Cemetery, MIs

James McKENZIE

Service No: 2089. Rank: Pte. Regiment: 5th Bn. Gordon Highlanders.

James was the son of the late Andrew and Elspet (m/s Hepburn) McKenzie of Copland Hill Peterhead, later Blackhouse, Peterhead.

Attested on the 14 Aug 1914, into B Coy in Peterhead, James was discharged from Scone Camp on the 9 Jun 1915 due to contracting tuberculosis. His medical records state that he was a delicate individual but on being discharged he was described as much

emaciated and had lost flesh. In permanent pain, James was classed as 100% disabled and unfit for work. He was granted a 20 shilling a week pension. James died at home, three years later of tuberculosis on the 26 Nov 1918 aged 27. The Commonwealth War Graves Commission, currently, does not record his death as a war death. James is buried in Constitution Street Cemetery, Peterhead.

References:
Death Certificate 1918, 232 01 0178
Battalion Roll 1914

Robert Andrew McKENZIE

Rank: 2Lt. Regiment: 9th Bn. King's Royal Rifle Corps.

Born in 1892, Robert was the only son of Roderick McKenzie, warder of HM Convict Prison, Peterhead. Prior to the war, Robert served his apprentice at the Burgh Surveyor's Office in Peterhead and latterly of St Andrews, Fife.

After training in Wales, Robert was gazetted into the KRRC. He was only at the front for a few months when he was killed in action on the 10 Nov 1917, aged only 25. Robert is buried in the White House Cemetery, St. Jean-Les-Ypres. This cemetery was begun in Mar 1915 and used until Apr 1918 by units holding this part of the line.

His medal card, which was compiled a few years after the war, suggests that Robert's father was a Robert McKenzie of 3 Cairview, Lawrencekirk, Kincardinshire.

References:
CWGC Casualty No 454766
Medal Card
Buchan Observer Dec 1917.

Sydney Keith McKESSAR*

Service No: 1615. Rank: Sgt. Regiment: 33rd Bn. Australian Imperial Force.

Born in Bulli, NSW, Australia in Mar 1896, Sydney was the son of Alexander and Maria McKessar, both natives of Peterhead who emigrated to Australia in the 1890's. Sydney was married to Jessie Muriel McKessar and they had one daughter named Enid McKessar.

Having enlisted on the 11 May 1916, Sydney arrived in France on the 5 Apr 1917 only to be killed on the 5 Jun 1917. He is buried in the Strand Military Cemetery.

After the war his wife Jessie remarried a returning soldier named Roy Monk.

References:
CWGC Casualty No 165353
Australian National Archive.

James Baxter McKINNON

Service No: 3321. Rank: Pte. Regiment: 4th Regiment. South African Infantry.

James was born about 1898 the son of John Hutton McKinnon and Elizabeth (m/s Wood) McKinnon of 16 Milner Rd., Woodstock, Cape Province and brother to John Hutton McKinnon all of whom originated from Peterhead.

James was killed at Delville Wood, Longueval, France on the 15 Jul 1916, aged 18. His body has never been recovered and his sacrifice is commemorated on the Thiepval Memorial, the memorial to the missing of the Somme which bears the names of more than 72,000 officers and men of the United Kingdom and South African forces who died in the Somme sector and have no known grave.

References:
CWGC Casualty No 803476

Alexander McLEAN

Service No: 2476. Rank: Pte. Regiment: 1st/5th Bn. Gordon Highlanders.

Born around 1883 and lived at 40 Merchant St, Peterhead, Alexander worked as a labourer at the Admiralty Works, Peterhead.

Having previously served in the Boer War, Alexander enlisted in the Gordon Highlanders in Peterhead. He was killed on the 3 Jun 1915 when shrapnel from a shell burst hit him and two others, killing them instantaneously. He was buried behind the firing trench and according to reports had met his death nobly. His body was not recovered and his name appears on the Le Touret Memorial which commemorates over 13,400 British soldiers who were killed in this sector of the Western Front and who have no known grave.

References:
CWGC Casualty 853877
Scotsman 12 Jun 1915

Charles Stobie McLEAN*

Service No: 229365. Rank: Pte. Regiment: 44th Bn. Canadian Infantry.

Born on the 18 Oct 1894 at Dunrossness, Charles was the son of Donald, a missionary and schoolmaster, and Mary McLean of The Schoolhouse, Fair Isle. He was the brother of Kenneth, Donald, Mary Helen, Euphenia, Louisa Elizabeth and Jane McFarland Mclean.

A sometime resident of Peterhead, Charles emigrated to Canada before enlisting into the Canadian Infantry at Winnipeg on the 2 Sep 1915. Charles was killed on the 22 Oct 1916 and is buried in the Warloy-Baillon Communal Cemetery Extension. This Cemetery contains 1,331 First World War Commonwealth burials.

References:
CWGC Casualty No 74742

Henry (Harry) Annand Firth McLEOD

Service No: S/22526. Rank: Pte. Regiment: 4th Bn Gordon Highlanders.

Born in the parish of Culter, Aberdeen in 1899, Harry was the second son of Mr and Mrs Alexander McLeod, of Castlebrae Cottage, Inverugie, Peterhead. Prior to the war, Harry was a farm servant in the Cromar district.

Harry enlisted into the Gordon Highlanders in Aberdeen and was killed in action on the 25 Jul 1918 aged only 19 years. The location of his grave is not known and his name appears on the Soissons Memorial which commemorates almost 4,000 officers and men of the United Kingdom forces who died during the Battles of the Aisne and the Marne in 1918 and who have no known grave.

References:
CWGC Casualty No 1759223

William James McLEOD

Service No: S/40581. Rank: Pte. Regiment: 2nd Bn. Gordon Highlanders.

Born in 1877 in Peterhead, William was the son of James and Christina Young (m/s Murray) McLeod of 67 Longate, Peterhead. He was the husband of Mary Helen McLeod whom he married in 1898. They had four children; Margaret Troup (later Henderson) Chrissie, Edith and Angus McLeod. William also had one brother and two sisters; Alexander, Christian and Maggie McLeod.

Prior to the war William was a cooper in Peterhead.

William enlisted in Leith and was killed on the 10 May 1917 aged 40 years. His body was never recovered and his sacrifice is commemorated on the Arras Memorial which commemorates almost 35,000 servicemen from the United Kingdom, South Africa and New Zealand who died in the Arras and have no known grave.

Upon William's death, his wife was an inmate of the Royal Asylum in Aberdeen and the children were under the care of Mrs James Ross (his sister) of 67 Longate, Peterhead.

References:
CWGC Casualty No 3077944
Service Record

George Smith McNAB

Service No: 3226/6. Rank: Pte. Regiment: Gordon Highlanders.
Service No: 266843. Rank: Pte. Regiment: 6th Bn. Gordon Highlanders.

 Born 2 Nov 1890 in Peterhead, George was the son of James and Mary Ann (m/s Finnie) McNab of 7 Back St, Peterhead. He was one of eleven children and his occupation was described as a painter. George married Elizabeth (Lizzie) Thomson on the 3 May 1916 and they one son, also named George Smith McNab. Later Lizzie lived at Barrhill, Culter, Peterculter, Aberdeenshire.

George enlisted into the Gordon Highlanders in Peterhead and was sent to France on the 2 Oct 1915. He was killed in action on the 31 Jul 1917 aged 26, during the 3rd Battle of Ypres (Passchendaele). His name is engraved upon the Ypres (Menin Gate) Memorial which lists the names of more than 54,000 officers and men whose graves are not known.

References:
CWGC Casualty No 1622342

David McWILLIAM

Service No: 2345/5. Rank: Pte. Regiment: 5th Bn. Gordon Highlanders.
Service No: 240543. Rank: LCpl. Regiment: 5th Bn. Gordon Highlanders.

Born in Peterhead around 1892, David was the third son of Ewan and Ann McWilliam of 22 Queen St. Peterhead. He was the brother of Ewan, Helen, Peter, Maggie, Andrew and Ann McWilliam. Prior to the war, David was a cooper with Messrs A. Wood and Sons, fishcurers.

David enlisted in Peterhead in 1914 and arrived in France on the 21 Aug 1915. He died on the 5 Dec 1917 during the Battle of Cambrai. David's name is inscribed upon the Cambrai Memorial, Louverval which commemorates more than 7,000 servicemen of the United Kingdom and South Africa who died in the Battle of Cambrai and whose graves are not known.

References:
CWGC Casualty No 1754986
Buchan Observer 18 Dec 1917

Donald McLeod McWILLIAM

Rank: Lt. Cmdr. Service: RNR – HMS Orama.

Donald was born about 1878 in Peterhead and was the son of James and Catherine McWilliam. He was the husband of Elspet Rolls (m/s Chisholm) McWilliam of 71 Grange Gardens, Peterhead.

A Merchant Seaman, Donald was employed by the Orient and Pacific Line. The war broke out whilst he was on leave in Aberdeen. Donald returned to London and was gazetted to HMS Orama. He saw action with the sinking of the SS Navarra and the German raider, the Dresden, off Juan Fernandez. Following the sinking of the Von Spee Squadron in the South Atlantic, Donald, now suffering from chronic dysentery, was placed on a passing steamer and sent home.

Donald died in London of dysentery on the 1 Mar 1916, aged 38. Following a large funeral in Peterhead, Donald was buried in Peterhead Cemetery.

References:
CWGC Casualty 326991
Buchan Observer 7 Mar 16 Page 4

Thomas George MILLER

Service No: 2966T. Rank: Stoker. Service: RNR – HMS Invincible.

Thomas was born about 1885 in Peterhead, the son of John and Catherine Miller of 1 Keith St., Peterhead. His siblings included; Alexander, William, John, Mary, George, Jessie, Lucy, James, Elizabeth, Oscar and

Albert Miller. Thomas later appears on the 1911 English Census where he is listed as a single man living in Dorset.

Thomas was another of the Peterhead sailors who were lost when HMS Invincible was sunk during the Battle of Jutland on the 31 May 1916, Thomas was aged 31 and his sacrifice is commemorated on the Portsmouth Naval Memorial.

References:
CWGC Casualty No 3037507

Alexander James Bolton MILNE*

Service No: 4381. Rank: Pte. Regiment: Gordon Highlanders.
Rank: 2Lt. Regiment 4th Bn. Gordon Highlanders.

Born in the Shetland Islands in 1887, Alexander was the son of the Rev. Alexander Allan Milne and Janet (m/s Bolton) Milne, later of Oakfield House, Doune, Perthshire.

Joining the Gordon Highlanders as an enlisted man, Alexander was later commissioned into the 4th Bn. He arrived in France on the 1 Dec 1915 and fell on the 22 Aug 1917 aged 30. Alexander was buried in the White House Cemetery, St. Jean-Les-Ypres which was begun in Mar 1915 and used until Apr 1918 by units holding this part of the line and was extended when graves were brought in from the battlefields around Ypres.

References:[2]
CWGC Casualty No 454805

Alfred MILNE

Service No: 4561. Rank: Pte. Regiment: 2nd Bn. Scots Guards.

Alfred died on the 16 May 1915 and is buried in the Terlincthun British Cemetery, Wimille The first rest camps for Commonwealth forces were established near Terlincthun in Aug 1914 and during the whole of the First

World War, Boulogne and Wimereux housed numerous hospitals and other medical establishments.

References:
CWGC Casualty No 4026502
Buchan Observer, Peterhead Roll of Honour 1919

James MILNE[3]

Service No: 930. Rank: Pte. Regiment: 2nd Bn. Gordon Highlanders.

Born in 1891, James was the son of Robert and Jane Milne, of Denside, Sandford, Boddam near Peterhead. He was the brother of Robert, Eliza, Francis, William and Mary Milne. His brother, William Milne fell in 1918.

James enlisted in Aberdeen and joined the BEF in France on the 7 Oct 1914. He was killed in action three weeks later on the 29 Oct 1914, aged 23. He died during the First Battle of Ypres and his sacrifice is commemorated on the Ypres (Menin Gate) Memorial, which now bears the names of more than 54,000 officers and men whose graves are not known.

References:
CWGC Casualty No 906974
Buchan Observer 31 Oct 1916 Page 4

James MILNE[3]

Service No: 240608. Rank: Pte. Regiment: 5th Bn. Gordon Highlanders.

Born in 1899 in Peterhead, James was the second son of Peter (occ fisherman) and Margaret (aka Maggie) (m/s Bruce) Milne of 12 Mid St., Buchanhaven. He was also the brother of Margaret M, Mary, Peter, John, Christina and William Milne.

James was killed, reportedly by accidentally drowning on the 7 Feb 1918. He is buried in the Doullens Communal Cemetery Extension No.1.

---

[2] Another soldier from Peterhead - Alexander John Buchan MILNE was severely injured by gassing in 1918. Former Dux of Peterhead Academy – no further information about his fate.

[3] There are two soldiers named Pte James Milne of the Gordon Highlanders with equal claim to be the soldier listed on the Peterhead Memorial. The details of both soldiers have been included here.

References:
CWGC Casualty No 83244
Buchan Observer Feb 1918.

James Gordon S. MILNE*

Service No: 3275. Rank: Pte. Regiment: 5th Bn. Gordon Highlanders.
Service No: 241018. Rank: Pte. Regiment: 5th Bn. Gordon Highlanders.

Born in Fraserburgh in 1879, James was the son of Alexander and Mary Milne. He was also brother to Elizabeth, Isabella W., Ritchie, Margaret, George, Mary J., Walter G., Joan M., Charles C.E. and Elize F. Milne.

James enlisted in Peterhead and after training in England arrived in France on the 12 Oct 1915. He fought for most of the Great War but sadly died of his wounds on the 2 Aug 1918 now aged 38. James is buried in the Royallieu French National Cemetery, Compiegne which was begun in Feb 1918, by No.16 French Hospital. After the Armistice, the cemetery was moved to the barracks at Royallieu.

References:
CWGC Casualty No 287270

James Smith MILNE

Service No: 3096. Rank: Pte. Regiment: 1st /5th Bn. Gordon Highlanders.

James was born in Peterhead in 1898 and was the fifth son of Henry T. and Mary Smith Milne, of 4 Port Henry Rd and later of 2 Backgate, Peterhead. He was also the brother of William, David John, Andrew, Henry, Mary, James and Alexanderina Milne. Prior to the outbreak of hostilities, James was a plumber and worked for Wm. Davidson, plumbers, Errol St. Peterhead.

James enlisted in Peterhead into the 5th Bn. Gordon Highlanders and joined up with the BEF on the 5 Dec 1915. He was killed in action at Mametz Wood on the 26 Jul 1916 aged only 18 years. James is buried in the Flatiron ("Flat Iron" to the troops) Copse Cemetery, Mametz.

References:
CWGC Casualty No 556929

John MILNE

Service No: 23188. Rank: L/Sgt. Regiment: 12th Bn. Highland Light Infantry.

Born in Peterhead in 1892, John was a resident of Inverurie and enlisted into the HLI in Aberdeen.

John arrived in France on the 26 Oct 1915 qualifying for the 1915 Star. He died of wounds on the 9 Apr 1917 aged 24. John is buried in the Faubourg D'amiens Cemetery, Arras.

References:
CWGC Casualty No 574513

Robert MILNE

Service No: 2380. Rank: Sgt. Regiment: 55th Bty. 33rd Bde. Royal Field Artillery.

Born in 1881, Robert was the son of Robert Milne and Margaret Smith and the husband of Elizabeth Durno Milne whom he married on the 31 Jan 1913 in Boddam. Robert's pre-war occupation was a prison guard.

Robert fell on the 27 May 1918 aged 37. His body was not recovered and his sacrifice is recorded on the Soissons Memorial which commemorates almost 4,000 officers and men of the United Kingdom forces who died during the Battles of the Aisne and the Marne in 1918 and who have no known grave.

References:
CWGC Casualty No 1759370
Buchan Observer Article 30 Apr 1918

William MILNE MM*

Service No: 3149. Rank: Pte. Regiment: 5th Bn. Gordon Highlanders.
Service No: 240964. Rank: L/Cpl. Regiment: 5th Bn. Gordon Highlanders.

Born in Old Deer in 1896, William was the son of Robert and Jane Milne, of Sandford, Boddam. He was the brother of James, Robert, Eliza, Francis and Mary Milne. His brother James fell in Oct 1914.

William enlisted into the 5th Bn. Gordon Highlanders in Peterhead and won the Military Medal in late 1917. He was killed in action on the 28 Jul 18 aged a mere 22 years. William is buried in the Bouilly Cross Roads Military Cemetery which was created in 1918 by the French Forces to contain British, French, Italian and German soldiers who had fallen in the vicinity.

References:
CWGC Casualty No 328863
MM – Soldiers Who Fell in the Great War

William MILNE CDG*

Rank: Maj. Regiment: 49th Bn. Machine Gun Corps.

Born in Boddam on the 14 Apr 1893, William was the son of George and Sarah Milne of Admiralty Cottages, Peterhead and later of 3 Claremont Place, Aberdeen. William was brother to Robert, Thomas, James and Margaret Milne.

Educated at Aberdeen University where he was enrolled in 1911 and graduated with a M.A in 1914. At the outbreak of war he joined the RAMC where he applied for a commission in a combatant unit. In Sep 1914 he was gazetted into the 14th Bn. HLI and was sent to Aberdeen to recruit for the regiment in the North. After training as a machine gunner, he was posted abroad as Machine Gun Officer with the 1st Bn. Dublin Fusiliers. He served through the whole of the Gallipoli Campaign and went to France in time to take part in the Somme battles of 1916. In recognition of his services and unflinching bravery in holding an important position in Belgium, he was decorated in Apr 1918 with the Croix de Guerre by a French General, and then promoted Major. A few days later, on 24 Apr 1918, he was severely wounded and captured at Kemmel Hill. He died as the result of his wounds at Soldau, Germany on the 25 Jul 1918. William is buried in Hamburg Cemetery which was used for the burial of over 300 Allied servicemen who died as prisoners of war. In 1923, it was decided that the graves of Commonwealth servicemen who had died all over Germany should be brought together into four permanent cemeteries.

References:
CWGC Casualty No 902501
Aberdeen University Roll of Honour.

William Leask MILNE

Service No: 2963. Rank: Cpl. Regiment: 5th Bn. Gordon Highlanders.
Service No: 292163. Rank: A/Sgt. Regiment: 7th Bn. Gordon Highlanders.

Born on the 4 Jul 1897, in Peterhead, William was the son of Alexander Milne Jnr and Georgina (m/s Birnie) Milne of 35 King St. and later of 3 Ellis Street, Peterhead. William was the brother to Alex, Donald, Maggie, and George Milne.

He enlisted in Peterhead, initially into the local 5th Bn. Gordon Highlanders before being transferred to the 7th Bn. as an A/Sgt. William was killed in action on the 23 Apr 1917 and his sacrifice is recorded on the Arras Memorial which commemorates almost 35,000 servicemen from the United Kingdom, South Africa and New Zealand who died in the Arras sector and have no known grave.

References:
CWGC Casualty No 781331

George Wallace MITCHELL

Rank: AB. Service: HM Water Tank Progress.

George was born in Peterhead in 1889, the son of Mrs Margaret Mitchell of 19 Chapel St., Aberdeen. He was the husband of Mary Christie Mitchell of 8 Newark Place, Port Glasgow.

HM Water Tanker Progress was a small harbour mooring boat or water carrier which sunk in the North Sea on the 21 Dec 1916. The bodies were washed up at Slains Castle, Cruden between the 8 and 10 Mar 1917. Six of the bodies have not been identified. There is a great deal of mystery over this incident as no local records remain. Indeed there was no knowledge of the incident amongst the local population. George died when the Progress was lost, aged 29, and is buried with his shipmates in the Cruden Parish Churchyard.

References:
CWGC Casualty No 326800

Herbert MITCHELL

Service No: 865. Rank: Spr. Regiment: 2nd /2nd (Highland) Field Coy. Royal Engineers.

Born on the 7 Jun 1894 in Peterhead, Herbert was the youngest son of David James and Margaret Jean (m/s Henderson) Mitchell of

Schoolhouse, Burnhaven, Peterhead. Herbert was the brother of David and Joseph William Mitchell. Prior to the war, Herbert was an apprentice engineer at the James Abernethy & Co Ferryhill Foundry.

Herbert enlisted in Aberdeen in Jan 1915 and arrived in France on the 3 May 1915. Having previously been injured, Herbert returned to the front and was killed by a trench mortar at Vimy on the 20 May 1916, age only 21. This young Sapper is buried in the Maroeuil British Cemetery.

References:
CWGC Casualty No 120954
Buchan Observer 30 May 1916 Page 4
Deaths & Page 5 Photo.

James MITCHELL

Rank: Skipper. Service: RNR - HMD Ocean Star.

James was born in 1876 and was the son of James Mitchell, of Peterhead and the husband of Jane Mitchell of 13 Victoria Rd., Peterhead.

James was killed when HMD Ocean Star was sunk by a mine explosion off the Isle of Wight on the 26 Sep 1917. Aged 41, James' sacrifice is commemorated on the Portsmouth Naval Memorial.

References:
CWGC Casualty No 3041373

John Harris MITCHELL

Service No: 204108. Rank: Pte. Regiment: 13th Bn. Canadian Infantry (Quebec Regiment).

John was born in Cruden, Aberdeenshire, on the 19 Sep 1890, the son of James and Eliza Ogilvie Mitchell of 37 St Mary St., Peterhead. He was the brother to Elizabeth, Christina, Anderson, Jemima, George (who fell in 1916), Andrew and Maggie Mitchell. His occupation was originally a farm servant. He emigrated to Canada in 1909 where he became a teamster (lorry driver).

John enlisted in Saskatoon on the 27 Dec 1915 but died of his wounds on the 9 Dec 1917 aged 27. James is buried in the Lijssenthoek Military Cemetery.

John's brother George was killed in action on the 1 Feb 1917. George does not appear on the Peterhead War Memorial or in the Buchan Observer 1919 Roll of Honour and so is

included in the epilogue to this book.

References:
CWGC Casualty No 432683
The War Book of Turriff & 12 Miles Round
Page 225
CEF Attestation Form.

Robert MITCHELL

Service No: 1461ES. Rank: Engineman. Service: RNR - HMD Laurel Crown.

Born in 1890, Robert was the son of James Mitchell of 16 Jamaica St, Peterhead and the husband of Mary Mitchell of 11 Maiden St., Peterhead. Robert and Mary had two children.

Robert was killed as a direct result of an explosion off the Orkney Islands caused by mines laid by U-75, the "Curt Beitzen" on the 22 Jun 1916. Robert was aged 26 and his body was never recovered. His sacrifice is commemorated on the Portsmouth Naval Memorial.

References:
CWGC Casualty No 3037527
Buchan Observer 4 Jul 1916 Deaths Page 4

James Allan MORRISON

Service No: 451901. Rank: Pte. Regiment: 58th Bn. Canadian Infantry (Central Ontario Regiment).

James was born on the 2 Jun 1886 in Peterhead, the fourth son of John (occ shoemaker) and Alexandrina Morrison of 8 Mid St., Buchanhaven, Peterhead. James was also brother to Alexander, Patrick, John, Beatrice, Catherine and Andrew Morrison.

James emigrated to Canada where he gain employment as a driver. He enlisted on 30 Jun 1915 at Niagara and died on the 8 Oct 1916 aged 28. His sacrifice is commemorated on the Vimy Memorial. After the war, Vimy Ridge was chosen as the site of the great memorial to all Canadians who served their country in battle during the First World War.

References:
CWGC Casualty No 1572132
Buchan Observer 21 Nov 1916.

John Smith MORRISON

Service No: 928. Rank: WO2. Regiment: 5th Bn. Gordon Highlanders.

Born in Peterhead in 1885, John was the son

of John and Elizabeth (m/s Smith) Morrison of 14 Maiden St. and later of 19 Windmill St., Peterhead. He was also the husband of Eliza J.F.D. (m/s Duthie) Morrison of 7½ Kirk St., Peterhead, whom he married in 1905. John was a plumber by trade but just prior to the war he was an officer at HM Convict Prison, Peterhead.

John enlisted in Peterhead in 1914 and arrived in France with the BEF on the 2 May 1915. At the age of 31, John was killed in action on the 31 Jul 1916 during the Third Battle of Ypres. His body has not been recovered and his name is inscribed on the Thiepval Memorial which bears the names of more than 72,000 officers and men of the United Kingdom and South African forces and have no known grave.

References:
CWGC Casualty No 1546003
Buchan Observer 29 Aug 1916.

Charles MUNDIE

Service No: 1875. Rank: LCpl. Regiment: 1st/5th Bn. Gordon Highlanders.

Born in Fraserburgh on the 16 Aug 1888, Charles was the son of Charles and Eliza (m/s Noble) Mundie, both natives of Fraserburgh. He was the husband of Helen Gibson (m/s Brand) Mundie of 34 St Andrew St., Peterhead, whom he married in 1913.

Charles enlisted into the Gordon Highlanders in Peterhead and was killed in action on the 13 Nov 1916, aged 29. Charles is buried in the Y Ravine Cemetery, Beaumont-Hamel.

References:
CWGC Casualty No 2742980

Angus Bain MUNRO

Service No: 2773. Rank: Pte. Regiment: 1st /5th Bn. Gordon Highlanders.

Born in Peterhead in 1888, Angus was the son of Angus and Sophia Rettie (m/s Massie) Munro and he was also the husband of Margaret Munro of 19 Longate, Peterhead. Angus had the following siblings - John Bain, Joseph Massie, James, Donald (died in infancy), Sophia, Alexander and Donald Munro.

After enlisting in Peterhead, Angus arrived in France on the 2 May 1915. He was killed in action during the Battle of Arras on the 26 Mar 1916 aged 27. Angus is buried in the Maroeuil British Cemetery. The cemetery was begun by the 51st Highland Division when Commonwealth forces took over the Arras front in Mar 1916. Almost half of the graves are those of Highland territorials.

References:
CWGC Casualty No 120971

Alexander MURRAY

Service No: 2883S. Rank: Stoker. Service: RNR – HMS Hawke.

Alexander was the son of William and Ann J. Murray of 8 Lily Terrace, West Rd., Peterhead.

HMS Hawke, a cruiser, was torpedoed and sunk by U-9 in the North Sea on the 15 Oct 1914. The torpedo ignited a magazine which and caused a tremendous explosion which ripped much of the ship apart. HMS Hawke sank in a few minutes, sending her captain, 26 officers and 497 men to their deaths. Alexander body was never recovered and his death is recorded on the Portsmouth Naval Memorial.

References:
CWGC Casualty No 2871732
Buchan Observer 10 Oct 1916 Page 4

Thomas Alexander MUTCH*

Service No: 217960. Rank: Driver. Regiment: 242nd Bde. Royal Field Artillery.

Born in Oldmeldrum, Aberdeenshire in about 1879, Thomas was the son of John and Christina W. Mutch. A former resident of Campbeltown, Aberdeen and Peterhead, Thomas was the husband of Penelope F. Mutch of 19 Albyn Grove, Aberdeen.

Thomas fell on the 18 Oct 1917, aged 38 and is interred in the La Clytte Military Cemetery which now has 1,082 casualties of the First World War buried or commemorated in this cemetery, 238 of the burials are unidentified.

References:
CWGC Casualty No 438644

Gordon Smith NAPIER

Service No: 2106. Rank: Pte. Regiment: 5th Bn. Gordon Highlanders.

Gordon was the son of Jonathan and Mary (m/s McPherson) Napier of 33 Queen St., Peterhead. Gordon was brother to James, Jonathon, Margaret, Stevenson, Mary, William, Lily Knox McPherson, and Isabella Napier.

Gordon died on the 6 Sep 1914 of pneumonia following a chill he contracted whilst on guard duty. In peace time he worked as a volunteer at St Margaret's Mission on Longate. After a highly impressive funeral in Peterhead, Gordon was laid to rest in Peterhead Cemetery still only 22 years old.

References:
CWGC Casualty No 327020
Buchan Observer 15 Sep 1914

James NICOL

Service No: Deal/10282 (S). Rank: Pte. Regiment: Royal Marine Light Infantry.

Born 26 Mar 1873 in the parish of St Nicholas, Aberdeen, James was the son of John and Mary Jane Nicol of Aberdeen. He was also the husband of Isabella Nicol and the father of John Nicol of 10 York St., Peterhead.

James initially enlisted into the 4th Bn. Gordon Highlanders and was discharged due to illness in 1915. As demands for more soldiers for France increased, James re-enlisted into the Royal Marine Light Infantry/Labour Corps. Whilst James was working at the RML Company RM Depot Deal, Kent, he died from disease on the 29 Jun 1917. James is buried in the Royal Naval Cemetery, Haslar, Gosport, Hampshire.

References:
CWGC Casualty No 3056002

James NICOL*

Service No: S/14197. Rank: Pte. Regiment: 7th Bn. Gordon Highlanders.

Born in Peterhead in 1885, James was the youngest son of Alexander and Margaret Nicol of Richmond Cottage, Cults, Aberdeenshire and later of Bellevue Cottage, Dales, Peterhead.

James was killed in action on the 31 Jul

1917, aged 22 years. He is buried at No-man's Cot Cemetery which has 79 WW1 burials most of which are of graves of the officers and men of the 51st Highland Division.

References:
CWGC Casualty No: 447484
Buchan Observer

James Ironside NICOL

Service No: 240698. Rank: LCpl. Regiment: 7th Bn. Gordon Highlanders.

Born in Lendrum Terrace, Stirling Hill, Boddam on the 9 Apr 1899, James was the son of Mary Jane Nicol, and the grandson of William Nicol of Lendrum Terrace, Stirling Hill, Boddam. Prior to the war, James lived in Gladstone Rd., Peterhead and worked at the Alexandra Sawmill, Peterhead.

James enlisted into the Gordon Highlanders in Peterhead and was killed in action on the 28 Jul 1918 aged 19 years. He is buried in the Chambrecy British Cemetery. This cemetery was made after the Armistice, by the concentration of graves from the surrounding battlefields and from the Courlandon Hospital (French Military) Cemetery.

References:
CWGC Casualty No 611270

Robert Robertson NICOL

Service No: 240841. Rank: Pte. Regiment: 1st/5th Bn. Gordon Highlanders.

Born on the 1 Nov 1895 at 16 Maiden St., Peterhead, Robert (aka Robin) was the son of Peter and Isabella (m/s Simpson) Nicol. He had three brothers; Peter, William and James Nicol. Robert also had a sister; Mrs Isabella (m/s Nicol) Palmer residing in the USA.

Robert enlisted into the Gordon Highlanders in Peterhead and was killed in action on the 9 Apr 1917, aged 21. He is buried in the Highland Cemetery, Roclincourt, which was extended when the battlefields were cleared after the 9 Apr 1917.

References:
CWGC Casualty No 262591

James McNab Smith OGSTON

Service No: S/3649. Rank: L Cpl. Regiment: 2nd Bn. Gordon Highlanders.

James was born on the 3 Jan 1891 in Peterhead and was the son of William Smith Ogston and Mary Ann (m/s McNab) Ogston of 5 Tolbooth Wynd, Peterhead, later of 23 Windmill St. He married Catherine Anne (Katie-Ann) McKinnon in Hartlepool in 1913. They had one daughter, Elizabeth Morrison Ogston born in 1915. James' twin brother William was also killed during WW1 (see below).

He enlisted in Aberdeen, and after training, James arrived in France on the 21 Jan 1915. He was killed in action on the 1 Jul 1916 and is buried in the Gordon Cemetery, Mametz. This cemetery was made by men of the 2nd Bn. Gordon Highlanders who buried some of their dead of 1 Jul 1916 in what had been a support trench.

References:
CWGC Casualty No 536244

William John Smith OGSTON

Service No: 45548. Rank: Gunner.
Regiment: Royal Garrison Artillery.

William was born on the 3 Jan 1891 and was the son of William Smith Ogston and Mary Ann (m/s McNab) Ogston of 5 Tolbooth Wynd, Peterhead, later of 23 Windmill St., Peterhead. James married Christine Winton on the 10 Sep 1910 and lived at 19 Port Henry Rd. They had a daughter Christine Winton Ogston born on the 8 Dec 1909. William's twin brother James was also killed in the war (See above).

William joined the Royal Regiment of Artillery in Hackney, Middlesex on the 24 Aug 1914 and served in England until 15 Jan 1916 when he joined the "Y" 12th Trench Mortar Bty of the Royal Garrison Artillery. William was killed in action on the 6 Apr 1917 and is buried in the Faubourg D'amiens Cemetery, Arras. The Commonwealth section of the Faubourg D'amiens Cemetery was begun in Mar 1916 and was enlarged after the Armistice when graves were brought in from the battlefields and from two smaller cemeteries in the vicinity.

References:
CWGC Casualty No 574652
Service Record

Peter PEDDIE

Service No: 3063. Rank: Pte. Regiment: 1st/5th Bn. Gordon Highlanders.

Born on the 25 Mar 1889 in Peterhead, Peter was the son of Peter and Margaret (m/s Garden) Peddie of 23 Windmill St., Peterhead. He was also the husband of Elizabeth Hill (m/s Grant) Peddie of 15 Chapel St., Peterhead whom he married on the 29 Dec 1912. Peter was from a large family and his siblings included: Samuel, James, George, Margaret, William, Anna Bella, Frederick B., Jane McP., Robert and Hora Peddie.

Two of Peter's brothers served in France and two others served on minesweepers. Prior to the war, Peter was employed at the Kirkburn Mills, Peterhead.

Peter enlisted into the Gordon Highlanders shortly after the outbreak of war. He was killed in action on the 13 Nov 1916 when the Gordon Highlanders lost 275 men at Mailly Wood and Beaumont- Hamel. Peter is interred in the Mailly Wood Cemetery, Mailly-Maillet, which the 51st Highland Division used following the capture of Beaumont-Hamel.

References:
CWGC Casualty No 111666
Buchan Observer 28 Nov 1916

George Gibson PENNANT

Service No: 903. Rank: Pte. Regiment: 5th Bn. Gordon Highlanders.
Service No: 351438. Rank: Cpl. Regiment: 16th Bn. Argyll and Sutherland Highlanders.

George was born in 1892, the son of Mary Ann Pennant, of Peterhead. On the 1 Jun 1904, George married Elsie Denes Pennant (later Browne) of Norwich and later of 37, Coleholm Rd., Great Yarmouth. They had four children; George Gibson, Elsie Jane and twin girls Helen J.D. and Mary Ann Pennant.

George joined the Army in 1909 and served in Scotland until he went to France on the 4 Aug 1918. He was promoted to A/Sgt in 1916 and was killed on the 24 Oct 1918 aged 36. He is buried in the Dottignies Communal Cemetery.

References:
CWGC Casualty No 479261
Service Record

Andrew PENNIE

Service No: 28192. Rank: Pte. Regiment: 1st Bn. Cameronians (Scottish Rifles).

Born on the 16 Dec 1885, Andrew was the son of Alexander Pennie, J.P. and Ann (m/s Robertson) Pennie of 5 Charlotte St.,

Peterhead, later of Cairnfield Cottage, Peterhead. Andrew was the brother to Mary, Maggie, Alexander, Willliam, John, Douglas, Lilly and Edward Pennie. His occupation prior to the war was a grocer.

Andrew enlisted into the Cameronians (Scottish Rifles) in Glasgow and was killed in action on the 21 Sep 1918 aged 31. He is buried in the Meath Cemetery, Villers-Guislain,. The cemetery contains 125 burials and commemorations of the First World War, the majority of whom belonged to the Cameronians, the Queen's Royal West Surreys and the London Regiment.

References:
CWGC Casualty No 246856
Birth Certificate

William Hay PHILIP

Service No: L/15589. Rank: Pte. Regiment: 4th Bn. Royal Fusiliers.

William was born in Peterhead in 1877, the son of Andrew Hay and Christina Wallace (m/s Cardno) Philip of Peterhead.

Enlisted in Dundee, William served in the 4th Bn. Royal Fusiliers which was one of the initial BEF Regiments. William was killed during the First Battle of Ypres on the 11 Nov 1914, aged 37. This battle was fought during Oct and Nov 1914, when a small British Expeditionary Force succeeded in securing the town before the onset of winter, pushing the German forces back to the Passchendaele Ridge. William's name is inscribed upon the Ypres (Menin Gate) Memorial which bears the names of more than 54,000 officers and men whose graves are not known.

References:
CWGC casualty No 1624090

William Sim PHILIPS

Service No: 9660. Rank: LCpl. Regiment: 1st Bn. Highland Light Infantry.

Born in Peterhead about 1885, William was the son of John and Margaret (m/s Sim) Philips. A professional soldier in the HLI. William enlisted in Hamilton on the 28 Dec 1904. He served in India but was court marshalled in 1910. William transferred to the Reserve in 1911 after almost 8 years service. He obtained employment in the Ordinance Stores in Stirling where he met and married Jessie Baxter Henderson on 11 Oct 1912 in Stirling. Jessie was the daughter of Archibald and Ann (m/s Baxter) Sim. They

emigrated to Grafton, Ontario, Canada and had one child together. Williams' father John Philips sailed with Captain David Gray on the SS Eclipse.

When the war broke out William returned to Scotland and enlisted into the HLI. He arrived in France with the BEF on the 4 Jan 1915 and was present at the Neuve Chapelle, Ypres and Hill 60 clashes. William died of his wounds on the 10 May 1915. He is buried in the Cabaret-Rouge British Cemetery, which was greatly enlarged in the years after the war when as many as 7,000 graves were concentrated here from over 100 other cemeteries in the area. For much of the twentieth century Cabaret Rouge served as one of a small number of 'open cemeteries' at which the remains of fallen servicemen newly discovered in the region were buried. Today, (2014) the cemetery contains over 7,650 burials of the First World War, over half of which remain unidentified.

References:
CWGC Casualty No 583684
Aberdeen City Roll of Honour
Service Record
Marriage Certificate.

Lewis Will PIRIE

Service No: 2264/5. Rank: Pte. Regiment: 5th Bn. Gordon Highlanders.
Service No: 240504. Rank: Pte. Regiment: 5th Bn. Gordon Highlanders.

Born in 1882 in Peterhead, Lewis was the youngest son of William and Mary (m/s Irvine) Pirie of 9 Errol St. Peterhead. He was also the husband of Eliza Bonnar whom he married in 1908. Lewis was the brother to William, John, Francis Finnie, Elizabeth Ann, James, Alexander and Maggie Pirie. Prior to the war he was a labourer in Peterhead harbour.

Enlisted in Peterhead, Lewis arrived in France on the 2 Aug 1915. Initially assumed to be a prisoner of war, he was actually killed in action on the 21 Mar 1918 aged 36, Lewis' sacrifice is commemorated on the Pozieres Memorial. This memorial commemorates over 14,000 casualties of the United Kingdom who have no known grave.

References:
Buchan Observer: 1914
CWGC Casualty No 1586835

Joseph PLUNKETT

Service No: 398. Rank: Pte. Regiment: 2nd Bn. Gordon Highlanders.
Service No: 50970. Rank: Pte. Regiment: 9th (Glasgow Highlanders.) Bn. Highland Light Infantry.

Joseph was born in 1891 in Airdrie, Lanarkshire and was the son of Joseph and Barbara Plunkett of 106 Beechwood Cottages, Uphall Station, Uphall, West Lothian. Joseph was also the husband of Helen Strachan (m/s Cameron) Plunkett of 6 Great Stuart St., Peterhead whom he married in Peterhead in 1916.

He enlisted into the 2nd Bn. Gordon Highlanders in Edinburgh and arrived in France on the 7 Oct 1914. Surviving nearly the entire war, Joseph transferred to the HLI before being killed on the 29 Sep 1918, aged 27. He is buried in Targelle Ravine British Cemetery, Villers-Guislain which was constructed in Sep and Oct 1918.

References:
CWGC Casualty No 315507

Ebenezer Oriston RALSTON

Service No: T4/142620. Rank: Pte. Regiment: Royal Army Service Corps.
Service No: 48031. Rank: Pte. Regiment: 18th Bn. Lancashire Fusiliers.

Born in 1888 in Elgin, Ebenezer was the son of Robert Ralston and the brother to Janet, David, Robert and Rachel Ralston, of Windmill St, Peterhead and later of 51 St Mary St., Peterhead. A long-time resident of Peterhead, Ebenezer enlisted in Aberdeen into the RASC.

After transferring to the Lancaster Fusiliers Ebenezer was killed in action on the 1 Jun 1918 aged 24. He is buried in the Martinsart British Cemetery which was used as a front-line cemetery from Sep 1918. The cemetery is unusual in that the graves are marked by stones made from red Corsehill or Locharbriggs sandstone, rather than the more usual Portland stone.

References:
CWGC Casualty No 181744

John McLean REID

Service No: 2348TS. Rank: Trimmer.
Service: RNR – HMD Forward III.

Born on the 8 Sep 1899 in Peterhead, John

was the son of James and Jemima (m/s McLean) Reid of 9 Great Stuart St., Peterhead and later of 4 Port Henry Rd., Peterhead.

John was serving aboard HMD Forward III when it was hit by a mine on the 31 Mar 1917. He was only 21 years old when he was killed by the explosion. The mine was laid by the U-boat UC-6 (Werner von Zerboni di Sposetti) in the North Sea off Suffolk. His sacrifice is commemorated on the Portsmouth Naval Memorial.

References:
CWGC Casualty 3041533

William Buchan REID

Service No: 1709. Rank: Pte. Regiment: Royal Army Medical Corps.

Born in 1894 in Peterhead, William was the son of Peter and Eliza Hay (m/s Buchan) Reid of 3 Gladstone Rd. Peterhead and he was also the brother to Eliza, Jane, Martha, Peter and Ann Reid.

William was an active member of the Aberdeen YMCA, Good Templars and Welcome Lodge. A popular young man, William was well-liked by his friends.

William enlisted in Aberdeen into the 1st /2nd Field Ambulance, RAMC and arrived in France on the 1 May 1915. He was killed in action on the 25 Jul 1916 aged only 21 years old. William is buried in the Mericourt-L'abbe Communal Cemetery Extension. The extension to the communal cemetery at Mericourt was begun in Aug 1915 and was used chiefly by field ambulances until Jul 1916.

References:
CWGC Casualty No 176747
Peterhead MI 543-583.
Aberdeen City Roll of Honour

William James REID

Service No: 2774. Rank: Pte. Regiment: 5th Bn. Gordon Highlanders.

Born in 1892 in Peterhead, William was the

son of William Reid (occ fisherman) & Mary Jane Brebner (later to marry David Mackie) of 70 Roanheads, Peterhead. He married Margaret Spence Masson on the 16 May 1915 in Peterhead. Prior to the war, William worked as a cooper with a local fish curing firm.

William enlisted in Peterhead and arrived in France with the BEF on the 5 Dec 1915. He was killed in action on the 30 Jul 1916 and his body was never recovered. William's sacrifice is commemorated on the Thiepval Memorial which bears the names of more than 72,000 officers and men of the United Kingdom and South African forces that died in the Somme sector and have no known grave.

References:
CWGC Casualty No 1550837
Buchan Observer 22 Sep 1916

William Alexander RETTIE

Service No: 3913. Rank: Pte. Regiment: 1st/5th Bn. Gordon Highlanders.
Service No: 231264. Rank: Pte. Regiment: 1st/5th Bn. Gordon Highlanders.

Born on the 17 Apr 1894 in Peterhead, William (aka Willie) was the son of Anne Smith Rettie of 70 Kirk St., Peterhead. He was a sawyer with Messrs J.B. Dickie & Co, Alexandra Sawmills, Peterhead before joining the Gordon Highlanders.

At the age 22, William was killed in action on the 31 Jul 1917 at the third Battle of Ypres. His body was never recovered and his name is honoured on the Ypres (Menin Gate) Memorial which bears the names of more than 54,000 officers and men whose graves are not known.

References:
CWGC Casualty No 910484
PJ 01 Sep 1917 Page 8
Buchan Observer 21 Aug 1917

William John RETTIE

Service No: 9702. Rank: LCpl. Regiment: 1st Bn. Scots Guards.

Born in Peterhead on the 23 Jul 1894, William was the son of Robert Cordiner Rettie and Annie Hope (m/s Grant) Rettie, later of 23 Hunter St., Glasgow. William's pre—war occupation was that of a gardener.

William enlisted into the Scots Guards in Glasgow and arrived in France on the 5 Jan

1915. He was killed in action less than three weeks later on the 25 Jan 1915, aged 20. William's body has never been found and his sacrifice is commemorated on Le Touret Memorial which commemorates over 13,400 British soldiers who were killed in this sector of the Western Front and who have no known grave.

References:
CWGC Casualty No 1561090

Alexander RITCHIE

Service No: S/17873. Rank: Pte. Regiment: 2nd Bn. Gordon Highlanders.

Enlisted in Aberdeen, Alexander was killed in action in the 3rd Battle of Ypres on the 4 Oct 1917. His death is commemorated on the Tyne Cot Memorial which now bears the names of almost 35,000 officers and men whose graves are not known.

References:
CWGC Casualty No 830837

David RITCHIE MM

Service No: 189184. Rank: Gnr. Regiment: C" Bty. 250th Bde. Royal Field Artillery.

Born in about 1894, David was the second son of William Alexander and Barbara Ritchie of 34 Tolbooth Wynd, Peterhead. Prior to the war, David was in the employment of Mr James Sutherland, Victoria Stables, Peterhead.

David enlisted in Glasgow and was killed very late in the war on the 1 Sep 1918, aged 24. Holder of the Military Medal, he is interred in the Suzanne Military Cemetery No.3.

References:
CWGC Casualty No 310422

Frank RITCHIE

Service No: T4/042743. Rank: Pte. Regiment: Army Service Corps (Horse Transport).
Service No: 20602. Rank: Pte. Regiment: West Yorkshire Regiment.
Service No: 55663. Rank: Pte. Regiment: 2nd/4th Bn. York and Lancaster Regiment.

Born in Peterhead on the 5 Oct 1898, Frank was the second son of William and Margaret (m/s McLean) Ritchie of 134 Queen St., Peterhead. He was the brother of Joseph George, John, Edward and Bella Ritchie. Frank's occupation was a blacksmith.

Frank joined the ASC on the 9 Jan 1915 and with his brother Joseph, was sent to England. On the 20 Sep 1915 aged only 17 years old, he arrived in France. His father then wrote to the Army explaining that his son was only 17. He was transferred back to England until he was no longer underage. His father wrote passionately that Frank was unsuitable for Foreign Service and he already had one son serving in Egypt. Frank was to return to France with the Yorks and Lancs Regiment in 1917 and was killed on the 25 Aug 1918, aged 20 years. Frank is buried Gomiecourt South Cemetery, Gomiecourt village was captured by the 3rd Division on 23 Aug 1918.

References:
CWGC Casualty No 569491
Peterhead MI B376-399
Service Record (includes father's letter)

Alexander Bruce ROBERTSON

Service No: 2604/5. Rank: Pte. Regiment: 5th Bn. Gordon Highlanders.
Service No: 240704. Rank: LCpl. Regiment: 7th Bn. Gordon Highlanders.

Alexander was born around 1894, the eldest son of George (occ cooper) and Elsie (m/s Bruce) Robertson of 1 Keith St., Peterhead and later of 6 Union St., Peterhead. In civilian life, Alexander was a cooper with Mr James Nicol, fishcurers, Peterhead.

He enlisted into the Gordon Highlanders in Peterhead and arrived in France on the 5 Dec 1915. Alexander was killed on the 24 Jul 1918 aged 24. His body has never been found and his sacrifice is commemorated on the Soissons Memorial which commemorates almost 4,000 officers and men of the United Kingdom forces who died during the Battles of the Aisne and the Marne in 1918 and who have no known grave.

References:
CWGC Casualty No 1759925
Peterhead MI C467-500

Alexander Walker ROBERTSON

Rank: Capt. Regiment: 2nd Bn. Gordon Highlanders.
Service No: 19726. Rank: LCpl. Regiment: 2nd Bn. Royal Berkshire Regiment.

Born in Peterhead on the 21 Dec 1876, Alexander was the eldest son of Lt. Col Robert Robertson of the 5th V Bn. Gordon Highlanders and Penelope Lucy Leslie Johnston (m/s Walker) Robertson. Together they had fourteen children and Alexander

was the first of three brothers to fall in WW1. He was educated at Glenalmond, Aberdeen Grammar School and Edinburgh University. A student of the Arts, Alexander became a partner in the firm of R. and A.V. Robertson, Solicitors, Peterhead before emigrating to Canada where he set up practice in Winnipeg.

From a young age, Alexander served as a Capt. in the 3rd V Bn. Gordon Highlanders. When the Boer War broke out he volunteered for active service and served as a Lt. with the 2nd Service Coy Gordon Highlanders. He was decorated with the Queen's Medal and three clasps for action at Natal, Transvaal and the Cape Colony.

In Dec 1915 Alexander returned from Canada and enlisted in the 2nd Bn. Berkshire Regiment where he served as an LCpl. He arrived in France in Apr 1916 and sadly fell on the 1 Jul 1916; his body has never been recovered.

Alexander's sacrifice is recorded on the Thiepval Memorial, the memorial to the missing of the Somme which bears the names of more than 72,000 officers and men of the United Kingdom and South African forces and have no known grave.

References:
CWGC Casualty No 1551937
Aberdeen University Roll of Honour
Additional Material by Mary Robertson

Charles Thomas Andrews ROBERTSON

Rank: Major. Regiment: 1st/5th Bn. Gordon Highlanders.

Born in Peterhead in 1886, Charles was the son of Lt Col Robert Robertson of the 5th V Bn. Gordon Highlanders and Penelope Lucy Leslie Johnston (m/s Walker)

Robertson. Charles was one of fourteen children and the third son to die in the war.

Charles was living in Singapore when the war broke out and returned home to be commissioned into the Gordon Highlanders. He arrived in France on the 3 May 1915 as a Lt. He was twice wounded and returned to the UK to recover from his injuries. On his return to France, Charles was again severely injured when he was captured with the fall of the Fresnoy Redoubt on 21 Mar 1918. Many thousands of the men who fought in March had become prisoners. The badly wounded among them had a very hard time. The German medical units were at full stretch and had difficulty tending to all their own wounded. Charles died in German hospital on the 23 Mar 1918, aged 32.

Charles is now buried at the Grand-Seraucourt British Cemetery; this Cemetery was made in 1920-26 by the concentration of graves from the battlefields and from other burial grounds near Aisne. Charles' medals were forwarded to Miss Charlotte Winifred Elaine Robertson (sister) at 28 Cleveland Gardens, Hyde Park, W2, London.

References:
CWGC Casualty No 580072
Buchan Observer Article 11 Jun1918
Additional material supplied by Carolyn Morrisey and Mary Robertson.

George (William) ROBERTSON*

Service No: 240691. Rank: Pte. Regiment: 2nd Bn. Gordon Highlanders.

Born in 1898, George was the son of James Robertson of Blackhills Farm, Peterhead.

George was killed in action in France on the 4 Oct 1917, aged 19 and his sacrifice is honoured on the Tyne Cot Memorial.

Note: Both the CWGC and the SNWM list this soldier's christian name as "William". The Buchan Observer and his medal card record his name as "George". His service number 240691 is common to the CWGC, SNWM and his medal records.

References:
CWGC Casualty No 831031
Medal Card
Buchan Observer Oct 1917

John ROBERTSON

Service No: 426. Rank: Driver. Regiment: Royal Field Artillery.

Service No: 636413. Rank: Bombardier. Regiment: "C" Bty. 256th Bde. Royal Field Artillery.

Born in Peterhead in 1893, John was the son of Capt. John Robertson of 146 Queen St., Peterhead. Prior to the war, he trained as an electrical engineer with Messrs James Simpson & Son, Peterhead and later in Edinburgh.

As a Territorial Reservist, John was mobilised in 1914 and arrived in France on the 24 Oct 1915. He died of his wounds on the 16 Aug 1917, aged 23 and is buried in the Brandhoek New Military Cemetery.

John's younger brother Andrew also fought with the Gordon Highlanders.

References:
CWGC Casualty No 430565

Leslie Johnston Walker ROBERTSON MC

Rank: Lt. Regiment: 3rd Bn. Gordon Highlanders.

Leslie was the son of Lt Col Robert Robertson of the 5th V Bn. Gordon Highlanders and Penelope Lucy Leslie Johnston (m/s Walker) Robertson. He and one of fourteen children and was their second son to fall in the war.

Leslie was commissioned 2Lt. into the 3rd Bn. Gordon Highlanders on the 29 Oct 1915 and he arrived in France on the 15 Sep 1916. Leslie was awarded Military Cross for conspicuous gallantry when he led his platoon to an objective, consolidated it and then led a bombing attack in which many of the enemy were killed or captured. Leslie was killed in action on the 3 Oct 1917 aged 25. He is buried in the Hooge Crater Cemetery which was begun in early in Oct 1917.

References:
CWGC Casualty No 459181
Aberdeen City Roll of Honour.
London Gazette 29 Oct 1915 Page 10658

George B. ROBSON

Service No: S/40075. Rank: Pte. Regiment: 2nd Bn. Gordon Highlanders.

Born in 1899, George was the son of Alexander and Helen Robson of B Street, Boddam near Peterhead. Prior to the war, he was a rope maker by trade.

George enlisted into the Gordon Highlanders

in Peterhead and was killed in action on the 16 Jun 1917. George's body has never been recovered and his sacrifice is recorded on the Arras Memorial which commemorates almost 35,000 servicemen from the United Kingdom, South Africa and New Zealand who died and have no known grave.

George lost one brother who fell in 1916 and another brother who was made a prisoner of war.

References:
CWGC Casualty No 1637480

James ROBSON

Service No: 2624. Rank: Pte. Regiment: 5th Bn. Gordon Highlanders.

Born in 1893 in Boddam, James was the 2nd son of Alexander and Helen Robson of B Street, Boddam and later of 12 Windmill St. Peterhead.

James enlisted in Peterhead and served with the Transport Section of the Gordon Highlanders. He died in the Dundee War Hospital on the 7 Mar 1916, aged 23, and is buried in Peterhead Cemetery.

His brother George died in 1917 and one other brother was a prisoner of war.

References:
CWGC Casualty No 327021
Buchan Observer 14 Mar 1916 page 4

Walter James ROBSON MM

Service No: 2745. Rank: Pte. Regiment: Gordon Highlanders.
Service No: 240766. Rank: Pte. Regiment: Gordon Highlanders.
Service No: WR/175924. Rank: Spr. Regiment: Royal Engineers.
Service No: 403988. Rank: Spr. Regiment: Royal Engineers.

Born in Longside in 1892, Walter was the son of Walter and Jane (m/s Forbes) Robson of 25 Broad Place[4], Peterhead and was also the husband of Ivy Agnes Robson of 44 Whapload Rd., Lowestoft, Suffolk. Walter was the brother of Ann, Alexander, William (below) and Bella Jane Robson. Prior to the war, he was in the employment of Mr James Reid, contractor, Peterhead.

After enlisting into the Gordon Highlanders, Walter arrived in France on the 2 May 1915.

Whilst in France, Walter was awarded the Military Medal for conspicuous bravery. He and a Sgt helped save 14 of his comrades by attacking 20 Germans who were lying in wait for them. He later transferred to the 51st Broad Gauge Operating Coy. Royal Engineers. Walter died of influenza in Calais on the 26 Oct 1918 aged 26, and is interred in the Les Baraques Military Cemetery, Sangatte.

References:
CWGC Casualty No 86345
Buchan Observer, Photo.

William ROBSON

Service No: 2266. Rank: Pte. Regiment: 1st/5th Bn. Gordon Highlanders.

Born in Peterhead in 1897, William (aka "Wilder") was the youngest son of Walter and Jane (m/s Forbes) Robson of 25 Broad Place[4], and later of 13 Backgate, Peterhead. He was also the brother of Ann, Walter James (above), Alexander and Bella Jane Robson.

William travelled to France with his brother Walter on the 2 May 1915 and was wounded at Bazentin-le-Grand. He was carried off the battlefield by his brother Walter only to die of his wounds on the 28 Jul 1916, aged only 19 years old. William is buried in the Heilly Station Cemetery, Mericourt-L'abbe.

References:
CWGC Casualty No 272372
Buchan Observer 15 Aug 1916

James ROSS

Service No: 3/7169. Rank: Pte. Regiment: 1st Bn. Gordon Highlanders.

Born in 1864 in the village of St Fergus near Peterhead, James was the son of James and Jane (m/s Johnston) Ross. James was a cooper by trade and he married Williamina Kemp on the 8 Aug 1888 in Peterhead. Their children included Mary Bella, Arthur, Elizabeth, Edith, James Allan, William Kemp (b. 28 Jul 1900) and Edward (b. 11 Jul 1902) Ross.

---

[4] Suspect this should read "Street"

At the outbreak of the war, James was already 50 years old, he told the attestation officer that he was 45 years old and was mobilised in Aberdeen on the 7 Oct 1914. He arrived in France on the 8 Nov 14 earning the 1914 Star, only to die nine days later 17 Nov 1914. His body has never been recovered and James' sacrifice is commemorated on the Ploegsteert Memorial.

James' widow was awarded a weekly pension of 18/6 a week for her and the two youngest boys.

References:
CWGC Casualty No 867874
Service Record

James Anderson SAMUEL

Service No: 1876. Rank: Pte. Regiment: 5th Bn. Gordon Highlanders.

Born in Peterhead, James was the son of Andrew and Barbara Jane (m/s Anderson) Samuel. Formerly from Peterhead, they lived at 9 Rugby Avenue, Rugby St., Hessle Rd., Hull. James was also the grandson of James Anderson of 1 Roanheads, Peterhead. He was a cooper by trade.

James enlisted in Peterhead in 1914 and arrived in France 5 May 1915. He was seriously wounded in July 1916. After recovering, he returned to the front, only to die of further wounds on the 13 Nov 1916 aged 20. James is buried in the Mailly Wood Cemetery where the 51st Highland Division fatalities were buried there following the capture of Beaumont-Hamel.

References:
CWGC Casualty No 111712

Thomas SANDY

Service No: 3532. Rank: Pte. Regiment: Gordon Highlanders.
Service No: 241150. Rank: Pte. Regiment: 5th Bn. Gordon Highlanders.

Born in Peterhead in 1894, Thomas was the son of Robert and Matilda Lily Sandy of 5 Constitution St., Peterhead. He was one of ten children.

Thomas enlisted in Peterhead into the Gordon Highlanders and was killed in action between the 21 Mar 1918 and 2 Apr 1918, aged 23. His body has not been recovered and his sacrifice is commemorated on the Pozieres Memorial which commemorates the 14,000 casualties of the United Kingdom and 300 of the South African Forces who have no

known grave.

References:
CWGC Casualty No 1587885

Alexander SCOTT*

Service No: 3201. Rank: L/Sgt. Regiment: 1st/5th Bn. Gordon Highlanders.

Born in New Pitsligo, Alexander was the youngest son of Charles and Mary Scott of Little Burnthill, Fraserburgh and later of Cowsrieve, Peterhead. He was also the brother of Charles, William and Lydia Scott.

Alexander enlisted in Peterhead in May 1915 and arrived in France on the 12 Oct 1915. He was killed on the 16 Dec 1916 by a shell explosion. Aged 32, Alexander is buried in the Adanac Military Cemetery (the name was formed by reversing the name "Canada"). This cemetery was started after the Armistice when graves were brought in from the Canadian battlefields around Courcelette and small cemeteries surrounding Miraumont.

References:
CWGC Casualty No 183952
Buchan Observer.

Campbell Lowe SCOTT

Rank: Lt. Regiment: 3rd Bn. Royal Scots.

Campbell was born in Peterhead on the 3 Feb 1894, the son of William Leslie Scott and Elizabeth Campbell Lowe Scott, of Willowbank, Peterhead. He was brother to William L. Scott who also fell in the war. Campbell studied Arts, at Aberdeen University (1912 – 15), with a view to becoming an advocate.

In Apr 1915, Campbell was commissioned 2Lt. and posted to the 14th Reserve Bn. and then to the 3rd Bn. Royal Scots. After serving in the UK, he was sent to Salonika in early 1917. He was attached to the 1st Bn. Royal Scots and then later to the 81st Trench Mortar Battery as the Bty Adjutant. Campbell saw action at Salonika, Struma and in the Vardar Valley. He met his death about midnight on 2 Sept 1918, whilst leading his gun team forward in the Vardar Valley, Macedonia. His Captain wrote: "He was an excellent officer, good, strict and popular; men of his type are few and far between. He was a thorough gentleman and a sportsman.

Campbell is buried in the Karasouli Military Cemetery in Greece. This cemetery was begun in Sep 1916 for the use of casualty clearing stations on the Doiran Front. At the Armistice, it contained about 500 burials but was greatly increased when graves were brought in from surrounding cemeteries.

References:
CWGC Casualty No 623839
Aberdeen University Roll of Honour
Aberdeen City Roll of Honour.

G. SCOTT

Rank: Pte. Regiment: 5th Bn. Gordon Highlanders.

To date, no evidence can be found identifying Pte G Scott. However, his sacrifice is honoured on the Peterhead War Memorial.

George Geddes SCOTT

Service No: 2123. Rank: Cpl. Regiment: 5th Bn. Gordon Highlanders.

Born in 1885 in Peterhead, George was the son of William and Elizabeth Scott of 39 Marischal St., Peterhead and the brother of Bessie, Williamina, Edith, Ida, Marion and William M. (who also fell in the Great War) Scott. A telegraph messenger by trade, George worked for Messrs Sinclair and Buchan, fishcurer, Peterhead.

George was a time-expired volunteer who re-joined at the outbreak of hostilities. Arriving in France on the 2 May 1915, George was killed in action on the 1 Dec 1916, aged 31. George's sacrifice is recorded on the Thiepval Memorial which bears the names of more than 72,000 officers and men of the United Kingdom and South African forces that died and have no known grave.

References:
CWGC Casualty No 811643

James Peter SCOTT

Service No: 29385. Rank: Pte. Regiment: 16th Bn. Canadian (Manitoba Regiment) Infantry.
Rank: Lt. Regiment: 79th Cameron Highlanders of Canada.
Rank: Capt. Regiment: Canadian Army Medical Corps.

James was born in Peterhead on the 15 May 1886, the son of James and Helen Webster (m/s Henderson) Scott of 8 St Mary St. Peterhead. He was the brother of John, Helen and Elizabeth Scott, all born in Peterhead. A solicitor by trade, James married Nellie Elizabeth Scott resident of Stanhope Terrace, Regents Park, London NW1.

Originally enlisted at Valcarties, Quebec, as a Pte into the 16th Bn. Canadian Infantry, James was later commissioned into the 79th Bn. Cameron Highlanders of Canada. He would then serve as a Quartermaster in the Canadian Army Medical Corps. James died of his wounds on the 16 May 1919 in Canadian Red Cross Hospital, St George, Hanover Square, London. He was buried in the Brookwood Military Cemetery, an area of land in Brookwood Cemetery (The London Necropolis) was set aside for the burial of men and women of the forces of the Commonwealth and Americans, who had died, many of battle wounds, in the London district.

References:
CWGC Casualty No 399525
Canadian War Project.

William Cowan SCOTT

Service No: S/13623. Rank: Pte. Regiment: 3rd Bn. Gordon Highlanders.

Born in 1883 in Peterhead, William was the son of Alexander and Mary Ann (m/s Thompson) Scott of 18 Prince St., Peterhead and the widower of Elizabeth Clark. He had six brothers and sisters including; Mary Ann, Johanna, Jane, Andrew, John and Harriet Scott.

William died on the 30 Sep 1918 by accidental drowning; his body was recovered in a tidal harbour near Peterhead on the 21 Oct 1918. William is buried in Peterhead Cemetery.

References:
CWGC Casualty No 326995
Death Certificate

William Leslie SCOTT

Rank: Lt. Regiment: 5th Bn. Gordon Highlanders.

Born on the 24 Dec 1892 in Peterhead, William was the son of William Leslie Scott and Elizabeth Campbell Lowe Scott, Willowbank, Peterhead. He was a student of Medicine at Aberdeen University in 1911-14.

When war broke out, William was entitled to remain at university but his desire to take an active part in the fighting was too strong for him. He obtained a commission in the 2nd/5th Bn. Gordon Highlanders in Dec 1914.

William was sent to France where he commanded the bombing section of his Battalion. He showed himself a leader of dauntless spirit, regardless of personal danger. A fellow-officer wrote William was a magnificent officer, and a very cheery trench companion. He was killed at Festuhert while entering a German trench with a party of bombers on 16 Jun 1915 still only 22 years old. William's brother Campbell also fell in the war.

William's sacrifice is commemorated on the Le Touret Memorial which commemorates over 13,400 British soldiers who were killed in this sector of the front and who have no known grave.

References:
CWGC Casualty No 1561784
Aberdeen University Roll of Honour.

William Milne SCOTT

Service No: 1554. Rank: Pte. Regiment: 5th Bn. Gordon Highlanders.

Born in 1898 in Peterhead, William was the son of William and Elizabeth Geddes Scott of Marischal St., Peterhead and the brother of Bessie, Williamina, Edith, Ida, Marion and George Scott (who also fell in the Great War).

After enlisting in Peterhead, William arrived in France on the 5 May 1915. He died of his wounds on the 4 Apr 1916 aged only 19 years. He had been wounded in both legs and both arms with his right leg having been amputated. William is buried on the Aubigny Communal Cemetery Extension.

References:
CWGC Casualty No 996401

Frederick Gordon SHAND

Service No: 2118. Rank: 2Lt. Regiment: Scottish Horse.
Rank: 2Lt. Regiment: Royal Field Artillery.

Born in 1891 in Peterhead, Frederick was the son of William and Elizabeth Shand, of Constitution St. Peterhead. He was also the brother of Margaret, Elizabeth, James, John and Christian Shand. Prior to the outbreak of hostilities, Frederick was employed by Messrs Gray and Gray, solicitors, Peterhead.

Originally commissioned into the Scottish Horse Regiment, he arrived in France on the 29 Sep 1917. Frederick later transferred to C Bty. 311th Bde. Royal Field Artillery and was killed on the 12 Oct 1918 aged 27. He had only recently returned to the front after leave in Peterhead. Frederick is interred in the Duisans British Cemetery, Etrun. From May to Aug 1918, the cemetery was used by divisions and smaller fighting units for burials from the front line.

References:
CWGC Casualty No 41204

William SHAND

Service No: TS1807. Rank: Saddler. Regiment: Army Service Corps.
Service No: 7220. Rank: Driver. Regiment: Royal Field Artillery.
Service No: T390332. Rank: Driver. Regiment: Army Service Corps.

Born in 1897, William was son of William (occ master shoemaker) and Christina (m/s Conner) Shand. He was also the husband of Mary Ann (m/s Geddes) Shand. They were married on the 11 Apr 1902 and they lived at 11 James St., Peterhead. William and Mary Ann had two boys, William (b.1905) and John (b. 1906).

William joined the ASC as a Saddler in 1914 only to be discharged six days later as being "Unlikely to become an efficient Soldier". Later in the war, when the demand for more men intensified, William enlisted into the RFA as a driver. Unfortunately William died of malaria on the 21 Oct 1918 whilst fighting the Turks in the Lebanon. He is buried in the Beirut War Cemetery which was begun in Oct 1918 and was later enlarged when graves were brought in from other burial grounds.

References:
CWGC Casualty No 896578
Service Record
Marriage Certificate

Kenneth SHEARER

Service No: 3/5261. Rank: Pte. Regiment: 3rd Bn. Gordon Highlanders.
Service No: 647. Rank: Pte. Regiment: 2nd Bn. Gordon Highlanders.

Born in 1892, Kenneth was the son of William and Margaret (m/s Roger) Shearer of 10 Threadneedle St. Peterhead. Kenneth had two brothers; James and John Shearer.

Kenneth joined the 3rd Bn. Gordon Highlanders in 1908 for a six year service. When he extended his service he was transferred to the 2nd Bn. In 1914, whilst in France, he suffered two separate gunshot wounds to the left foot. Later, on the 25 Sep 1915 at Vermelles, Kenneth received a rifle bullet to the right side of his chin (medical report lists a number of horrific injuries to his lower face) leaving him only able to eat minced food. By Oct 1915, Kenneth was now dangerously ill and was evacuated to England, only to be discharged from the Army on the 29 Aug 1916. Kenneth returned to Peterhead and in 1917 he married Catherine Buchan. Sadly, Kenneth passed away on 2 Feb 1919 as a result of pneumonia no doubt attributable to his war service. Kenneth's sacrifice is not listed with the CWGC.

References:
Service Pension Record
Death Certificate

Maxwell SHEPHERD

Service No: 1826. Rank: Pte. Regiment: Gordon Highlanders
Service No: 20169. Rank: LCpl. Regiment: Machine Gun Corps (Infantry).

Maxwell was born on the 1 Aug 1896 in the Maud Poorhouse; his mother was Margaret Shepherd, a domestic servant. Later Maxwell was fostered by Mr. and Mrs. William Mutch of 7 Water Lane, Aberdeen. Prior to the war Maxwell was a farm servant with Mr J. Ritchie, farmer, Clerkhill, Peterhead.

Maxwell enlisted into the Gordon Highlanders in Peterhead and was then transferred to the 23rd Coy MGC (Infantry). Maxwell was taken prisoner during the German offensive to capture Brie and its nearby strategically important bridge. He died in a Germany hospital on the 27 Mar 1918. Maxwell was only 22 years old and is now buried in the Brie British Cemetery.

References:
CWGC Casualty No 265285
Birth Certificate
Buchan Observer Article 2 Jul 1918

Norman SHEWAN

Service No: 3705: Rank: Pte. Regiment: 3rd Bn. London Regiment, Royal Fusiliers.

Norman was born in Shanghai in 1876, the eldest son of Andrew Gordon and Agnes (m/s Barnet) Shewan. He was also the husband of Amy Amelia Goldstone of St Mary's, Essex whom he married in 1903. They had a daughter together named Grace. Prior to the war, Norman worked as a ship's carpenter in Peterhead.

Described as a "Clean, Willing and Good Soldier, Sober and intelligent", Norman was medically discharged from the Army on 14 Jan 1916 due to the physical stress of active service aggravated by gas poisoning. This refers to an incident between Richeburg and Lavant when Norman was "slightly gassed by our own side". He became progressively unfit and was discharged from the Army. Norman died on the 16 Apr 1916 due to complications brought on by his injuries. He is buried in Peterhead Old Churchyard.

References:
Buchan Observer 25 Apr 1916 Page 4
St Peter's MIs

William James SIM

Service No: S/21688. Rank: Pte. Regiment: 7th Bn. Seaforth Highlanders.
Service No: 1/16507. Rank: Pte. Regiment: Territorial Bn.

Born in Peterhead in 1898, William was the son of John and Annie (m/s Chisholm) Sim of 21 Kirk St., Peterhead. He was the brother of Minnie, Marjorie, John and Hugh Sim. Prior to the war, William was an apprentice mason with Mr William West, builder, Constitution St., Peterhead.

William enlisted in Aberdeen and died of his wounds on the 19 Oct 1917 after being fatally injured whilst acting as a stretcher-bearer. He was aged only 19 years and is interred in the St. Julien Dressing Station Cemetery.

References:
CWGC Casualty No 447196

George SIMPSON

Service No: 2595. Rank: Pte. Regiment: 1st /5th Bn. Black Watch (Royal Highlanders). Service No: 202785. Rank: Pte. Regiment: 4th/5th Bn. Black Watch (Royal Highlanders).

George was born in Fyvie, Aberdeenshire and enlisted into the Black Watch (Royal Highlanders) in Forfar.

A one-time resident of Peterhead he was posted to France on the 13 Mar 1915 and was killed in action on the 27 Sep 1917. George's sacrifice is recorded on the Tyne Cot Memorial which has the names of almost 35,000 officers and men whose graves are not known.

References:
CWGC Casualty No 3064900

John Alexander SIMPSON

Service No: 2495. Rank: Pte. Regiment: 1st/5th Bn. Gordon Highlanders.

Born in the parish of Newmachar in 1896, John (aka Jack) was the son of William (occ blacksmith) and Mary Simpson, of 4 Smithy Lane, Longside, then later of 61 Kirk St., Peterhead. He was also the younger brother of William Simpson.

John enlisted in Peterhead and arrived in France on the 5 Dec 1915. He was killed in action on the 13 Nov 1916 aged 20. John was buried in the Y Ravine Cemetery, Beaumont-Hamel. The village of Beaumont-Hamel was attacked and reached on 1 Jul 1916, by units of the 29th Division but it could not be held. It was attacked again and captured, with the Ravine, by the 51st Highland Division on 13 Nov 1916.

References:
CWGC Casualty No 2743031

William SIMPSON

Service No: 5786. Rank: Pte. Regiment: 3rd Bn. Scots Guards.

Born in 1885 in St Fergus, Aberdeenshire, William was the youngest son of James and Sophia (m/s Dow) Simpson. He was a brother to Margaret, James, Elspet, Sarah, Mary-Jane, Alexander and George Simpson. William was married to Jessie Ann Murray of 2 Back St. Peterhead.

William served for many years in the Scots Guards (Reserve) before enlisting in the Great War, he arrived in France on the 7 Oct 1914 qualifying for the 1914 Star. William was medically discharged from the Army on the 20 Apr 1917 and died of pulmonary tuberculosis on the 10 Nov 1920.

References:
Service Pension Record
Death Certificate 1920 232/01 0194

William SIMPSON*

Service No: 2176. Rank: Tpr. Regiment: Scottish Horse Yeomanry.

Born in Udny, Aberdeenshire, William enlisted in Peterhead and was posted to the Balkans on the 1 Sep 1915.

William was killed in action at Gallipoli on the 17 Sep 1915. He is believed to be interred in the Green Hill Cemetery which has 2,971 servicemen of the First World War buried or commemorated in this cemetery. 2,472 of the burials are unidentified but special memorials commemorate a number of casualties known or believed to be buried among them.

References:
CWGC Casualty No 602499

William Barclay Moir Davie SINCLAIR

Service No: 3023.Rank: Pte. Regiment: 5th Bn. Gordon Highlanders.

Born on the 6 Sep 1896 in Peterhead, William was the youngest and seventh son of John & Jane (m/s Buchan) Sinclair of 42 Broad St., Peterhead and then of 28 Balmoor Terrace, Peterhead. He was one of ten children born to John and Jane who themselves were married in 1874 in Boddam. Prior to the war William was in the employment of his father.

He enlisted in Peterhead and was shipped out to France on the 5 Dec 1915. William was killed in action during the Battle of the Somme on the 30 Jul 1916 and the location of his body remains unknown. William's sacrifice is commemorated on the Thiepval Memorial which bears the names of more than 72,000 officers and men of the United Kingdom and South African forces that died in the Somme sector and have no known grave.

References:
CWGC Casualty No 1553108
Buchan Observer 15 Aug 1916.

William Will SINGER*

Service No: 1393. Rank: Trooper. Regiment: 2nd/1st Bn. Lothian and Border Horse.

Born in 1891 in Aberdeen, William was the son of William Murray and Ann Amelia Grant (m/s Will) Singer. He was also the brother of Mary Isabella, Amelia Margaret, Susan Silver and Janetta Taylor Singer.

A sometime resident of Peterhead, William died at Edinburgh City Hospital on the 22 Jan 1916 of tuberculosis. He is buried in the Aberdeen (Allenvale) Cemetery.

References:
CWGC Casualty No 326427

George R. SKELTON

Service No: S/8359. Rank: Pte. Regiment: 1st Bn. Gordon Highlanders.

George was born in 1888 in the parish of Old Machar, Aberdeen, and was the son of Joseph and Mary (m/s Urquhart) Skelton of Woodside, Aberdeen and later of 2 Low Street, Peterhead. George was brother to James, Patrick, Mary Ann, Jeannie, Joseph F., Helen and Mary C. Skelton. Prior to the war, George worked as a general labourer on nearby farms.

After enlisting in Glasgow, George arrived in France on the 13 Apr 1915. He was killed in action on the 18 Jul 1916. George's sacrifice is honoured on the Thiepval Memorial which bears the names of more than 72,000 officers and men of the United Kingdom and South African forces who died in the Somme sector.

References:
1891, 1901 Census Returns
CWGC casualty No 1553187

James SKELTON

Service No: 51196. Rank: Pte. Regiment: 18th Bn. Highland Light Infantry.

James was born in 1885 in the parish of Woodside, Aberdeen, the son of Joseph and Mary (m/s Urquhart) Skelton. He married Jane A. Skelton of 2 Low Street, Peterhead and they had three children; Joseph, James and Helen Skelton. Stepdaughter Bella B. Thomson also lived with the family. By 1918, James is listed as the husband of Annie Dodds Skelton of 49 West End, Tweedmouth, Berwick-on-Tweed. Prior to the war, James worked as a labourer at the Admiralty Works

in Peterhead harbour.

Enlisted in Edinburgh, James was killed in action on the 30 Sep 1918, aged 36. His body was never recovered and his death is commemorated on the Tyne Cot Memorial which lists almost 35,000 officers and men whose graves are not known.

References:
1891, 1911 Census Returns
CWGC Casualty No 3065022

Alexander Davidson SLESSER (SLESSOR)

Service No: 24786. Rank: Pte. Regiment: 1st Bn. King's Own Scottish Borderers.

Born in 1887 in Grasie, New Deer and baptised at Longside, Alexander was the son of Alexander Irvine Slessor and Jane Carle Burnett of Yonderton, Hatton. He was also the husband of Christian Wallace Slessor, of 57 Longate, Peterhead and later of 98 Main St. Buckie.

Alexander enlisted in Aberdeen and died of his wounds on the 9 May 1918 aged 31. He is buried in the Boulogne Eastern Cemetery which, until Jun 1918, the fatalities from the hospitals at Boulogne were buried in the Cimetiere de L'Est.

References:
CWGC Casualty No 45748
Buchan Observer 21 May 1918

Alexander Ogilvy SMITH

Service No: 2506. Rank: Pte. Regiment: 5th Bn. Gordon Highlanders.

Born in 1897 in Peterhead, Alexander was the son of Alexander (occ. prison warder) and Elspet Smith. He was also the brother of Helen I., Edmund C. and John F. Smith. Prior to the war, Alexander was a farm servant in Fyvie, Aberdeenshire.

After enlisting in Peterhead, Alexander arrived in France on the 5 Dec 1915 only to be killed in action on the 13 Nov 1916 at Beaumont-Hamel. Alexander is buried in the Mailly Wood Cemetery which was used by the 51st Highland Division buried in it following the capture of Beaumont-Hamel.

References:
The War Book of Turriff & 12 Miles Round
Page 255
CWGC Casualty No 111737

Edgar Clarence Thayton SMITH*

Service No: 4213. Rank: Pte. Regiment 5th Bn. Gordon Highlanders.

Edgar was born in Staplehurst, Kent in 1891, the eldest son of Ephraim and Annie Smith of 16 Maiden St. Peterhead. He was the brother of Annie, Edith, Ephraim, William and Sidney Smith. Before the war, Edgar was in the employment of Messrs Patterson & Co. London House, Peterhead. He was married to S. A. Budd (formerly Smith), of Alvington Cottage, Wray Park Rd., Reigate, Surrey.

Edgar enlisted into the 5th Bn. Gordon Highlanders in late 1915 and was killed near Courcelette on the 29 Nov 1916, aged 21. He is buried in the Adanac Military Cemetery at Miraumont (the name was formed by reversing the name "Canada") which was made after the Armistice when graves were brought in from the Canadian battlefields around Courcelette and small cemeteries surrounding Miraumont.

References:
CWGC Casualty No 183996
Buchan Observer 5 Dec 1916

George Birnie SMITH

Service No: 6444. Rank: Pte. Regiment: Gordon Highlanders.
Service No: 202805. Rank: Pte. Regiment: 2nd Bn. Gordon Highlanders.

Born in Peterhead in 1895, George was the youngest son of William Smith (occ blacksmith) of Cowsrieve, Peterhead, George enlisted into the Gordon Highlanders in Peterhead.

George was reported missing on the 26 Oct 1917 and his death was not confirmed until Sep 1918. His body was never recovered and his sacrifice appears upon the Tyne Cot Memorial which bears the names of almost 35,000 officers and men whose graves are not known.

References:
CWGC Casualty No 3065357

George Douglas SMITH

Service No: 2400. Rank: Pte. Regiment: 5th Bn. Gordon Highlanders.
Service No: 240575. Rank: A/Sgt. Regiment: 5th Bn. Gordon Highlanders.

Born in 1893 in Aberdeen, George was the son of George and Mary Ann Smith and the

brother of Jessie Smith.

George enlisted into 5th Bn. Gordon Highlanders on the 19 Oct 1914 age 20. He was listed as an engineer residing at 12 Lodge Walk, Peterhead.

There is no evidence that George served overseas and he was released from active service on 2 Nov 1915 to be employed in shipbuilding in Greenock. He was later discharged on the 26 Aug 1918 suffering from tuberculosis and no longer fit. George died five months later in Forfar.

George's mother's address on his death certificate is recorded as 12 Lodge Walk, Peterhead.

References:
Death Certificate.
1911 Census – 12 Lodge Walk

James Malcolm SMITH*

Service No: 54322. Rank: Pte. Regiment: 12th Bn. Highland Light Infantry.

Born in Peterhead in 1898, James was the son of William and Marianne Smith of School House, Blackhills, Peterhead and later of Coronation St., Wick, Caithness. Prior to the war, James was employed by the Bank of Scotland.

James had only been at the front for a few months when he died of his wounds on the 30 Oct 1918 aged 20 and he is buried in the Terlincthun British Cemetery, Wimille. The cemetery at Terlincthun was begun in Jun 1918 when the space available for service burials in the civil cemeteries of Boulogne and Wimereux were exhausted.

References:
CWGC Casualty No 4027253

John SMITH

Service No: 25449. Rank: Pte. Regiment: 1st/5th Bn. Royal Scots Fusiliers.

Born in Aberdeen in 1891, John was the son of John and Charlotte (m/s Williamson) Smith and the husband of Williamina (m/s Craighead) Smith, of 10 Love Lane, Peterhead. John and Williamina had three children including William and James Williamson Smith plus one unknown child.

John fell on the 20 Sep 1918 and is buried in the Sunken Road Cemetery, Boisleux-St. Marc which was begun by the hospitals in

May 1917 and used until July when it began to be shelled. It was completed the following Sep and Oct.

References:
CWGC Casualty No 285153

George STEPHEN (McLEAN)

Service No: 23018. Rank: Pte. Regiment: 1st Bn. King's Own Scottish Borderers.

Born in 1897 in Peterhead, George was the fifth son of James Cordiner Stephen (occ cooper) and Christina (m/s McLeman) Stephen of 38 Maiden St., Peterhead. George was also the brother to James, Elizabeth Ann, Robert, Jessie Pye, Daniel McLeman, Alexander, Jane and Christina Stephen. In civilian life he was cooper with Mr C.M. Bruce, fishcurer, Peterhead.

George enlisted and served under the name of George McLEAN. The reasons for this are unknown. Whilst serving with C Coy, 1st Bn. KOSB he died on the 12 May 1918 still aged only 20. George is buried in the Cinq Rues British Cemetery, Hazebrouck which was used chiefly by the field ambulances and fighting units of the 29th Division from Apr to Aug 1918.

References:
CWGC Casualty No 69489

James STEPHEN

Service No: 21271/DA. Rank: Deckhand. Service: RNR – HMS Victory.

Born on the 20 Apr 1877 in Peterhead, James was the son of David and Helen Stephen of 1 Well Street, Buchanhaven, Peterhead. He was also the brother to David, Andrew, Marjory, Alexander, Jane, Adam, Helen and George W. Stephen.

Whilst serving with the RNR aboard HMS Victory, James died of disease on the 8 Sep 1918 and is buried in Peterhead Cemetery.

References:
CWGC Casualty No 326997

James STEPHEN

Service No: 2080. Rank: Pte. Regiment: 5th Bn. Gordon Highlanders.
Service No: 240417. Rank: Pte. Regiment: 1st/5th Bn. Gordon Highlanders.

Born in Peterhead in 1897, James was the son of Andrew and Sarah Morrison Stephen of 12 Ellis St., Peterhead.

James enlisted in Peterhead into the 5th Bn. Gordon Highlanders and arrived in France on the 2 May 1915. James was listed as missing, believed killed at Cardonette on the 26 Mar 1916, aged only 18 years old. He was later buried in the Arras Road Cemetery which was begun by the 2nd Canadian Infantry Brigade soon after the 9 Apr 1917. In 1926, it started to be enlarged with the addition of 993 from other cemeteries mainly from North and East Arras.

References:
CWGC Casualty No 279518

Robert McKenzie STEPHEN

Service No: S/23397. Rank: Pte. Regiment: 7th Bn. Gordon Highlanders.

Born in 1900 in Boddam, Robert was the youngest son of George and Annie (m/s Stephen) Stephen of 3E Street, Boddam and later of 42 Broad St., Peterhead. He was also brother to John W., Isabella H., Christian C. and Alexander Stephen. He had just completed an apprenticeship with Messrs J.E. Hutchison & Son, grocer, Queen St., Peterhead when the war broke out.

Robert was killed in action on the 24 Jul 1918 at Marfaux near Rheims, France, aged only 18 years. Robert's body was never recovered and his sacrifice is commemorated on the Soissons Memorial which lists almost 4,000 officers and men of the United Kingdom forces who died during the Battles of the Aisne and the Marne in 1918 and who have no known grave.

References:
CWGC Casualty No 1760287

Peter STEWART

Service No: 2393. Rank: Pte. Regiment: 5th Bn. Gordon Highlanders.

Peter lived at Berefold near the Toll of Birness, Aberdeenshire and enlisted in Ellon into the 5th Bn. Gordon Highlanders. He arrived in France on the 5 May 1915 and fell on the 27 Jul 1916 with no known grave. His sacrifice is commemorated on the Thiepval Memorial which bears the names of more than 72,000 officers and men of the United Kingdom and South African forces that died in the Somme sector and have no known grave.

References:
CWGC Casualty No 1554617

Alexander STRACHAN

Service No: 5009/DA. Rank: Deckhand.
Service: RNR - HMS Canopus.

Born in Peterhead on the 14 May 1903, Alexander was the son of James Strachan of Roanheads, Peterhead.

Having served aboard HMD Peace (PD.130), Alexander died of disease on 10 Nov 1918 whilst aboard the accommodation ship HMS Canopus. Alexander was only 15 years old at the time. He is buried in the Peterhead Old Cemetery.

References:
CWGC Casualty No 326999

Benjamin STRACHAN

Service No: 2041/SA(PO). Rank: Second Hand. Service: RNR - HMD Era II.

Born on the 9 Oct 1882 in Buchanhaven, Benjamin was the son of Arthur and Elizabeth (m/s Buchan) Strachan aka "Betsy". He was the husband of Mary Ann (m/s Tait) Strachan, of The Ives, Ugie St., Peterhead. They had a daughter Elizabeth Strachan b. 1916, who later married David Stephen. Benjamin was also the brother of Arthur, George, Joseph, Mary, William and Alex Strachan.

Whilst serving aboard HMD Era II, Benjamin was taken seriously ill. Sadly he died of disease in Aberdeen on the 27 Feb 1918 aged 35. Benjamin is buried in the Old Peterhead Churchyard.

References:
CWGC Casualty No 327000

James STRACHAN

Service No 2974 Rank: Pte. Regiment: 5th Bn. Gordon Highlanders.
Service No: S/40262. Rank: Pte. Regiment: 6th Bn. Gordon Highlanders.

James was born in 1898 in Peterhead and was the son of Andrew Strachan of 12 Ugie Street, Buchanhaven, Peterhead. Prior to the war, James was a baker.

He enlisted into the 5th Bn. Gordon Highlanders on the 15 Jan 1915 in Peterhead. In Sep 1916, James was posted to the 2nd Bn. Gordon Highlanders. He was severely injured in Apr 1917 with a gunshot wound to the buttocks. He remained in hospital till Jul 1917.

Five months later he was posted again, this time to the 1st /6th Bn. Gordon Highlanders. On the 21 Mar 1918 James was listed as missing in action and later confirmed dead on that date. His body was never recovered and his sacrifice is listed on the Arras Memorial. This memorial commemorates almost 35,000 servicemen from the United Kingdom, South Africa and New Zealand who died in the Arras sector and has no known grave.

His father, Andrew moved on to Kirkton, Duffton, Aberdeenshire and then on to 67 Commercial St. Lossiemouth.

References:
CWGC Casualty No 1671428
Service Record

Robert STRACHAN

Service No: 2666. Rank: Pte. Regiment: 5th Bn. Gordon Highlanders.

Robert was born in Peterhead and was a resident of Roanheads. He enlisted into the 5th Bn. Gordon Highlanders in Peterhead.

Robert was killed on the Courcelette Firing Line on the 2 Dec 1916 from a shell explosion. His body was never recovered and his sacrifice is commemorated on the Thiepval Memorial. This memorial to the missing of the Somme bears the names of more than 72,000 officers and men of the United Kingdom and South African forces who died in the Somme sector and have no known grave.

References:
CWGC Casualty No 1554966

Wilfred Alfred STRACHAN

Rank: Engineer. Service: Admiralty Civilian.

Born in Peterhead on the 22 Jan 1889, William was the son of William Buchan Gray Strachan and Jane Ann (m/s Sangster) Strachan of 31 King St., Peterhead. William was a brother to George, John, Elizabeth, Harry, Marjory D., Ernest

Rose and Mary Strachan. Additionally he had four other siblings who all died in infancy.

William was employed by Fairfield Shipbuilding Co. building HM Submarine "K.13." The K.13 sank during sea trials as a result of an accident on the 29 Jan 1917. Thirty-two of the eighty man crew died before rescuers could arrive 57 hours after the accident. William is buried in the Faslane Cemetery This cemetery contains 33 First World War Graves, of which 31 are connected with the sinking of HM Submarine "K.13" in the Gareloch.

References:
CWGC Casualty No 2752926

Leslie STRATH*

Rank: Labourer. Service: RNAS Lenabo.

Born in 1901 in Peterhead, Leslie was the son of George and Maggie (m/s Kidd) Strath of 50 Queen St. Peterhead. He was the brother of George and Janet Strath.

Leslie died at the RNAS Lenabo, near Longside as a result of an accident. At the age of 15, he fell from a ladder to the ground below, a distance of 130 feet.

References:
BO 1919 Peterhead Roll of Honour
Death Certificate

James STRONACH

Service No: 2749. Rank: Pte. Regiment: 5th Bn. Gordon Highlanders.

James was born in 1895 in Peterhead, the son of Alexander and Mary (m/s Chalmers) Stronach of 44 Longate, Peterhead. He was also the brother to William, Mary, David, Barbara and Chrissie Stronach. A butcher by trade, James enlisted on the 21 Dec 1914, into the 5th Bn. Gordon Highlanders.

James was then discharged from the Army because of sickness on the 29 Oct 1915 without going to France. He was awarded the Silver War Badge in 1917 and died in Peterhead on the 3 Feb 1920 of Pulmonary tuberculosis. He is buried in Peterhead Cemetery.

References:
Service Pension Records
Death Certificate

Andrew SUMMERS

Service No: S/40132. Rank: Pte. Regiment: 8th/10th Bn. Gordon Highlanders.

Born in Peterhead on the 21 May 1895, Andrew was the son of Andrew and Lizzie Summers of 2 Harbour St., Peterhead and later of Cruden. He was also the brother to Jemima, Jessie and Isabella Summers.

Andrew enlisted in Peterhead and died of his wounds on the 11 Apr 1917, aged 22. He is buried in the Duisans British Cemetery, Etrun. Most of the graves relate to the Battles of Arras in 1917.

References:
CWGC Casualty No 41367
Birth Certificate

George Edward SUMMERS

Service No: 892102. Rank: Pte. Regiment: 190th Bn. Canadian Infantry.

Born in Winnipeg on the 21 Mar 1892, George was the Son of George and Elizabeth Summers of 762 Spruce St., Winnipeg, formerly of Aberdeenshire, Scotland. He was the husband of Hattie Bertrice (formerly Summers), of Erno, Ontario.

George died back in Winnipeg on the 28 Nov 1918 of injuries sustained in action and is buried in the Winnipeg (Brookside) Cemetery.

References:
CWGC Casualty No 4012642

William Cay SUMMERS

Service No: 204897. Rank: Pte. Regiment: 15th Bn. Canadian Infantry (Central Ontario Regiment).

Born on the 21 Apr 1892, William was the youngest son of George and Ann (m/s Cay) Summers, of Cruden, then of 21 Castle St., Peterhead and latterly of 2 Seagate, Peterhead. He was also a brother to Jane Mitchell, Margaret Dow, Maggie, George Dow, Andrew, Joseph Cay and Charles Summers.

After emigrating to Canada, William enlisted in Saskatoon on the 25 Jul 1916. After a year at the front, William was listed as "missing presumed a prisoner of war". However he had been hit by an enemy shell and died of his wounds on the 5 Apr 1918. He is buried in the Duisans British Cemetery, Etrun

References:
CWGC Casualty No 41370
Buchan Observer Article 7 May 1918

George Francis SUTHERLAND

Service No: 2164. Rank: Trooper. Regiment: 13th Bn. Scottish Horse.
Service No: 315714. Rank: Pte. Regiment: Black Watch (Royal Highlanders).

Born in 1894 in Glasgow, George was the second son of George and Marjory Cameron Sutherland, of The Retreat, Scone, Perthshire. The family moved to Peterhead and his father was the Clerk of Works at HM Convict Prison, Peterhead. George's brothers and sisters were; Maggie, Andrew, Christian and Patrick Sutherland. Prior to enlisting, George was an engineer at the Caledonian Railway Works, Perth.

After enlisting into the Scottish Horse, George was posted to the Balkans on the 18 Aug 1915. He then served in Flanders and died of his wounds 26 Jul 1918, aged 24. He is buried in the Janval Cemetery, Dieppe. Dieppe was used by Commonwealth forces as a minor base from Dec 1914 onwards.

References:
CWGC Casualty No 239080

John Wilson SUTHERLAND

Service No: 6810. Rank: Pte. Regiment: 8th /10th Bn Gordon Highlanders.
Service No 384344 Rank: Pte. Regiment: 129th Coy. Labour Corps.

Born in Leith, Midlothian in 1874, John was the son of John and Margaret Sutherland and the husband of Christina Sutherland of 39 North St., Peterhead.

John enlisted in the Gordon Highlanders but was later posted to the Labour Corps. In 1917, men were transferred to the Labour Corps if their medical rating fell below A1. John died on the 7 Nov 1917, aged 43 and is buried in the Wimereux Communal Cemetery.

References:
CWGC Casualty No 85074

Thomas SUTHERLAND

Service No: 2789/S(PO). Rank: Stoker.
Service: RNR – HMS Thalia.

Born 20 Sep 1891 in Glasgow, Thomas was the son of Thomas and Jane (m/s Reid)

Sutherland and the husband of Mary Sutherland of 7 James St., Peterhead. Thomas was also the brother of Elspet and James Sutherland.

Whilst serving with HMS Thalia, Thomas died at home of disease on the 28 Apr 1919, aged 27 and is buried in the Peterhead Cemetery.

References:
CWGC Casualty No 327001

D. TAYLOR

Pte D. Taylor 1st /5th Bn. Gordon Highlanders, his death is honoured on the Peterhead War Memorial.

James Hutchison TAYLOR

Service No: S/23402. Rank: Pte. Regiment: Black Watch (Royal Highlanders).
Service No: S/41675. Rank: Pte. Regiment: 4th Bn. Gordon Highlanders.

Born on the 2 Sep 1898 in Peterhead, James was the son of Robert Turner and Anne (aka Bessie) (m/s Hutchison) Taylor of 3 Lodge Walk, Peterhead.

James enlisted in Aberdeen into the Black Watch (Royal Highlanders) before being posted to the 4th Bn. Gordon Highlanders. He was killed in action on the 22 Mar 1918 aged 19 years and his body was not recovered. James' sacrifice is recorded on the Arras Memorial which commemorates almost 35,000 servicemen from the United Kingdom, South Africa and New Zealand who died in the Arras sector.

References:
CWGC Casualty No 1672023
Buchan Observer Article 30 Apr 1918

John TAYLOR

Service No: 3666. Rank: Pte. Regiment: 1st Bn. Gordon Highlanders.
Service No: 241234. Rank: Pte. Regiment: 7th Bn. Gordon Highlanders.

Born in Peterhead and enlisted in Aberdeen into the 1st Bn. Gordon Highlanders, John was killed in action on the 14 Apr 1918. John's body was never found and his sacrifice is recorded on the Ploegsteert Memorial. This memorial commemorates more than 11,000 servicemen of the United Kingdom and South African forces who have no known grave.

References:
CWGC Casualty No 869143

John Robert TAYLOR

Service No: S/43332. Rank: Pte. Regiment: 1st Bn. Gordon Highlanders.

Born on the 22 Jul 1891 at 79 King St., Peterhead, John was the son of Christine Taylor who married William Graham of 10 Love Lane, Peterhead. John was also the husband of Isabella Duncan Kinmond (m/s Wyness) Taylor of 50 Queen St., Peterhead whom he married in 1914. Prior to the war, John was employed by J.B. Dickie & Co. Alexandra Sawmills, Peterhead.

John enlisted in Peterhead and was killed in action on the 13 Nov 1916 still aged only 25. His body was never recovered and his sacrifice is commemorated on the Thiepval Memorial, the memorial to the missing of the Somme, which bears the names of more than 72,000 officers and men of the United Kingdom and South African forces who have no known grave.

References:
CWGC Casualty No 815138

Robert Mutch TAYLOR*

Service No: 12437. Rank: Pte. Regiment: 6th Bn. Gordon Highlanders.

Born on the 12 Jul 1888 in Elgin, Robert was the son of John Robb and Mary Ann (m/s Campbell) Taylor, later of Ben Nevis, Hopeman, Morayshire. He was also the brother of William G. and Agnes Taylor.

A one-time resident of Peterhead, Robert was killed during the Beaumont-Hamel offensive on the 13 Nov 1916. He is buried in the Mailly Wood Cemetery, Mailly-Maillet which the 51st Highland Division used following the capture of Beaumont-Hamel.

References:
CWGC Casualty No 111779
Birth Certificate

Robert Nicol TAYLOR

Service No: S/24480. Rank: Pte. Regiment: Argyll & Sutherland Highlanders.
Service No: S/42269. Rank: Pte. Regiment: 9th Bn. Seaforth Highlanders.
Born in Peterhead in 1899, Robert was the

son of Robert Slater and Annie (m/s Keiller) Taylor of 25 St. Peter St., Peterhead.

Robert initially enlisted into the A&SH in Aberdeen, before being posted to the 9th Seaforth Highlanders. He died of his wounds on the 14 Aug 1918 aged 18. Robert is buried in the Terlincthun British Cemetery, Wimille, which was begun in Jun 1918 when the space available for service burials in the civil cemeteries of Boulogne and Wimereux was exhausted.

References:
CWGC Casualty No 4027420

Thomas W. TAYLOR

Service No: 2156. Rank: Pte. Regiment: 5th Bn. Gordon Highlanders.
Service No: 240454. Rank: Pte. Regiment: 1st/5th Bn. Gordon Highlanders.

Born in Peterhead, Thomas was the son of Alexander and Mrs Taylor of 9 Pool Lane, Keith Inch, Peterhead.

Thomas enlisted in Peterhead and arrived in France on the 21 Aug 1915. He was killed between the 9 Apr 1917 and the 11 Apr 1917 during the attack on Roclincourt and is interred in the Roclincourt Valley Cemetery.

References:
CWGC Casualty No 190422

Alexander Bruce TENNANT*

Service No: 2847. Rank: Pte. Regiment: Lovat Scouts.
Service No: 5333. Rank: Pte. Regiment: 1st Bn. Queen's Own Cameron Highlanders.
Service No: S/40561. Rank: Pte. Regiment: 1st Bn. Queen's Own Cameron Highlanders.

Born in Peterhead in 1894, Alexander was the son of George and Margaret (m/s Robb) Tennant and the brother of Amelia and George Tennant. The family later moved to Glasgow.

Alexander was killed on the 18 Apr 1918 and has no known grave. His sacrifice is honoured on the Loos Memorial which commemorates over 20,000 officers and men who fell in the area from the River Lys to the old southern boundary of the First Army, east and west of Grenay.

References:
CWGC Casualty No 1770503
Birth Certificate

James Matthew THIRD

Service No: 29606. Rank: Fusilier. Regiment: Royal Scots Fusiliers.
Service No: S/17646. Rank: Pte. Regiment: 9th Bn. Seaforth Highlanders.

Born in Old Deer on the 16 Mar 1886, James was the son of Elspet Third and the husband of Elizabeth Gordon (m/s Duthie) Third of 16 Chapel St., Peterhead and later of 22 North St., Peterhead. James and Elizabeth (Betsy) had two sons James Matthew Third, born 1914 and William Noble Duthie Third, born 1917. In civilian life James was a carter with Mr James Sutherland, Victoria Stables, Peterhead.

James enlisted in Aberdeen into the Royal Scots Fusiliers before being transferred to the Seaforth Highlanders. He fell on the 23 Mar 1918 and his body has never been recovered. His sacrifice is commemorate on the Pozieres Memorial which honours over 14,000 casualties of the United Kingdom and 300 of the South African Forces who have no known grave.

References:
CWGC Casualty No 1589437

David A. THOIRS

Service No: 10312. Rank: Pte. Regiment: 6th Bn. King's Own Scottish Borderers.

Born in 1881 in Edinburgh and sometime resident of Berwick, David was the son of James and Margaret (m/s Mitchell) Thoirs, of Windmill St., Peterhead. He was also the brother of Alexander Jamison, Mary Ann and Margaret Thoirs.

David enlisted in Berwick into the 1st Bn. KOSB and arrived in Egypt on the 16 Nov 1914. David was listed as missing presumed dead on the 3 May 1917 aged 36. His sacrifice is honoured on the Arras Memorial which commemorates almost 35,000 servicemen from the United Kingdom, South Africa and New Zealand who died in the Arras sector and has no known grave.

References:
CWGC Casualty No 777156

Robert THOM

Service No: 240783. Rank: Pte. Regiment: 2nd Bn. Gordon Highlanders.

Born and enlisted in Peterhead, Robert was the husband of Mrs Thom of 3 Tanfield Place, Peterhead. Prior to the war he was a carter with Mr James Sutherland of Peterhead.

Robert was killed in action on the 26 Oct 1917. His sacrificed is honoured on the Tyne Cot Memorial which names almost the 35,000 officers and men whose graves are not known.

References:
CWGC Casualty No 827404

Alexander John THOMSON

Service No: S/19588. Rank: Pte. Regiment: 8th/10th Bn. Gordon Highlanders.
Service No: S/41414. Rank: Pte. Regiment: 8th Bn. Black Watch (Royal Highlanders).

Born in Peterhead on the 10 Jun 1899, Alexander was the fourth son of Allan and Margaret (m/s Baxter) Thomson of 7 Low St., Burnhaven, Peterhead. Alexander was one of ten children of which three sons were killed in action and one seriously injured. His siblings were: Allan (KIA) James (KIA), William (injured), George, Walter (died in infancy), Alice Mary, Arthur, Margaret Helen, Ann and Norman Davidson Thomson. Prior to the war, Alexander worked as a farm servant in the district.

Alexander enlisted into 8th/10th Bn. Gordon Highlanders before being posted to the 8th Bn. Black Watch (Royal Highlanders). He was killed in action on the 19 Jul 1918, nine days before his brother Allan was killed. He fell during the ill-fated Meteren engagement in which over two hundred members of the Black Watch (Royal Highlanders) were killed or injured. Alexander's sacrifice is honoured on the Ploegsteert Memorial which commemorates more than 11,000 servicemen of the United Kingdom and South African forces who died in this sector and have no known grave.

Alexander's father had passed away two months earlier on the 10 May 1918.

References:
CWGC Casualty No 866410
Gordon Highlander's Website

Allan THOMSON DCM, MM

Service No: 2171. Rank: Pte. Regiment: 5th Bn. Gordon Highlanders.
Service No: 240460. Rank: Sgt. Regiment: 1st/5th Bn. Gordon Highlanders.

Born on the 26 Oct 1895 in Peterhead, Allan was the eldest son of Allan & Margaret (m/s Baxter) Thomson of 7 Low St., Burnhaven, Peterhead. Allan was one of ten children of which three sons were killed in action and one seriously injured. His siblings were: James (KIA), William (injured), Alexander John (KIA), George, Walter (died in infancy), Alice Mary, Arthur, Margaret Helen, Ann and Norman Davidson Thomson. Prior to the war, Allan was a blacksmith with Mr Whyte, Sandford, Peterhead.

Allan initially joined the F Coy of the 5th Bn. Gordon Highlanders because the two Peterhead Companies were full. In 1914, he was sent to Bedford, England for training before arriving in France on the 2 May 1915. A fierce and courageous soldier, Allan was awarded both the Military Medal and the Distinguished Conduct Medal in Apr 1918. The citation reads:

"For conspicuous gallantry and devotion to duty. On finding that the platoon on the flank was held up by machine gun fire, he crawled along the parapet, and, single-handedly, rushed the machine gun and captured it, killing the crew. His conduct during the whole operation was an inspiration to his men."

Allan was killed during the attack on Buzancy on the 28 Jul 1918, only nine days after his brother Alexander was killed. Allan is buried in the Buzancy Military Cemetery which was made by the 15th Division; the original graveyard contained 96 burials. After the Armistice, graves were brought in from the surrounding battlefields.

Alexander's father had passed away two months earlier on the 10 May 1918.

References:
CWGC Casualty No 274995
Gordon Highlanders Website

George THOMSON

Service No: 1742. Rank: Pte. Regiment: 5th Bn. Gordon Highlanders.
Service No: 240261. Rank: Pte. Regiment: 1st/5th Bn. Gordon Highlanders.

Born on the 27 Oct 1896 at Crookedneuk, Longside, George was the second son of George and Mary (m/s Norrie) Thomson of 37 St Mary St., Peterhead. George was also the brother of Frank, Robina, Mary and Alice Thomson. In civilian life, George worked as a farm servant at Corskellie, Lonmay.

George enlisted into the A Coy, 5th Bn. Gordon Highlanders in Strichen and arrived in France on the 5 May 1915. George fell on the 6 Dec 1917 aged a mere 21 years old. He is buried in the Bancourt British Cemetery.

References:
CWGC Casualty No 206400

James THOMSON

Service No: 1816. Rank: Pte. Regiment: 1st/5th Bn. Gordon Highlanders.

Born in Peterhead in 28 Oct 1896, James was the second son of Allan & Margaret (m/s Baxter) Thomson of 7 Low St., Burnhaven, Peterhead. James was one of ten children of which three sons were killed in action and one seriously injured. His siblings were: Allan (KIA), William (injured), Alexander John (KIA), George, Walter (died in infancy), Alice Mary, Arthur, Margaret Helen, Ann and Norman Davidson Thomson. Prior to the war, James worked as a farm servant in the district.

Of his four brothers James was the first to enlist in late 1914; sadly he also was the first to die. James arrived in France on the 2 May 1915 before being killed in a mine explosion on the 26 Mar 1916 aged 19 years. James is buried in the Maroeuil British Cemetery. This cemetery was begun by the 51st Highland Division when Commonwealth forces took over the Arras Front in Mar 1916. Almost half of the graves are those of Highland territorials.

References:
CWGC Casualty No 121098

John THOMSON

Service No: 4864. Rank: Pte. Regiment: 48th Bn. Australian Imperial Force.

Born in Peterhead in about 1888, John was the son of George and Elsie Craig Thomson. He emigrated to Australia where he married Otina Marie Thomson of Alberton, South Australia (SA) later of Glanville, SA. They had one child together – name unknown. John's occupation was listed as a sail maker.

John enlisted into the AIF on the 31 Mar 1917. He sailed for England on HMAT Borda on the 26 Jun 1917. John arrived in France on the 29 Jan 1918 and was killed in action during the Battle of Amiens on the 8 Aug 1918. His sacrifice is commemorated on the Villers-Bretonneux Memorial which is the Australian National Memorial erected to commemorate all Australian soldiers who fought in France and Belgium during the First World War.

References:
CWGC Casualty No 1452429
National Australian Archive

John THOMSON

Service No: 1913. Rank: Pte. Regiment: 1st/5th Bn. Gordon Highlanders.

Born in Peterhead in about 1898, John was the only son of the late John Thomson of Peterhead.

John enlisted in Maud and arrived in France on the 5 Dec 1915. He was killed during the Beaumont-Hamel Offensive on 13 Nov 1916, aged 18. John is buried in the Y Ravine Cemetery, Beaumont-Hamel. There are now over four hundred 1914-18 war casualties buried in this site.

References:
Peterhead War Memorial Website - Anne Park
CWGC Casualty No 2743055

Laurance THOMSON

Service Number: 2777. Rank: Pte. Regiment: 5th Bn. Gordon Highlanders.
Service Number: 240785. Rank: Cpl. Regiment: 1st/5th Bn. Gordon Highlanders.

Born in 1887, Laurance was the son of Laurance Murphy and Sarah R. (m/s Clark) Thomson and also was the husband of Bella (m/s Findlay) Thomson later Lumsden of 8 St Andrew St., Peterhead. Laurance and Bella were married on the 18 Apr 1913 in Aberdeen and had two children.

After enlisting into the Gordon Highlanders, Laurance arrived in France on the 2 May 1915. He died of gas poisoning on the 9 Aug 1918, aged 31, at the British 63rd Casualty Clearing Station. There are now over one hundred 1914-18 war casualties buried in this cemetery. The majority belonged to the 15th (Scottish) and 34th Divisions, who fell in Jul and Aug 1918.

References:
CWGC Casualty No 287225
Marriage Certificate

William THOMSON

Service No: 1907. Rank: Pte. Regiment: 5th Bn. Gordon Highlanders.
Service No: 240342. Rank: Pte. Regiment: 1st/5th Bn. Gordon Highlanders.

Born and enlisted in Peterhead, William was killed in action on the 21 Mar 1918 and his sacrifice is honoured on the Pozieres Memorial which commemorates over 14,000 casualties of the United Kingdom and 300 of the South African Forces who have no known grave.

William was also awarded the Territorial Force War Medal.

References:
CWGC Casualty No 1589546

William THOMSON

Service No: 886296. Rank: Pte. Regiment: 46th Bn. Canadian Infantry.

Born on the 24 Feb 1892 at 29 Queen St. Peterhead, William was the son of James Thomson, a Great North of Scotland Railway signalman and Mary (m/s Mutch) Thomson of 70 Queen St., Peterhead. He was also brother to Jane and George Thomson. William emigrated to Canada to work as a farmer in Saskatchewan.

He enlisted on the 19 Oct 1915 at Prince Albert in Saskatchewan, Canada before being killed on the 12 Apr 1917. William is buried in the Canadian Cemetery No.2, Neuville-St. Vaast. This cemetery was established by the Canadian Corps after the successful storming of Vimy Ridge on 9 Apr 1917.

References:
Canadian Archive – Attestation Paper
CWGC Casualty No 2955060
Birth Certificate.

William THOMSON

Service No: 1808D. Rank: Seaman. Service: RNR – HMS Bulwark.

Born on the 27 Jul 1873, William was the son of George and Amelia Thomson, of Peterhead and the nephew of Mrs Mary Stewart of 5 Maiden St. Peterhead.

William was killed when HMS Bulwark blew up suddenly on the 26 Nov 1914 whilst moored off Sheerness, Kent. She was destroyed by a large internal explosion with the loss of 736 men. William's body was never recovered and his sacrifice is honoured on the Portsmouth Naval Memorial which commemorates those members of the Royal Navy who had no known grave, the majority of deaths having occurred at sea where no permanent memorial could be provided.

References:
CWGC Casualty No 2872190

William John THOMSON

Service No: 2533DA. Rank: Deckhand. Service: RNR – HMD Nina. (PD.497).

Born on the 8 Aug 1894 in Peterhead, William was the son of William John and Mary Thomson, of 9, Almanythie Rd., Peterhead.

William died on the 2 Aug 1917 aged 23 years when HMD Nina caught fire and blew up in the English Channel. William's sacrifice is honoured on the Portsmouth Naval Memorial which commemorates those members of the Royal Navy who have no known grave.

References:
CWGC Casualty No 3041738

William TOCHER

Service No: 241260. Rank: Pte. Regiment: 5th Bn. Gordon Highlanders.

Born in Peterhead in 1895, William was the son of Christopher Burnett Tocher and Isabella Rennie Tocher of 2 Seagate, Peterhead. He was also brother of Mary Jane, Margaret Ann, John Edward, Elizabeth Bella Taylor Anderson and Christopher Burnett Tocher.

William enlisted in Aberdeen and was killed in action on the 30 Aug 1917, aged 22. His sacrifice is recorded on the Tyne Cot Memorial which bears the names of almost 35,000 officers and men whose graves are not known, most of whom died during the Passchendaele offensive.

References:
CWGC Casualty No 827865
PJ 22 Sep 17 Page 4: Peterhead

James Arthur Gall TRAIL

Service No: 2461. Rank: Pte. Regiment: 1st/5th Bn. Gordon Highlanders.

Born in Peterhead in about 1893, James was the second son of Isabella Chalmers Trail of 4 Weavers Lane, Peterhead and the grandson of Simon Trail, fruiterer, Queen St. Peterhead.

James enlisted into D Coy of the 5th Bn. Gordon Highlanders in Peterhead in Nov 1914. After training in England he arrived in France on the 5 Dec 1915. He was killed in action on the 1 Sep 1916 as a result of a shell burst. James was aged 23 at the time and is buried in the Cite Bonjean Military Cemetery, Armentieres. This cemetery was continually used by the near-by field ambulances and fighting units.

References:
CWGC Casualty No 277522

Thomas TRAYNOR

Service No: 2922S. Rank: Stoker. Service: RNR – HMS Hawke.

Thomas was born on the 4 Oct 1899 in Glasgow, the son of Francis and Margaret (m/s Ward) Traynor. Thomas married Margaret Stewart Walker and was a resident of Windmill St, Peterhead. Prior to the war, Thomas was a driver aboard a Buckie drifter. Following the war, his wife Margaret moved to Lowestoft, England.

Thomas was killed when HMS Hawke was sunk by a German submarine on the 15 Oct 1914. His sacrifice is listed upon the Portsmouth Naval Memorial.

References:
CWGC Casualty No 2872224
Buchan Observer 20 Oct 1914

Kenneth URQUHART

Service No: 4041. Rank: LCpl. Regiment: 1st/4th Bn. Gordon Highlanders.

Kenneth was born in 1886 at Brightmony, Auldearn, Nairn, the son of Alexander and Elsie Urquhart, of Standalane, Cawdor, Nairn.

He was the brother of Hector Urquhart. Kenneth enlisted in Aberdeen and died of his wounds on the 8 Apr 1916, aged 30, He is buried in the Aubigny Communal Cemetery Extension. From Mar 1916 to the Armistice, Aubigny was held by Commonwealth troops and burials were made in the Extension until Sep 1918.

References:
CWGC Casualty No 996759

Alexander Jamison WALKER

Service No: 3/6093. Rank: Pte. Regiment: 1st Bn. Gordon Highlanders.

Born in Burnhaven, Peterhead in 1893, Alexander was the son of Christina Simpson Walker, who lived in New Aberdour and later of 126 Wellington Rd., Aberdeen. Alexander was the husband of Agnes Boynes C. McIntosh whom he married in 1914 in Aberdeen.

Enlisted in Aberdeen, Alexander arrived in France on the 19 Dec 1914 and barely six months later died on the 2 Jun 1915 now aged 21. His body has never been located and is honoured on the Ypres (Menin Gate) Memorial which now bears the names of more than 54,000 officers and men whose graves are not known.

References:
CWGC Casualty No 912535

David WALKER

Service No: 2530. Rank: Pte. Regiment: 5th Bn. Gordon Highlanders.
Service No: 592640. Rank: Pte. Regiment: Labour Corps.

Born in 1886 in Peterhead, David was the son of Robert and Annie (m/s Mackie) Walker and the husband of Mary Bruce of 38 Windmill St., Peterhead. He was also the brother to Alexander, James, Daniel, Jane and Robert Walker. Prior to the war, David was a carter in Peterhead.

David enlisted into the Gordon Highlanders and after training arrived in France on the 4 Dec 1915. Due to disability, he was later transferred to the Labour Corps. David died at the General Hospital, Lincoln, Lincolnshire, England on the 14 Jul 1918 aged 32. He is buried in the Old Peterhead Cemetery.

References:
CWGC Casualty No 327003

Robert WALKER*

Service No: 3126. Rank: Pte. Regiment: 5th Bn. Gordon Highlanders.
Service No: 240960. Rank: Pte. Regiment: 2nd Bn. Gordon Highlanders.

Robert enlisted into the 5th Bn. Gordon Highlanders at Peterhead in mid-1915 and proceeded to France with the draft in Dec 1915.

He was wounded at High Wood on the 30/31 Jul 1916. In mid-1917 he was transferred to the 2nd Bn. On 26 Oct 1917, the British launched what became known as the Second Battle of Passchendaele, (26 Oct - 10 Nov 1917). Robert was one of over a hundred men of the battalion who died on that first day and most the bodies were never recovered. (Other Peterhead men killed on that day were George D. Watson, George Smith, Robert Thom and John S. Baird).

Robert's sacrifice is honoured on the Tyne Cot Memorial which now bears the names of almost 35,000 officers and men whose graves are not known.

References:
Material Supplied by Carolyn Morrisey.
CWGC Casualty No 825738

W. WALKER

Pte W. Walker 1st Bn. Gordon Highlanders. His sacrifice is honoured on the Peterhead War Memorial.

William Saddler WALKER

Service No: 2221. Rank: Cpl. Regiment: 5th Bn. Gordon Highlanders.

Born on the 13 Aug 1895 at 1 Port Henry Lane[5], Peterhead, William was the son of William and Dorothy Halcrow (m/s Cooney) Walker. He was also the brother of Elizabeth, Margaret and Charlotte Walker.

William enlisted in Peterhead and joined the BEF in France on the 2 May 1915. He was killed in action during the attack on Beaumont-Hamel on the 13 Nov 1916 and

---

[5] Should read Port Henry Road

his body has never been recovered. William's sacrifice is recorded upon the Thiepval Memorial which is the memorial to the missing of the Somme. It bears the names of more than 72,000 officers and men of the United Kingdom and South African forces who have no known grave.

References:
CWGC Casualty No 818601
Birth Certificate

George Jenkin WALLACE

Service No: 2586. Rank: Pte. Regiment: Gordon Highlanders.
Service No: 408277. Rank: Pte. Regiment: Labour Corps.
Service No: 238220. Rank: Pte. Regiment: 23rd Bn. Lancashire Fusiliers.

Born in 1889 in Peterhead, George was the son of Alexander Robb and Christian (m/s Cow) Wallace of Peterhead. George was also the brother to Jessie (later Mrs Butham, of Bean St. Hull), Margaret Strachan and Mary Wallace.

George died of his wounds on the 9 Dec 1918, aged 29. He is buried in the St. Andre Communal Cemetery. This cemetery was used by German hospitals during the greater part of the war and by No.11 Casualty Clearing Station after the British occupation of Lille.

References:
CWGC Casualty No 278873

John Moffat WALLACE*

Service No: 5977 Rank: Gnr. Regiment: Royal Canadian Horse Artillery.

Born on the 25 May 1881, John was the son of Mr and Mrs Robert Wallace of Stirling, Scotland. He emigrated to Canada in the years prior to the war.

John, now a teamster, enlisted on the 20 Sep 1914 at Valcartier, Quebec. He died of his wounds on the 25 Aug 1916 aged 35 years. John is buried in the Mont Huon Military Cemetery, Le Treport.

References:
CWGC Casualty No 120413

Robert (WATTERS) WATERS

Service No: S/5360 Rank: LCpl. Regiment: 10th Bn. Gordon Highlanders.

Service Returns state that Robert was born around 1895 in St Andrew's, Fife and enlisted in Glasgow. A some-time resident of Peterhead, he enlisted into the Gordon Highlanders.

Robert arrived in France on the 8 Jul 1915 and was killed in action very soon afterwards on the 25 Sep 1915. Robert's body has never been recovered and his sacrifice is honoured on the Loos Memorial. This memorial commemorates over 20,000 officers and men who have no known grave.

References:
Service Returns 1915.
Material provided by Carolyn Morrisey
CWGC Casualty No 736800

George Duncan WATSON

Service No: 240840. Rank: Pte. Regiment: 2nd Bn. Gordon Highlanders.

Born on the 11 Aug 1897 in Windmill St. Peterhead, George was the son of Alexander and Isabella Duncan (m/s Kinghorn) Watson. George was also brother to Alexander, Mary Jane and James Clark Watson.

George enlisted in Peterhead and was killed on the 26 Oct 1917. His body has not been recovered and George is honoured on the Tyne Cot Memorial which bears the names of almost 35,000 officers and men whose graves are not known.

References:
CWGC Casualty No 826194
Birth Certificate

Alexander George WATT

Service No: 3305. Rank: Pte. Regiment: 4th Regiment, South African Infantry.

Born about 1876, Alexander was the son of George and Margaret (m/s Milne) Watt of Peterhead and the husband of Lizzie Watt of Malvern, Durban, South Africa. He was also a brother to James, Joseph, Ellen, Christian, Georgina, Robert, George, Margaret and Ellenora Watt.

Alexander served in the German West and East Africa; in Egypt and in the South African Campaign. He was seriously injured on the 17 Jul 1916 in France and died of his wounds in London on the 24 Jul 1916, aged 40. His body was returned to Peterhead to be buried in the Old Churchyard.

References:
CWGC Casualty No 327029
South African War Project

John C. WATT*

Born in about 1897, John was the only son of John C. and Violet Watt of 50 Queen St., Peterhead. He had a least two sisters; Violet and Bella Watt. Prior to the war, John was an apprentice cooper with J. & S. Buchan, fishcurers, Peterhead.

John enlisted in 1914 into the Gordon Highlanders. In Apr 1918, John was listed as missing - presumed a prisoner of war. Correspondence was received from John whilst he was a prisoner. His death was listed on the 1919 Peterhead Roll of Honour as occurring in 1918. No other information is available about his fate.

John does not appear in any CWGC records

References:
Buchan Observer 1918

Harry (Henry) WATT

Service No: 2830. Rank: Pte. Regiment: 5th Bn. Gordon Highlanders.
Service No: 240808. Rank: Pte. Regiment: 1st/5th Bn. Gordon Highlanders.

Harry was born in Peterhead on the 5 May 1895, the son of Joseph and Annie (m/s Robertson) Watt of 71 Kirk St. Peterhead and later of 16 St Mary St., Peterhead. Prior to the war, Harry was employed in the Peterhead office of Messrs Richard Irvin & Sons, fishsalesmen.

Harry was one of up to sixteen children. These include; Joseph (b.1888), Chrissie (b.1890), George (b.1891), Alexander George (b.1892),Arthur (b.1894), Mary (b.1895), Douglas (b.1899), James Webster (b.1900), Alfred (b.1901), James Robertson (b.1902), William Davie (b.1904), Bertie (b.1906) and Bessie (b.1906) Watt. Four of the Watt brothers joined the Colours during the course of the Great War.

Harry enlisted in Peterhead shortly after the outbreak of war. Following training in England, he arrived in France on the 2 May 1915. Harry was killed in action at Ypres on the 31 Jul 1917 aged 22. His body was not recovered and he is honoured on the Ypres (Menin Gate) Memorial which now bears the names of more than 54,000 officers and men whose graves are not known.

References:
CWGC Casualty No 910565
Buchan Observer 21 Aug 1917
Public Family Tree

Robert Gordon Grant WATT

Service No: 2148. Rank: Pte. Regiment: 1st/5th Bn. Gordon Highlanders.

Born in Gordonston, Clatt near Huntly on the 22 Jun 1895, Robert was the natural son of Elsie Watt and the adopted son of Mr and Mrs John Milner of 7 Lily Terrace, West Rd., Peterhead. The family previously lived at 7 Gordon House, Cairntrodlie, Peterhead. Prior to the war, Robert was a carter with Mr J. Reid of Peterhead.

Robert enlisted in Peterhead soon after the outbreak of war and following training in England he arrived with the BEF in France on the 2 Aug 1915. Robert died of his wounds on the 15 May 1916 aged 21. He is buried in the Aubigny Communal Cemetery Extension. From Mar 1916 to the Armistice, Aubigny was held by Commonwealth troops and burials were made in the Extension up until Sep 1918.

References:
CWGC Casualty No 996832
Birth Certificate

William WATT

Service No: 2317. Rank: Pte. Regiment: 1st/5th Bn. Gordon Highlanders.

Born at Millbrex, New Deer, Aberdeenshire in 1896, William was the youngest son of Samuel and Jane (m/s Montgomerie) Watt of 20 Constitution St., Peterhead. He was also the brother of May (b.1882), Annabella (b.1885), John (b.1886), Henrietta (b.1888), Jessie Rollo (b.1890), George (b.1892), James (b.1885) and Elizabeth (b.1899) Watt.

William enlisted in Peterhead and after training, arrived in France on the 2 May 1915. He was killed by shrapnel in the trenches near Sector G3, Authuille-Hamel on the 17 Sep 1915, aged 19. William is buried in the Peronne Road Cemetery, Maricourt which was originally known as Maricourt Military Cemetery No.3.

References:
CWGC Casualty No 311525
Gordon Highlanders Website

W. WATT

Pte W. Watt, Gordon Highlanders, his sacrifice is honoured on the Peterhead War Memorial

Frank WEBSTER

Service No: 1482. Rank: Pte. Regiment: 5th Bn. Gordon Highlanders.
Service No: 240144. Rank: A/Cpl. Regiment: 1st/5th Bn. Gordon Highlanders.

Born in Peterhead in 1895, Frank was the son of John and Maggie Webster, of 4a Cairntrodlie, Peterhead and later of Benwells, Kirk Square, Peterhead. Frank was also the younger brother of James, Harry, Lily, Maxwell Allen and Lottie Webster. Prior to the war, Frank was an apprentice in the employment of Mr James McGee, fishcurer, Peterhead.

Soon after the commencement of hostilities, Frank joined the Gordon Highlanders in Peterhead. After training in England, Frank arrived in France on the 2 May 1915. Whilst attached to the 153rd Trench Mortar Bty, Frank died of wounds on the 26 Jun 1917, aged 22 years. He is buried in the Poperinghe New Military Cemetery.

References:
CWGC Casualty No 139638

James McBean WELSH

Service No: 1631/U. Rank: Engineman.
Service: RNR – HMS Pembroke.

Born in Peterhead in 1883, James was the son of Henry and Christina (m/s Milne) Welsh and the husband of Alice Rose Welsh of 66 Kirk St., Peterhead. James was also the brother to Janet, Helen, Maggie, Elizabeth, John, Alexander, Lydia, Peter, Christina and Henrietta Welsh.

Whilst serving aboard HMS Enterprise, James was taken ill and sadly died at home of pulmonary tuberculosis on the 18 Jun 1918 aged 35. James is buried in Peterhead Old Cemetery.

References:
CWGC Casualty No 327032
Death Certificate

James WHYTE*

Service No: 3207. Rank: Pte. Regiment: 5th Bn. Gordon Highlanders.
Service No: 240977. Rank: Cpl. Regiment: 5th Bn. Gordon Highlanders.

Born in Boddam in about 1895, James was the son of James and Mary Whyte of Sandford Lodge, Peterhead. He was also the husband of Eleanor C. Whyte of 11 Love Lane, Peterhead and later of 2, Market Terrace, Strichen, Aberdeenshire. Prior to the war, James worked on local farms.

James enlisted into the Gordon Highlanders in Peterhead and after training was sent to France on the 12 Oct 1915. James was badly wounded in Dec 1917 but later returned to the front. He was killed between 21 Mar 1918 and 2 Apr 1918 and has no known grave. James' sacrifice is honoured on the Pozieres Memorial which commemorates over 14,000 casualties of the United Kingdom and 300 of the South African Forces who have no known grave and who died on the Somme.

References:
CWGC Casualty No 851170

David Kelly WILL

Service: S/3556. Rank: Pte. Regiment: 3rd Bn. Gordon Highlanders.
Service: S/3556. Rank: Pte. Regiment: 9th Bn. Gordon Highlanders.

Born in Peterhead about 1894, David was the second son of James and Mary Ann (m/s Kelly) Will of 22 Chapel St., Peterhead. He was also the brother to James Kelly (who also served with the Colours), Catherine, William Kelly (KIA), Mary, John and Alexander Geary Will.

A resume of David's war record show:

4 Sep 1914 - Enlisted in Aberdeen into 3rd Bn. Gordon Highlanders.
3 Jan 1915 - Arrived in France.
14 Jun 1915 - Wounded, Gunshot Wound at Ypres and returned to England.
02 Sep 1915 - Embarked at Folkestone to join the 9th Bn. Gordon Highlanders.
12 Sep 1915 – Wounded, Gassed.
27 Apr 1917 - Wounded and posted Missing aged 23.

David's body has never been recovered and his sacrifice is honoured on the Arras Memorial which commemorates almost 35,000 servicemen from the United Kingdom, South Africa and New Zealand who died in

95

the Arras sector and have no known grave.

References:
CWGC Casualty No 774295
Service Record.

William Kelly WILL

Service No: 241689. Rank: Pte. Regiment:
5th Bn. Gordon Highlanders.
Service No: 241689. Rank: Pte. Regiment:
1st Bn. Gordon Highlanders.

Born in Peterhead on the 11 Dec 1897, William was the third son of James and Mary Ann (m/s Kelly) Will, of 22, Chapel St., Peterhead. He was brother to James Kelly (who also served with the Colours), David Kelly (KIA), Catherine, Mary, John and Alexander Geary Will. William was a cooper in Peterhead prior to the outbreak of war.

On the morning of 26 Sept 1917 the 1st Bn. Gordon Highlanders began an advance on Zonnebeke during the Third Battle of Ypres. All of those shown as missing with William on the Casualty List are later included on the memorial to the missing at Tyne Cot which now bears the names of almost 35,000 officers and men whose graves are not known. It appears William name had been missed out or not confirmed at that point. William's name was later added to the memorial following a petition made by Mr James Grant, who kindly allowed William's photograph to be used here.

References:
CWGC Casualty No 75227962
Mr James Grant.

Alexander WILLIAMSON

Rank: Merchant Seaman. Service: Royal Naval Reserve.

Born in around 1875 in Peterhead, Alexander was the son of Alexander (occ. Seaman) and Isabella (m/s Batty) Williamson of 2 Backgate, Peterhead, and was also the husband of Amelia (m/s Davis) Williamson. Alexander had seven younger brothers, these include: George, James, Robert and Charles (KIA) Williamson, plus three more unknown. Amelia and Alexander had six children

together including Amelia, John Massie and Margaret Williamson.

Alexander died at 18 Castle St. Peterhead on the 21 Jun 1919 of pneumonia and is buried in Constitution St. Cemetery, Peterhead.

References:
Death Certificate.

Charles WILLIAMSON

Service No: S/3650. Rank: LCpl. Regiment: 9th Bn. Gordon Highlanders.

Born in Peterhead in about 1890, Charles was the youngest and eighth son of Alexander and Isabella (m/s Batty) Williamson of 84 Longate, Peterhead and later of 2 Backgate, Peterhead. He was also brother to Alexander, George, James and Robert (plus three more). Prior to the war he was a cooper with William Bruce, fishcurer, Peterhead.

Charles initially joined the 5th Bn. Gordon Highlanders and arrived in France on the 9 Jul 1915. During the war he was posted to the 9th Bn. Gordon Highlanders before being killed on the 22 Aug 1917, aged 27. His body has never been recovered and his sacrifice is recorded on the Tyne Cot Memorial which bears the names of almost 35,000 officers and men whose graves are not known.

References:
CWGC Casualty No 877389

William Millar WILLIAMSON

Service No: 2408. Rank: Pte. Regiment: 5th Bn. Gordon Highlanders
Service No: 240579. Rank: Pte. Regiment: 6th Bn. Gordon Highlanders.

Born on the 6 Dec 1895 at 28 York St., Peterhead, William was the son of Alexander Leslie (occ master blacksmith) and Mary (m/s Lawrence) Williamson of 27 Prince St. and later of Rose St, Peterhead. He was also a brother to Annie M., Jessie W., Maggie B., Lizzie R., Alexander J., Robert and Thomas G. Williamson. Prior to the war, William was a blacksmith in the employ of his father.

William enlisted in Peterhead soon after the outbreak of war and arrived in France on the 2 May 1915. Later he was posted to the 6th Bn. Gordon Highlanders before being killed in action on the 11 Apr 1918. His body has never been recovered and his sacrifice is remembered on the Loos Memorial which commemorates over 20,000 officers and men who have no known grave.

References:
CWGC Casualty No 737435
Buchan Observer Article 21 May 1918
Birth Certificate

Andrew WILLOX*

Service No: 1586. Rank: Piper. Regiment: 5th Bn. Gordon Highlanders.

Born in 1883 in Stuartfield near Old Deer, Aberdeenshire, Andrew was the son of John Willox and the grandson of James and Jane Willox of Blackhills, Peterhead.

Andrew arrived in France on the 2 May 1915 with the 5th Bn. Gordon Highlanders and fell during the 3rd Battle of Ypres on the 31 Jul 1916, aged 23 years. Andrew's body was not recovered and his sacrifice is honoured on the Thiepval Memorial which is the memorial to the missing of the Somme and bears the names of more than 72,000 officers and men of the United Kingdom and South African forces who died and have no known grave.

References:
CWGC Casualty No 822482

Charles WILLOX

Service No: 135460. Rank: Gnr. Regiment: 238th Bde. Royal Garrison Artillery.

Born in Peterhead on the 1 Dec 1896, Charles was the son of James Simpson Willox and Jane (m/s Robertson) Willox of Lower Grange, Peterhead. Charles had two brothers named John R. and Norman B. Willox and a sister named Betsy Willox.

Charles enlisted in Peterhead on the 8 Dec 1915, Charles was posted to 3 Depot, RFA on the 30 Dec 1916. During the war, Charles received at least two gunshot wounds and also received a pension for being gassed twice in 1917 and 1918. Towards the end of the war, Charles was a patient of the Queen Mary's Military Hospital in Whalley. He was discharged from the Army in 1919 with a 20% disability pension of 5 shillings and sixpence per week.

Charles died on the 18 Apr 1920 as a result of injuries sustained after being gassed during the war.

References:
Anne Park
Buchan Observer 20 Apr 1920
Service Record

James WILLOX

Service No: 2622. Rank: Pte. Regiment: 5th Bn. Gordon Highlanders.
Service No: 240692. Rank: A/Sgt. Regiment: 1st/5th Bn. Gordon Highlanders.

James was born in Peterhead in 1895, the son of James and Isabella (m/s Will) Willox of 41 Windmill St., Peterhead. He was also brother to John Kelman and Bella Willox.

After enlisting in Peterhead, James arrived in France on the 2 May 1915. He died on the 24 Jun 1917 aged 20, at the 3rd Canadian Casualty Clearing Station. James is buried in the Lijssenthoek Military Cemetery which was first used by the French 15th Hopital D'Evacuation and in Jun 1915.

References:
CWGC Casualty No 150540

William WILLOX

Service No: 73. Rank: Pte. Regiment: 2nd Bn. Gordon Highlanders.

Born in Peterhead on the 20 Apr 1890, William was the eldest son of Andrew Robertson and Annie (m/s Colvin) Willox of Nether Park, Lonmay formerly of Peterhead. He was also the brother to Margaret Yeats, Mary Ann, Jessie, Anderina and Sarah Willox.

Whilst serving with A Coy, 5th Bn. Gordon Highlanders, William went to France on the 7 Oct 1914 with his regiment from India. He was wounded at Ypres and invalided home. William returned to the front in Feb 1915 with the 2nd Bn., only to be killed in action on the 17 Mar 1915, aged 24. William's last resting place has not been discovered and his sacrifice is honoured on the Ypres (Menin Gate) Memorial which bears the names of more than 54,000 officers and men whose graves are not known.

References:
CWGC Casualty No 911324
Buchan Observer 1915.

William Cordiner WILSON

Service No: S/43285. Rank: Cpl. Regiment: 1st Bn. Gordon Highlanders.

Born in Peterhead in 1891, William was the son of William and Mary (m/s Cordiner) Wilson of 71 King St., Peterhead. He was also the eldest brother of Maggie M., George and Elizabeth Wilson.

Having enlisted into the Gordon Highlanders in Peterhead, William fell on the 13 Nov 1916 aged a mere 19 years. His body was never recovered and his sacrifice is commemorated on the Thiepval Memorial, the memorial to the missing of the Somme which bears the names of more than 72,000 officers and men of the United Kingdom and South African forces who died in the Somme sector and have no known grave.

References:
CWGC Casualty No 822908
1911 Scottish Census

William Webster WISEMAN

Service No: 2087. Rank: Pte. Regiment: 5th Bn. Gordon Highlanders.
Service No: 240419. Rank: A/Cpl. Regiment: 5th Bn. Gordon Highlanders.

Born in Peterhead in 1894, William was the son of Joseph and Elizabeth (m/s O'Brien) Wiseman of 22 Backgate, Peterhead. He was the younger brother of Anne, Peter, Jane, James Chalmers, Joseph, Isabella and George Wiseman. Prior to the outbreak of hostilities, he was in the employment of Mr James Sutherland, Victoria Stables, Peterhead.

William enlisted into the 5th Bn. Gordon Highlanders in Peterhead soon after the start of the war. He arrived in France on the 2 May 1915 and was killed at the Chemical Works, during the Battle of Arras on the 17 May 1917. He was aged 23 years and his body was not recovered. His sacrifice is honoured on the Arras Memorial which commemorates almost 35,000 servicemen from the United Kingdom, South Africa and New Zealand who died in the Arras sector and have no known grave.

William's bother, George Wiseman was made a prisoner of war after the Battle of Mons.

References:
CWGC casualty No 774866

Ronald John WISHART

Service No: 1015982. Rank: Pte. Regiment: 72nd Bn. Seaforth Highlanders of Canada Canadian Expeditionary Force.

Ronald was born on the 21 Feb 1890, the son of Robert and Margaret Wishart of Alloa, Clackmannanshire formerly of Aberdeen. He was married to Nora Hutchison of Innesfallen, Peterhead. Ronald later emigrated to Canada where he became an accountant at the Royal Bank of Canada, Vernon, BC.

Ronald enlisted in Valcartier, Quebec and died of his wounds on the 12 Oct 1918 aged 27. Ronald is buried in the Etaples Military Cemetery. The area around Etaples was the scene of immense concentrations of Commonwealth reinforcement camps and hospitals.

References:
CWGC Casualty No 497948

William Hutchison Leask WOOD

Service No: 3582. Rank: Pte. Regiment: Gordon Highlanders.
Service No: 241179. Rank: Signaller. Regiment: 1st Bn. Gordon Highlanders.

William (aka "Dickie") was born on the 5 May 1897, the son of James and Helen (m/s Milne) Wood of Ellis St. Peterhead. In civilian life William was employed with Mr L Gellatly, commission agent, Harbour St., Peterhead.

He was wounded in Mar 1918 and returned to England for treatment. On his return to the front, William was killed on the 27 Sep 1918. He is buried in the Lowrie Cemetery, Havrincourt. Most of the men buried in the cemetery died in Sep 1918.

References:
CWGC Casualty No 301699

Robert WRIGHT*

Service No: 815. Rank: Pte. Regiment: 1st Bn. Gordon Highlanders.

Born in Kemnay, Aberdeenshire and enlisted in Maud, Robert was a sometime resident of Peterhead.

Robert arrived in France on the 13 Aug 1914 and was killed in action on the 26 Aug 1914. His sacrifice is honoured on the La Fertésous-Jouarre Memorial which commemorates 3,740 officers and men of the British Expeditionary Force (BEF) who fell at the battles of Mons, Le Cateau, the Marne and the Aisne between the end of Aug and early Oct 1914 and have no known graves.

References:
CWGC Casualty No 724722

Wilson George YOUNGSON

Service No: 3036. Rank: Pte. Regiment: 1st/5th Bn. Gordon Highlanders.

Known as George, he was born in Peterhead in 1893 the son of Wilson and Isabella Leith (m/s Gray) Youngson, of 10 Seagate, Peterhead. He was also the brother of Maggie, Jeanie, Mary and Joanna Youngson.

George enlisted into the Gordon Highlanders in Peterhead in Dec 1914. Prior to which, he was a painter in the employ of Mr Ferguson, painter, Peterhead.

George died of his wounds on the 20 Mar 1916 aged 23 years when the dugout he was taking cover in was hit by an aerial torpedo. He is buried in the Aubigny Communal Cemetery Extension.

References:
CWGC Casualty No 996986

Alexander Forman YULE

Rank: Pte. Regiment: Royal Army Medical Corps (TF).
Rank: Pte. Regiment: 72nd Regiment (Seaforth Highlanders of Canada) CEF
Service No: 75677. Rank: Pte. Regiment: 29th Bn. Canadian Infantry.

Born in Fraserburgh on the 7 Mar 1890, Alexander was the son of William and Christian (m/s Donaldson) Yule of 10 High St., Burnhaven, Peterhead. He was the brother of Elspet Smith, William, Robert Donaldson (died in Australia), John Donaldson, Margaret, Charles Scott and James Yule. Prior to the Great War, Alexander was employed as a confectioner in Rose St. Peterhead. He also worked for the Great North British Railways.

After emigrating to Canada, Alexander worked as a fireman in the BC Fire Brigade. He enlisted in Vancouver, BC on the 1 Mar 1915 and was killed on the 10 Sep 1916. Alexander is buried in the Sunken Road Cemetery, Contalmaison. The Sunken Road Cemetery was made in Jul-Oct 1916, during the middle of the Somme offensive. There are now over two hundred 1914-18 war casualties buried in this cemetery.

References:
CWGC Casualty No 613802
Canada World War 1 Project

James YULE

Service No: 2430. Rank: LCpl. Regiment: 5th Bn. Gordon Highlanders.
Service No: 240592. Rank: Cpl. Regiment: 1st/5th Bn. Gordon Highlanders.
Service No: 34559. Rank: Pte. Regiment: 5 A.C. Labour Centre, Labour Corps.

James was the son of James and Jessie (m/s McLennan) Yule and the husband of Mary Ann Smith (m/s Johnston) Yule of 72 Longate, Peterhead. James and Mary had at least four children: Alexander, Elizabeth, James (Enstone) and William Sinclair Yule.

James joined the BEF in France on the 2 May 1915. During the war, James was injured and was posted to the Labour Corps. He died at home in Peterhead on the 5 Sep 1918, aged 38 and was buried in the Peterhead Cemetery.
References:
CWGC Casualty No 327005

Robert Donaldson YULE

Service No: 2339. Rank: Pte. Regiment: Australian Infantry Base Depot.

Born in Fraserburgh in 1885, Robert was the son of William and Christian (m/s Donaldson) Yule, of 10 High St., Burnhaven and later of Blair Athol, Queensland. He was also the brother of Elspet Smith, William, John Donaldson, Margaret, Alexander Forman (killed in the war), Charles Scott and James Yule.

Robert emigrated to Australia in 1909 and enlisted on the 27 Jan 1916 at Rockhampton, Perth, WA. Robert was accidentally killed on 4 Feb 1916, when a limb of tree was blown down by a cyclone at Fraser Hill Camp, Brisbane. Robert is buried in the Brisbane General (Toowong) Cemetery which has 270 Commonwealth burials of the 1914-1918 War.

References:
CWGC Casualty No 134075
National Australian Archives.

William YULE*

Service No: SS/5170. Rank: Pte. Regiment:
Army Service Corps.
Service No: A/202720. Rank: Rifleman.
Regiment: 11th Bn. Kings Royal Rifle Corps.

William was the son of Alexander and
Elizabeth Abernethy formerly Yule of 56
Harlington Terrace, Weston, South Shields,
England.

A former resident of Peterhead, William
joined up with the BEF in France on the 2 Jan
1915 and was killed on the 7 Nov 1917 when
he received a gunshot wound to the head.
William is buried in the Fins New British
Cemetery, Sorel-Le-Grand.

References:
CWGC Casualty No 555354

EPILOGUE

MEN NOT FOUND ON THE PETERHEAD
WAR MEMORIAL OR THE 1919
PETERHEAD ROLL of HONOUR

The following men are not recorded on the
Peterhead War Memorial nor are they listed
on the Buchan Observer's 1919 Peterhead
Roll of Honour. However, records show that
these men, who also gave their lives for this
country, either lived or worked here; some
were educated here at the Peterhead
Academy and some are sailors who originate
from far-away towns and cities and are
buried here. The vast majority of these men
are honoured on nearby local village
memorials or in their home towns.

ANDERSON, Robert – Son of J.R. Anderson,
Longate, Peterhead, 1st Canadian Div.

BARNET, William - S/6637 Pte. 1st Bn. Gordon
Highlanders.

BEER, Charles Wilson – 512/SA Second Hand.
RNR HMT Raven. Drowned in Peterhead Harbour
(Feb 1915).

BIRNIE, John – Signalman, Cameroonians (SR)
son of Maitheson Birnie late of Peterhead.

BUCHAN, John - S/240954 Piper 5th Bn. Gordon
Highlanders.

BUCHAN, Robert - TF/263149 Pte. 17th Bn. Royal
Sussex Regiment.

CATTO, John - 2127 Pte. 5th Bn. Gordon
Highlanders.

CARMICHAEL, James – Assistant Engineer RNR
HMS Princess Irene.

CHALMERS, Joseph - S/6134 LCpl. 9th Bn.
Gordon Highlanders.

COURT, W.H. 22796 Stoker 1st Class RNR HMS
Lilac.

CRANNA, William George – 74051 Pte. 1st Bn.
Machine Gun Corps (Infantry).

COW, William – (Skimmer) 16 Castle St.
Peterhead. Lost with the Gebruder.

CUNNINGHAM, J. – 178563 Leading Seaman
RNR HMT Daniel Stroud.

DAVIDSON, George Andrew – 106179 Pte. 1st
Bn. Canadian Mounted Rifles.

DAWSON, James Herbert – 1334/TS Trimmer
RNR HMT Onward. Drowned in Peterhead
Harbour(Feb 1915).

DICKENSON, (THOMPSON) C.T. – 297595 PO.
RNR HM Motor Lighter.

DUNCAN, Charles – Pte Gordon Highlanders, 88
Longate, Peterhead.

DUNCAN, William Hardy - 10986 Pte. Royal
Scots Fusiliers.

EWAN, John - S/17308 Pte. 6th Bn. Gordon
Highlanders.

FARQUHAR, John – 296540 Pte (2nd Class) Royal
Air Force.

FERGUSON, Roderick Mackenzie – 2Lt. 4th Bn.
Gordon Highlanders.

FRASER, John B. – Sgt Maj. Lancaster Fusiliers
son of Alex. Fraser of Cocklaw, Peterhead.

GEDDES, John – Pte. Gordon Highlanders. Bro. of
Mrs John Robb, Constitution St. Widower and
father of three.

GIBSON, George – Pte. Canadian Infantry.
Grandson of James Milne, 3 Maiden St. Peterhead.

GILL, Arthur – 241460 Pte. 1st/5th Bn. Gordon
Highlanders.

GILL, George - 6/3022 Pte. 2nd Bn. Canterbury
Regiment, NZEF.

GILL, William – Pte. Gordon Highlanders, Love
Lane Peterhead.

GORDON, William D. - Pte. Son of John Gordon
Menie, Belhelvie.

GRANT, Peter – Local Man who received a head
injury and disappeared after the war.

GRANT, Lewis Alexander – 241194 Sgt. 1st/5th
Bn. Gordon Highlanders.

GRAY, Robert – Pte Gordon Highlanders son of
Robert Gray, 22 Queen St. Peterhead.

GRAY, Taylor David - 307564 Pte. 8th Bn. Royal Warwickshire.

HALL, Herbert John – 2Lt. 5th Bn. Gordon Highlanders.

HARVEY, C. - Cook SS Bel-lily.

HARVEY, J.W. – 6772/DA Deck Hand HMT Emilion.

HIRD, William James - 7179 CSM. 1st Bn. Gloucester Regt.

JACK, John Reid – 1674 Pte. 1st Bn. Ayrshire Yeomanry.

KIDD, James Alexander – 1577 Sgt 1st/5th Bn. Gordon Highlanders.

LAIRD, John – 133734 Gnr. 55th Bty. 33rd Bde Royal Field Artillery.

LEITCH, James - S/41580 Pte. 5th Bn. Queen's Own Cameron Highlanders.

McPHERSON, William – 1st RN Bde, MIA near the Dardanelles. Lived in Glasgow.

McROBBIE, G. C. – LCpl Gordon Highlanders, Fairview Roanheads.

MITCHELL, George Ogilvie – 132531 Pte. 73rd Bn. Canadian Infantry. Son of James and Eliza Mitchel KIA 1 Feb 1917.

MUNRO, Norman McLeod – 5th Bn. Gordon Highlanders, Son of John Ross Munro, blacksmith KIA, 31 Jul 16.

OLDHAM, George – Cpl. Queen Victoria Rifles, son of Mr and Mrs James Oldham, Buenos Aires, late of Peterhead.

RIDDLE, John Dean – 2Lt. 1st/5th Bn. Gordon Highlanders.

SAUL, Herbert Lepard – 2Lt. 7th Bn. Suffolk Regt. Husband of Elsie West, Balmoor.

SELBIE, Alexander Baird – 3546 Pte. 1st/5th Bn. Gordon Highlanders.

SELLAR, Colin Philip - S/42519 Pte. 1st/4th Gordon Highlanders.

SELLAR, John – Lt. 6th Bn. Seaforth Highlanders.

SIMPSON, George Shewan – Canadian Infantry (mother was from Peterhead).

SMITH, John - 352171 Pte. 11th Bn. Royal Scots Fusiliers. Formerly 133760 Royal Field Artillery.

SMITH, George – Carpenter, SS Powhatan. Son of Alexander and Helen Smith and husband of Jeanie Cowie. Roanheads.

SUTHERLAND, John – 242038 Pte. 5th Bn. Gordon Highlanders.

TAYLOR David Gray – 307564 Pte. 1st /8th Royal Warwickshire Regiment. Formerly Royal Engineers.

THOMSON, Adam Howie – 2Lt. 191 Sqn. Royal Air Force.

THOMSON, John – 240256 Cpl. 5th Bn. Gordon Highlanders.

TITFORD, M. – 1472/X Seaman RNR HM Yacht Moonson (from Newfoundland).

TORBET, F.J. – 2127/ES Engineman HMD Girl Rhoda.

WALLACE, John – Spr, Canadian Engineers. Son of John Wallace late of Peterhead. KIA 1 Oct 1918.

WARREN, J.F. – M/5781 Armourer. RN HMS Lilac.

WATT, Douglas Gordon – 2Lt. 3rd Bn. Gordon Highlanders.

WATT, John – 4505 Pte. 1st/4th Bn. Gordon Highlanders.

WATTS, W. – Extra Hand. Trawler Windward Ho.

WOOD, William - S/14801Pte. 1st Bn. Gordon Highlanders.

YEATS, William - Lt. 2nd Bn. Australian Infantry, A.I.F.

During 1918 and for the next few years many memorials were written to the fallen. This one has been selected to represent all those heartfelt poems of sacrifice and remembrance. This lad was not an officer nor was he holder of any gallantry medal – he simply was a Peterhead loon who sacrificed his future. Our debt to him and all the other men of Peterhead who gave their lives, is to remember their sacrifice.

John McLean Reid
1889 – 1917

Our loss can never be told
I miss you more as the days grow old.

Oft when I sit in sorrow and woe
There comes a dream of long ago

And unknown to the world you stand by my side
And whisper "Dear Mum death cannot divide"

When last we saw his smiling face
He was so strong and brave;

We little thought how soon he'd lie
In a hero's ocean grave.

Dearly loved and deeply mourned
Now asleep with Jesus.

(*Written by his mother and published in the Buchan Observer 1918*)